Economic Autonomy and Democracy
Hybrid Regimes in Russia and Kyrgyzstan

How do individuals decide to exercise their democratic rights? This book argues that they first assess their economic autonomy, meaning their ability to make a living independent of government authorities. Before individuals consider whether their resources and organizational abilities enable them to act on their interests, they calculate the risk of political activism to their livelihood. This is particularly evident in regions of the world where states monopolize the economy and thus can readily harass activists at their workplaces. Economic autonomy links capitalism and democracy through individuals' calculations about activism. Accounts of activists' decisions about establishing independent media, leading political organizations, and running for office, and descriptions of government harassment in Russia and Kyrgyzstan, along with examples from most regions of the world, illustrate these arguments. A lack of economic autonomy and the interaction among democratic rights help explain the global proliferation of hybrid regimes, governments that display both democratic and authoritarian characteristics.

Kelly M. McMann is an assistant professor of political science at Case Western Reserve University. Her work appears in the edited volumes *The Transformation of Central Asia: States and Societies from Soviet Rule to Independence* (2003) and *Everyday Life in Central Asia: Past and Present* (forthcoming). She has conducted field research in the capital cities and outlying regions of Russia, Kazakhstan, and Kyrgyzstan and survey research in Kazakhstan, Kyrgyzstan, and Uzbekistan. Grants from the National Science Foundation, the National Endowment for the Humanities, the National Council for Eurasian and East European Research, the International Research & Exchanges Board, and the Institute for the Study of World Politics have funded her research.

Economic Autonomy and Democracy

Hybrid Regimes in Russia and Kyrgyzstan

KELLY M. McMANN
Case Western Reserve University

CAMBRIDGE UNIVERSITY PRESS
Cambridge, New York, Melbourne, Madrid, Cape Town, Singapore, São Paulo

Cambridge University Press
40 West 20th Street, New York, NY 10011-4211, USA

www.cambridge.org
Information on this title: www.cambridge.org/9780521857611

First published 2006

Printed in the United States of America

A catalog record for this publication is available from the British Library.

Library of Congress Cataloging in Publication Data

McMann, Kelly M., 1970–
Economic autonomy and democracy : hybrid regimes in Russia and Kyrgyzstan / Kelly
M. McMann.
    p.   cm.
Includes bibliographical references and index.
ISBN 0-521-85761-9
1. Democracy – Russia (Federation)   2. Democracy – Kyrgyzstan.   3. Political
participation – Russia (Federation)   4. Political participation – Kyrgyzstan.
5. Russia (Federation) – Politics and government – 1991–   6. Kyrgyzstan – Politics and
government – 1991–   7. Russia (Federation) – Economic conditions – 1991–
8. Kyrgyzstan – Economic conditions – 1991–   I. Title.

JN6699.A15M39   2006
320.947–dc22   2005022523

ISBN-13   978-0-521-85761-1 hardback
ISBN-10   0-521-85761-9 hardback

To Ellen and John McMann

Contents

Figures

Tables

Acknowledgments

Aigul, Almazbek, Nadezhda, and the other citizens of Russia and Kyrgyzstan who shared their stories with me are the foundation of this book. To these activists, politicians, bureaucrats, and businesspeople I owe the greatest debt. In addition to these individuals, eight families in Russia and Kyrgyzstan were particularly instrumental. Without their friendship, living in these countries would not have been nearly as enjoyable or educational. Their hospitality extended beyond food and shelter. They treated me as one of their own, including me in momentous occasions, such as the weddings of dear friends, and routine activities, such as the slaughtering of lambs! Sadly, the possibility that some of these individuals could face negative repercussions for their openness and hospitality has deterred me from revealing their identities.

Two individuals, Edward Gibson and Zvi Gitelman, provided inspiration for this project during my graduate studies at the University of Michigan. Ed's outstanding seminar on democratization prompted me to shift my focus from ethnic conflict to democratic development. Zvi's enthusiasm for field research and foreign languages was a useful reminder that, despite its stumbling blocks, graduate study is an extraordinary experience that few are so fortunate to have.

Pauline Jones Luong and Henry Hale have been generous with their advice and time and have provided ongoing encouragement since I left Ann Arbor. Each has been an excellent mentor. These individuals and the community of post-Soviet politics scholars I have come to know have made the start of my career particularly stimulating and enjoyable.

During this project, certain people offered particularly useful advice or opportunities from which I benefited tremendously. These individuals include Alfred Evans, Mark Beissinger, the late Leonid Gordon, Ted Hopf, the late Harold Jacobson, Joel Moses, Tokonai Ozhukeeva, Nikolai Petrov, and Sergei Zasorin.

Institutional support has been superb. The faculty and staff of the Department of Political Science and the Center for Russian and East European Studies at the University of Michigan ensured that my graduate studies were invigorating and pleasant. I am particularly grateful for the numerous grants the University of Michigan provided to fund this project. During my time at Harvard University's Davis Center for Russian and Eurasian Studies, Timothy Colton, John Schoeberlein, Lisbeth Tarlow, and Joshua Tucker made me feel welcome and provided a stimulating environment in which I was able to refine my ideas. Most recently, I have benefited from the support of the Department of Political Science and the College of Arts and Sciences at Case Western Reserve University. The current and former department chairs, Joseph White and Vincent McHale, respectively, have ensured that I have had the time and resources necessary to conduct research for this project and write this book. A fellowship from the Institute for the Study of World Politics funded the field research. This material is based upon work supported by the National Science Foundation under Grant No. SBR-9729989. Any opinions, findings, and conclusions or recommendations expressed in this material are those of the author and do not necessarily reflect the views of the National Science Foundation.

Numerous research assistants at the universities mentioned helped me collect information and edit this book. I am grateful to Gulnora Aminova, Christopher Beattie, Christopher Erenburg, Joshua Ehrenreich, Amanda Gibson, Philip Kehres, Inna Oskova, Marlene Torres, Sarah Tremont, and Brittany Williams for their assistance.

Many scholars commented on various versions of this book, and I am grateful to them for their thoughts and time. Members of my dissertation committee – Samuel Eldersveld, Zvi Gitelman,

Katherine Verdery, and William Zimmerman – provided extensive, helpful suggestions at the early stage of this project. Douglas Blum, Melissa Caldwell, Gerald Easter, Pauline Jones Luong, and Valerie Sperling offered useful assessments of the first complete draft. Todd Eisenstadt, Henry Hale, Heather Hill, Debra Javeline, Kathryn Lavelle, Emery Lee, Frances Lee, Ellen Lust-Okar, Sharon Werning Rivera, Bruce Rutherford, Richard Snyder, and members of Harvard's Post-communist Politics and Economics Workshop shared their insights about portions of the manuscript. I also appreciate the comments that two anonymous reviewers for Cambridge University Press provided. In the final stage of the project, Lewis Bateman provided invaluable advice about the publishing industry.

I thank two publishing houses and the Slavic Research Center of Hokkaido University for permission to reproduce information from my earlier publications. Data about candidates' nominations in Table 4.6 and information in Table 5.2 appeared in "The Personal Risks of Party Development," in *Dilemmas of Transition in Post-Soviet Countries*, edited by Joel C. Moses, 163–186 (Chicago: Burnham Inc. Publishers, 2003), now a Rowman and Littlefield title. Sections of Appendix A and Table B.5 appeared in "International Influences on Russian Regional Democratization," in *Slavic Eurasia's Integration into the World Economy and Community*, edited by Shinichiro Tabata and Akihiro Iwashita, Slavic Eurasian Studies, no. 2, 413–434 (Sapporo: Slavic Research Center, Hokkaido University, 2004). Tables A.1, A.3, and A.5 were reprinted with permission from *Post-Soviet Geography and Economics*, Vol. 41, No. 3, 155–182 (© V. H. Winston & Son, Inc., 360 South Ocean Boulevard, Palm Beach, FL 33480. All rights reserved.)

On a personal note, I dedicate this book to my parents in recognition of two important gifts they gave me: an excellent college education and the choice of a career. This good fortune early in life has enabled me to pursue my interests. I would also like to thank my husband's parents, Penelope and Theodore York, for providing a peaceful retreat and stimulating conversation during the research and writing of this book. I am grateful to our close friends Todd Gorman and Scott Miller for keeping my husband company during my long absences. They, along with their spouses and children, Nathalie Turgeon, Emma and Noah

Gorman, and Lisa Cosimi, have also provided lively respites from my work. My young daughter, Marie, has supplied daily breaks from writing, rejuvenating me each time with a single smile.

It is fitting that I thank my husband, Gregory York, last, for he has excelled in all these roles: as friend, motivator, mentor, advisor, advocate, editor, and companion. For this I am extremely grateful.

Notes on Transliteration

Throughout this book, I have used the Library of Congress system of Russian transliteration. However, for well-known names and words, I use the more common spelling (for example, Yeltsin instead of El'tsin and oblast instead of oblast'). I transliterated Kyrgyz and Uzbek names and words from their Russified forms unless another version was standard.

Economic Autonomy and Democracy
Hybrid Regimes in Russia and Kyrgyzstan

Capitalism, Democracy, and Economic Autonomy

"My wife asked me to not be involved in politics so that I could feed our family," a middle-aged man in the former Soviet Union recounted to me in 1997. This simple, pragmatic statement reveals a fundamental way in which capitalism influences democracy. Specifically, capitalism acts on democracy through individuals' assessments of their economic autonomy, or their ability to earn a living independent of the state. With the end of Soviet communism in 1991, this man became actively involved in democratic politics. He founded a branch of a political party, which supported candidates for regional and national elections. "When I created the party, I did not think there would be risks," he explained. He had assumed that greater political freedom in the late Soviet period meant that he no longer had to fear government reprisals for oppositional activity. He was wrong. Provincial authorities fired this man from his job as a school director three times between 1991 and 1997 as punishment for his political activism. Meanwhile, his organization dwindled from 100 to 12 members as others faced similar workplace harassment. Unable to find a job beyond the reach of local officials, the man decided to abandon the party. He and his fellow leaders dissolved the organization, even though the party was thriving in other regions of the country.

This story is typical of the accounts I heard from current and former activists in post-Soviet countries. The common theme is that when one's livelihood and one's political activism collide, the latter suffers. To be precise, these accounts illustrate that economic autonomy is the foremost means by which capitalism increases people's capacity to exercise their democratic rights. Furthermore, they suggest that investigations of capitalism and democracy should not concentrate exclusively on socioeconomic groups but should also consider individuals. The importance of individual assessments of economic autonomy is easy to grasp, but this link between capitalism and democracy has been overlooked in previous scholarship.

CAPITALISM AND DEMOCRACY

Existing studies of capitalism and democracy acknowledge both compatibility and tension between the two systems. As Charles Lindblom noted in *Politics and Markets* in 1977, "liberal democracy has arisen only in nations that are market-oriented."[1] Moreover, scholars have described how the two systems share many characteristics, including uncertain outcomes and pluralism.[2] Yet, debate continues as to whether capitalism is a net benefit to democracy. Research suggests that capitalism promotes the right to participate in democratic institutions; however, it both supports and undermines people's capacity to exercise that right.

Capitalism has directly contributed to the creation and maintenance of democratic rights. Historically, capitalist development produced a new economic class that demanded democratic rights.[3] "[Democracies] were established to win and protect certain liberties: private property, free enterprise, free contract, and occupational choice," Lindblom

---

[1] Charles Lindblom, *Politics and Markets: The World's Political Economic Systems* (New York: Basic Books, 1977), 165.

[2] In market and electoral competitions, the outcomes are not predetermined but uncertain. In other words, a business may succeed or fail; a candidate may win or lose. Market economies and democratic systems also exhibit "extremes of pluralism," meaning that each system is decentralized, with power and resources widely distributed. See V. Bunce, "Elementy neopredelennosti v perekhodnyi period," *Polis* 1 (1993), 44–51; Friedrich A. von Hayek, *The Road to Serfdom* (Chicago: University of Chicago Press, 1980); Lindblom, *Politics and Markets*; Adam Przeworski, *Democracy and the Market: Political and Economic Reforms in Eastern Europe and Latin America* (Cambridge: Cambridge University Press, 1991).

[3] Robert Dahl, *Democracy and Its Critics* (New Haven, CT: Yale University Press, 1989), 252; Barrington Moore, *Social Origins of Dictatorship and Democracy: Lord and Peasant in the Making of the Modern World* (Boston: Beacon Press, 1966); Dietrich Rueschemeyer, Evelyne Huber Stephens, and John D. Stephens, *Capitalist Development and Democracy* (Chicago: University of Chicago Press, 1992).

explains.[4] In the modern era, business continues to support democratic rights as a means of maintaining these liberties.[5]

However, although capitalism promotes democratic rights, it does not necessarily enable people to use those rights. On the one hand, the pluralistic nature of capitalism enhances the capacity to exercise democratic rights.[6] Political resources that are helpful to exercising rights, such as money, knowledge, status, and access, are held not by a single authority in capitalist systems but are distributed throughout society.[7] Moreover, these resources increase the organizational capacity of non-state actors, allowing them to protect these rights against government encroachment.[8]

On the other hand, the division of labor in capitalist societies creates differences in status and opportunity that result in some groups having greater political resources than others.[9] For example, Lindblom identified the "privileged position" of business in America that stems from the larger amounts of money, status, and access companies enjoy. Corporations can use their funds for political influence, companies' tax payments make governments beholden to them, and consequently businesses have greater access to government officials. Businesses can even circumvent democratic means of influencing government officials.[10]

---

[4] Lindblom, *Politics and Markets*, 169.

[5] Ibid., 164.

[6] Robert Dahl, *After the Revolution? Authority in a Good Society*, Rev. ed. (New Haven, CT: Yale University Press, 1990).

[7] Dahl, *Democracy and Its Critics*, 252.

[8] Lindblom, *Politics and Markets*, 170–174, 179; Max Weber, *Economy and Society: An Outline of Interpretive Sociology* (Berkeley: University of California Press, 1978), 143.

[9] Dahl, *Democracy and Its Critics*, 326; Robert Dahl, *Democracy, Liberty, and Equality* (Oslo: Norwegian University Press, 1986), 10–11; Robert Dahl, *A Preface to Economic Democracy* (Berkeley: University of California Press, 1985), 55; Robert Dahl and Charles Lindblom, *Politics, Economics, and Welfare: Planning and Politico-Economic Systems Resolved into Basic Social Processes* (New York: Harper, 1953), 281–282; Robert Dahl, *Toward Democracy – a Journey: Reflections, 1940–1997* (Berkeley: University of California, 1997), 147.

[10] Scholars who acknowledge the inequality of resources have explained the coexistence of the two systems in different ways. According to Lindblom, businesses' support for democratic rights and their ability to indoctrinate the public enable capitalism and democracy to function together. Similarly, Claus Offe and John Keane have attributed the coexistence of the two systems to an accord between labor and capital, which party systems support by keeping anticapitalist issues off the agenda. See Lindblom, *Politics and Markets;* Claus Offe and John Keane, *Contradictions of the Welfare State* (Cambridge, MA: MIT Press, 1984).

The contradictory influences of capitalism are perhaps best reconciled in a quotation by Robert Dahl, a scholar who early in his career argued that capitalism had a purely beneficial impact on democracy but then acknowledged its negative influences. "In the twentieth century, the existence of a market-oriented capitalist economy in a country has been favorable to democratization up to the level of polyarchy [or democracy as we know it]; but it is unfavorable to democratization beyond the level of polyarchy."[11] In other words, capitalism facilitates the creation of contemporary democracy, but it impedes the full realization of democratic ideals.

ECONOMIC AUTONOMY

This book argues that economic autonomy is the foremost means by which capitalism enhances people's ability to exercise their democratic rights, whether in advanced democracies or hybrid regimes, governments that exhibit both democratic and authoritarian characteristics. Economic autonomy is a product of capitalism, and it is essential to the practice of democracy. Economic autonomy results from capitalism because in a capitalist economy the market, not the state, generates opportunities for earning a living. Most citizens make a living through private ventures, with minimal interference from the state.[12] In turn, economic autonomy allows people to engage in the political activities that are essential to the operation of democratic institutions.

The calculation of whether one's economic autonomy is sufficient to protect one from government harassment comes before consideration of interests, resources, and organizational capacity – the focus of other studies that examine the impact of capitalism on democracy. Democratic interests and resources are not sufficient for political activism. The ability to make a living independent of the state is critical to the practice of democracy; otherwise, citizens will avoid activism for fear of economic reprisals by the government.

The idea of economic autonomy encourages us to refocus the debate from socioeconomic classes to individuals. Previous studies argued that capitalist development provides classes with the resources and

[11] Dahl, *Toward Democracy*, 147.
[12] Bunce, "Elementy."

organizational capacity to act against dominant groups in pursuit of their pro-democratic interests.[13] The pro-democratic leanings of one's strengthened social class may be sufficient to motivate an individual to join peers in a single street protest. However, for long-term political engagement, individuals calculate their own economic risks before acting. The accounts of post-Soviet citizens in this book illustrate that decisions by individuals, not characteristics of classes, are the first link in the chain between capitalism and democracy.

The concept of economic autonomy emphasizes how state economic monopolies compromise democratic rights. In the former Soviet Union and in other regions of the world where states play significant economic roles, economic autonomy is highly salient. Where the state does not have an economic monopoly, individuals may not consciously calculate their economic autonomy because the idea of economic dependence on government authorities is foreign to them. Yet, a decrease in economic autonomy in these places would hinder democratic participation nonetheless. Regardless of geographic location, economic autonomy is a concept that illuminates when people participate.

AN EMPIRICAL PUZZLE

"A Few Miles Apart, 2 Russias Contend for Nation's Future"... "Democratic Norms Under Assault in Russian Far East."[14] In the 1990s, headlines such as these revealed the real-world puzzle from which my argument about economic autonomy emerged. Media accounts and case studies suggested that Russia had only pockets of democracy across its vast territory. Opposition candidates in one region ran without negative repercussions, but those in another region lost

---

[13] Moore, *Social Origins of Dictatorship and Democracy*; Rueschemeyer et al., *Capitalist Development and Democracy*. Eva Bellin also contends that group interests motivate pressure for democracy, but she finds that support for democracy cannot be assumed under conditions of late-developing capitalism. See Eva Bellin, "Contingent Democrats: Industrialists, Labor, and Democratization in Late-Developing Countries," *World Politics* 52 (January, 2000), 175–205; Eva Bellin, *Stalled Democracy: Capital, Labor and the Paradox of State-Sponsored Development* (Ithaca, NY: Cornell University Press, 2002).

[14] Michael Specter, "A Few Miles Apart, 2 Russias Contend for Nation's Future," *New York Times*, May 25, 1996, 1; Jeffrey Lilley, "Eastern Model: Democratic Norms under Assault in Russian Far East," *Far Eastern Economic Review* (April 7, 1994), 28.

their jobs. Journalists in one province reported freely, but those in another censored their remarks. Political groups in one region operated openly, but those in another disbanded because of harassment.

This patchwork of democracy is not unique to Russia. In countries such as Mexico, India, Spain, Chile, and Brazil, democracy has also developed unevenly.[15] Even in older democracies, democracy may be weaker in some regions. Prime examples are the American South historically and southern Italy to this day.[16] Yet, the unevenness in established democracies is not nearly as great as in countries that only recently introduced democratic institutions, such as Russia. In Russia, only a small percentage of regions can be considered democracies. Scholars have provided country-specific descriptions of the uneven development of democracy, yet no theories have incorporated these findings.

Democratization theories tell the story of democratic development solely from a national perspective. One school of thought, "crafting" theories,[17] explains democratization through interactions among elites,

---

[15] Jonathan Fox, "The Difficult Transition from Clientelism to Citizenship," *World Politics* 46 (January, 1994), 151–184; Patrick Heller, "Degrees of Democracy: Some Comparative Lessons from India," *World Politics* 52 (July, 2000), 486–501; Juan J. Linz and Amando de Miguel, "Within-Nation Differences and Comparisons: The Eight Spains," in *Comparing Nations: The Use of Quantitative Data in Cross-National Research*, ed. Richard L. Merritt and Stein Rokkan (New Haven, CT: Yale University Press, 1966), 307; Marcus J. Kurtz, "Free Markets and Democratic Consolidation in Chile: The National Politics of Rural Transformation," *Politics and Society* 27 (June, 1999), 275–301; Guillermo O'Donnell, "On the State, Democratization and Some Conceptual Problems: A Latin-American View with Glances at Some Postcommunist Countries," *World Development* 21 (August, 1993), 1358–1361; Jeffrey Rubin, *Decentering the Regime: Ethnicity, Radicalism, and Democracy in Juchitâan, Mexico* (Durham, NC: Duke University Press, 1997); Simon Schwartzman, "Regional Contrasts within a Continental-Scale State: Brazil," in *Building States and Nations: Analyses by Region*, ed. S. N. Eisenstadt and Stein Rokkan (Beverly Hills, CA: Sage Publications, 1973), 226.

[16] V. O. Key and Alexander Heard, *Southern Politics in State and Nation* (Knoxville: University of Tennessee Press, 1984); Alexander P. Lamis, "The Two-Party South: From the 1960s to the 1990s," in *Southern Politics in the 1990s*, ed. Alexander P. Lamis (Baton Rouge: Louisiana State University Press, 1999), 1–49. Also, see Robert D. Putnam, Robert Leonardi, and Raffaella Nanetti, *Making Democracy Work: Civic Traditions in Modern Italy* (Princeton, NJ: Princeton University Press, 1993).

[17] John Higley and Michael Burton, "The Elite Variable in Democratic Transitions and Breakdowns," *American Sociological Review* 54 (February, 1989), 17–32; Giuseppe Di Palma, *To Craft Democracies: An Essay on Democratic Transitions* (Berkeley: University of California Press, 1990); Mattei Dogan and John Higley, *Elites, Crises, and the Origins of Regimes* (Lanham, MD: Rowman and Littlefield Publishers, 1998);

whereas the other attributes democratization to socioeconomic conditions.[18] Both schools devote almost no attention to subnational politics, focusing instead on national elites, processes, and conditions. At most, crafting theories allow a subnational civic movement to play a role in negotiated transition, and socioeconomic theories lead a scholar to footnote that a region is a socioeconomic outlier. Overall, crafting theories seem implicitly to assume democracy will develop evenly throughout a country once transition occurs in a national capital. Socioeconomic theories seem implicitly to assume that aggregate characteristics will enable democracy to be consolidated equally successfully across regions.

Studies that do focus on subnational politics give little attention to questions of democratization. In 1974, Mark Kesselman and Donald Rosenthal lamented the myopia of subnational investigations: These studies considered center–periphery relations only from a legal perspective, they ignored the influence of rural and national governments on urban politics, and they rejected cross-national research.[19] Since then, many of these problems have been overcome, but theories of subnational political development still have not emerged.[20] Instead, since the

John Higley and Richard Gunther, *Elites and Democratic Consolidation in Latin America and Southern Europe* (Cambridge: Cambridge University Press, 1992); Juan J. Linz and Alfred C. Stepan, *Problems of Democratic Transition and Consolidation: Southern Europe, South America, and Post-communist Europe* (Baltimore: Johns Hopkins University Press, 1996); Przeworski, *Democracy and the Market*; Guillermo O'Donnell, Philippe C. Schmitter, and Laurence Whitehead, *Transitions from Authoritarian Rule*, 4 vols. (Baltimore: Johns Hopkins University Press, 1986); Dankwart A. Rustow, "Transitions to Democracy: Toward a Dynamic Model," *Comparative Politics* 2 (April, 1970), 337–363.

[18] Carles Boix and Susan C. Stokes, "Endogenous Democratization," *World Politics* 55 (July, 2003), 517–549; Robert Dahl, *Polyarchy: Participation and Opposition* (New Haven, CT: Yale University Press, 1971); Karl W. Deutsch, "Social Mobilization and Political Development," *American Political Science Review* 55 (September, 1961), 493–514; Alex Inkeles, "The Modernization of Man," in *Modernization: The Dynamics of Growth*, ed. Myron Weiner (New York: Basic Books, 1966), 138–150; Seymour M. Lipset, "The Social Requisites of Democracy Revisited: 1993 Presidential Address," *American Sociological Review* 59 (February, 1994), 1–22; Seymour M. Lipset, "Some Social Requisites of Democracy: Economic Development and Political Legitimacy," *American Political Science Review* 53 (1959), 69–105.

[19] Mark Kesselman and Donald B. Rosenthal, *Local Power and Comparative Politics* (Beverly Hills, CA: Sage Publications, 1974), 10–12, 14.

[20] This inattention to subnational variation is not surprising considering that scholars created these theories to explain differences in democratic development among

mid-1970s, scholars of comparative politics have been examining the subnational level through the lenses of federalism, elite values, decentralization, local government law, and urban politics.[21] In the 1990s and the first years of the new century, there has been a reemphasis on subnational politics, and the topics have expanded to include elections, political movements, state institutions, and economic policy.[22] Over the years, Americanists have paid greater attention to the subnational level, but they tend to ask questions about the status quo instead of change over time: Who controls local polities? How can

countries. Moreover, the national approach may reflect a certain pragmatism: As Dahl acknowledged, investigating democracy in all subnational units, from municipal governments to trade unions, would be a Herculean task. Even a focus on subnational governments can prove more difficult because in the provinces government restrictions on fieldwork may be more severe and suspicion of foreigners may be greater. Finally, this preference for the national level over the subnational level mirrors a pattern found throughout the discipline of political science. See Dahl, *Polyarchy*, 14.

[21] For example, see Betty M. Jacob, Krzysztof Ostrowski, and Henry Teune, *Democracy and Local Governance: Ten Empirical Studies* (Honolulu: University of Hawai'i, 1993); Daniel Elazar, *Exploring Federalism* (Tuscaloosa: University of Alabama Press, 1987); Henry Teune, "Local Government and Democratic Political Development," *The Annals of the American Academy of Political and Social Science* 540 (July, 1995), 10–23; International Studies of Values in Politics Project, *Values and the Active Community: A Cross-National Study of the Influence of Local Leadership* (New York: Free Press, 1971).

[22] Caroline Beer, "Assessing the Consequences of Electoral Democracy: Subnational Legislative Change in Mexico," *Comparative Politics* 33 (July, 2001), 421–440; Rebecca Bill Chavez, "The Construction of the Rule of Law in Argentina: A Tale of Two Provinces," *Comparative Politics* 35 (July, 2003), 417–437; Kent Eaton, "Designing Subnational Institutions: Regional and Municipal Reforms in Postauthoritarian Chile," *Comparative Political Studies* 37 (March, 2004), 218–244; Frances Hagopian, *Traditional Politics and Regime Change in Brazil* (Cambridge: Cambridge University Press, 1996); Elizabeth J. Remick, "The Significance of Variation in Local States: The Case of Twentieth Century China," *Comparative Politics* 34 (July, 2002); Karen L. Remmer and François Gelineau, "Subnational Electoral Choice: Economic and Referendum Voting in Argentina, 1983–1999," *Comparative Political Studies* 36 (September, 2003), 801–821; Karen L. Remmer and Erik Wibbels, "The Subnational Politics of Economic Adjustment: Provincial Politics and Fiscal Performance in Argentina," *Comparative Political Studies* 33 (May, 2000), 419–451; Rubin, *Decentering the Regime*; Richard Snyder, "After Neoliberalism: The Politics of Reregulation in Mexico," *World Politics* 51 (January, 1999), 173–204; Richard Snyder, *Politics after Neoliberalism: Reregulation in Mexico* (Cambridge: Cambridge University Press, 2001); Yang Zhong and Jie Chen, "To Vote or Not to Vote: An Analysis of Peasants' Participation in Chinese Village Elections," *Comparative Political Studies* 35 (August, 2002), 686–712.

average citizens participate? How do different levels of government interact?[23]

With respect to Russia, neither media accounts nor academic studies offer an explanation for subnational variation in democracy. Media reports supply descriptions of one or two regions, but no generalizations about the uneven development. Many scholarly works provide a comprehensive picture of politics in a single Russian province or city.[24] However, because each study explores different aspects of democracy and uses different measures, it is difficult to draw general conclusions. Another set of works has explored subnational political development across multiple regions. These investigations have provided valuable data and analysis about single aspects of democracy, such as the emergence of democratic movements, administrative control over elections, variation in electoral outcomes, political parties, legislative–executive relations, and the effectiveness of government institutions.[25] Yet, these

[23] Robert Dahl, *Who Governs? Democracy and Power in an American City* (New Haven, CT: Yale University Press, 1989); Gerald Frug, *Local Government Law* (St. Paul, MN: West, 1988); Key and Heard, *Southern Politics*; Paul E. Peterson, *City Limits* (Chicago: University of Chicago Press, 1981); Clarence N. Stone, *Regime Politics: Governing Atlanta, 1946–1988* (Lawrence: University Press of Kansas, 1989). Nancy Burns's work on the creation of special districts and municipalities is an exception to this rule. Unfortunately, her study offers little insight into the uneven development of democracy because she focuses on the establishment of new political entities instead of change in existing ones. See Nancy Burns, *The Formation of American Local Governments: Private Values in Public Institutions* (Oxford: Oxford University Press, 1994), 25.

[24] Single case studies of Russian regions and cities are too numerous to list here, but most have appeared in the journals *Europe–Asia Studies*, *Post-Soviet Affairs*, and *Eurasian Geography and Economics* and in edited volumes, including: Theodore H. Friedgut and Jeffrey W. Hahn, eds., *Local Power and Post-Soviet Politics* (Armonk, NY: M. E. Sharpe, 1994); Timothy J. Colton and Jerry F. Hough, *Growing Pains: Russian Democracy and the Election of 1993* (Washington, DC: Brookings Institution Press, 1998). Also, see Robert W. Orttung, *From Leningrad to St. Petersburg: Democratization in a Russian City*, 1st ed. (New York: St. Martin's Press, 1995); Nicolai N. Petro, *Crafting Democracy: How Novgorod Has Coped with Rapid Social Change* (Ithaca, NY: Cornell University Press, 2004).

[25] M. Steven Fish, *Democracy from Scratch: Opposition and Regime in the New Russian Revolution* (Princeton, NJ: Princeton University Press, 1995); G. V. Golosov, "Electoral Systems and Party Formation in Russia: A Cross-Regional Analysis," *Comparative Political Studies* 36 (October, 2003), 912–935; Grigorii Golosov, *Political Parties in the Regions of Russia: Democracy Unclaimed* (Boulder, CO: Lynne Rienner Publishers, 2004); A. Konitzer-Smirnov, "Incumbent Electoral Fortunes and Regional Economic Performance during Russia's 2000–2001 Regional Executive Election Cycle," *Post-Soviet Affairs* 19 (January–March, 2003), 46–79; Valentin Mikhailov, "Regional

studies do not provide a comprehensive picture of democratic activity. A small number of scholars have investigated subnational political differences systematically and comprehensively; however, they have asked other questions: How did provincial regimes differ during the perestroika era? What were the consequences of these Soviet-era differences? How can the democratic and authoritarian outcomes of transition from communist regimes best be characterized? What accounts for differences in the power of regional political machines?[26] Scholars of comparative, American, and post-Soviet politics have yet to offer a theory of democracy's uneven development within countries.[27]

THE INVESTIGATION

The news articles and case studies about Russia suggest that it is a good place to begin studying the uneven development of democracy. But, how can we ensure that findings in Russia apply outside the country?

Elections and Democratisation in Russia," in *Russian Politics under Putin*, ed. Cameron Ross (Manchester: Manchester University Press, 2004), 198–220; Bryon J. Moraski, "Electoral System Design in Russian *Oblasti* and Republics: A Four Case Comparison," *Europe–Asia Studies* 55 (2003), 437–468; Joel C. Moses, "Political–Economic Elites and Russian Regional Elections 1999–2000: Democratic Tendencies in Kaliningrad, Perm and Volgograd," *Europe–Asia Studies* 54 (2002), 905–931; Joel C. Moses, "Voting, Regional Legislatures and Electoral Reform in Russia," *Europe–Asia Studies* 55 (2003), 1049–1075; Steven L. Solnick, "Gubernatorial Elections in Russia, 1996–1997," *Post-Soviet Affairs* 14 (1998), 48–80; Kathryn Stoner-Weiss, *Local Heroes: The Political Economy of Russian Regional Governance* (Princeton, NJ: Princeton University Press, 1997). Also, Ralph S. Clem and Peter R. Craumer have published numerous analyses of subnational electoral outcomes in *Post-Soviet Geography and Economics*.

[26] Henry E. Hale, "Explaining Machine Politics in Russia's Regions: Economy, Ethnicity, and Legacy," *Post-Soviet Affairs* 19 (2003), 228–263; Joel Moses, "Soviet Provincial Politics in an Era of Transition and Revolution, 1989–91," *Soviet Studies* 44 (1992), 479–509; Mary McAuley, "Politics, Economics, and Elite Realignment in Russia: A Regional Perspective," *Soviet Economy* 8 (January–March, 1992), 46–88; Vladimir Gel'man, "Regime Transition, Uncertainty and Prospects for Democratisation: The Politics of Russia's Regions in a Comparative Perspective," *Europe–Asia Studies* 51 (September, 1999), 939–956; Vladimir Gel'man, Sergei I. Ryzhenkov, and Michael Brie, *Rossiia regionov: transformatsiia politicheskikh rezhimov*, ed. Vladimir Gel'man, Sergei I. Ryzhenkov, and Michael Brie (Moscow: Ves' Mir, 2000).

[27] Samuel Eldersveld, "The Comparative Development of Local Political Systems," in *Nation, Power, and Society: Essays in Honor of Jerzy J. Wiatr*, ed. Aleksandra Jasinska-Kania and Jacek Raciborski (Warsaw: Wydawnictwo Naukoe Scholar, 1996), 344–345.

The first step is to investigate the same puzzle in a very different country – the Kyrgyz Republic (Kyrgyzstan). The inclusion of both Russia and Kyrgyzstan helps guarantee that my conclusions apply to countries with a variety of institutional structures, socioeconomic levels, and cultural heritages. Through a combination of survey research in each country and fieldwork in four of their regions, it is possible to study the uneven development of democracy in a more systematic and comprehensive manner than earlier studies. A second step toward increasing generalizability is to apply the theory of economic autonomy developed from these post-Soviet states to other regions of the world. The remainder of this chapter describes the design of the project in the post-Soviet states and other parts of the world and concludes with an outline of the contents of the book.

Russia and Kyrgyzstan

Previously, Russia and Kyrgyzstan were two of 15 republics in the communist Soviet Union. Today, both are independent countries that have introduced democratic institutions. Despite their shared Soviet history and experiments with democracy, Russia and Kyrgyzstan are quite different institutionally, economically, and culturally.

Experiments with Democracy. In the Soviet Union in the late 1980s, national leaders in Moscow inadvertently initiated an extraction from the old regime through the policies of glasnost (openness) and perestroika (restructuring). In the republics, elites, such as Boris Yeltsin, and movements, such as the popular fronts, pushed the political transformation further. Even in republics, such as the Kirghiz Soviet Socialist Republic (today Kyrgyzstan), where greater political freedom did not become linked to demands for more autonomy, elites, including later president Askar Akaev, and groups, such as Erk Kyrgyzstan (Free Kyrgyzstan), advocated greater political liberalization. Although the center initiated the transformation, the periphery fueled it, resulting in the destruction of the old regime and the disintegration of the Soviet Union in December 1991.

With sovereignty came a new phase in the experiments with democracy. The countries now had the right to determine whether to further develop, maintain, or destroy nascent democratic institutions and practices. Presidents Yeltsin of Russia and Akaev of Kyrgyzstan made commitments to further democratization, yet even in the early 1990s, while these pledges held, democracy did not develop evenly throughout the countries.

Institutional Differences. The patchwork of democracy is particularly surprising in Kyrgyzstan because the country has a unitary system of government. One would expect that the intentions of the national leader would have had great influence on local reform. By contrast, Russia has a federal system of government, so the uneven development of democracy is not as unexpected.

The Russian constitution describes Russia as a federation, and during the 1990s Russia increasingly evolved into a federation as regional leaders became more powerful and developed their own policies.[28] As early as 1992, Moscow gave the regions greater responsibilities, namely for social welfare and price subsidies. Moreover, regional leaders started to claim control of local natural resources, branches of banks, and law enforcement agencies. Provincial leaders also began to develop relations with foreign countries, rent out property owned by the federal government, sell licenses previously under the national purview, and in a few cases use alternative currencies.

In the early 1990s, some Russian regions began to elect their executives. By the late 1990s, all provinces had elected their leaders, and elections became customary. Although Yeltsin removed two elected governors in October 1993, this practice ended with the adoption of the new constitution in December 1993. Deputies in regional legislatures were also elected, although the regional executives tend to overshadow the legislative branches. Regions gained additional authority by signing bilateral treaties with Moscow in the mid-1990s, although many agreements have not been fully implemented. Since coming into office in 2000, President Vladimir Putin has attempted to recapture authority from subnational leaders – an issue we will revisit in Chapter 5.

In contrast, Kyrgyzstan's constitution in the mid-1990s labeled the country a "unitary republic" and granted no autonomous powers to

---

[28] Subnational autonomy extends to lower levels of government as well. Territories generally elect local executives and legislatures, and local governments, provincial capitals in particular, have claimed greater authority for themselves.

subnational governments. The presidential administration appoints and frequently dismisses regional executives and, in the past, their lower-level counterparts. In practice, regional executives are the most powerful officials at the provincial level. Citizens elect deputies to their regional *kenesh* (council), but the presidential administration must approve the selection of the chairperson. Moreover, the role of the councils is to approve and implement policy rather than to create it. A deputy in the province of Osh confirmed this role, saying, "The laws are made by the Zhogorku Kenesh [national parliament]. We simply review laws."[29]

In sum, central authority in Kyrgyzstan manifests itself through the appointment of executives and *kenesh* chairs and through the minimal responsibility granted to the elected representative bodies. Through a constitutional referendum in 2002, the national government devolved some authority to local governments and representative bodies. Chapter 5 explores the impact of this change.

Economic Differences. Russia and Kyrgyzstan also differ socioeconomically, as the data in Table 1.1 indicate. Thanks to the Soviet education system, literacy remains high in both countries, but other measures indicate that Kyrgyzstan is significantly less economically developed. In Kyrgyzstan, most people lack modern conveniences, many live in rural areas and work in agriculture, and half are poor. By contrast, nearly half of Russia's citizens have some modern amenity, a majority live in cities and work in the industrial or service sectors, and only one-third are poor. Socioeconomic theories of democratization would predict a greater likelihood of democracy in Russia than in Kyrgyzstan. For this reason also, these two states are interesting choices for exploring uneven democratic development within countries.

Kyrgyzstan is less economically developed because of its nomadic heritage and its poor resource endowment. The ancestors of

[29] Author's interview (81) with a deputy in the oblast parliament, Osh oblast, May 20, 1998. In the footnotes throughout the text, I cite the number of the interview, the position of the person, the location, and the date. I do not include the individual's name or other identifying information unless the person is a representative of a foreign group or a provider of background information in the capital cities or abroad. I take this approach in order to protect individuals from negative repercussions as a result of granting an interview. Representatives of foreign groups and providers of background information in the capital cities and abroad are not at risk.

TABLE I.I. *Socioeconomic Indicators for Russia and Kyrgyzstan*

Measures	Russia	Kyrgyzstan
Radios[a] (percentage of population owning, 1997)	42	11
Passenger cars (percentage of population owning, 1997)	12	3
Telephone lines[b] (percentage of population owning, 1997)	19	8
Urbanization (percentage of urban population, 1997)	73	35
Agricultural employment (percentage of employed, 1997)	12	48
Poverty[c] (percentage of population, 1993–1999)	31	51
Ratio of costs to income[d] (percentage, 1996)	45	100

Note: Comparable data for the two countries are not available in all cases, so I provide a variety of data, the aggregate of which suggest that Kyrgyzstan is less developed than Russia. Figures are rounded to whole numbers.

[a] A radio receiver used for broadcast to the general public.

[b] A line connecting a customer's phone to the public switched telephone network. Cell phones are becoming increasingly common among the urban elite in both countries, but they are out of reach for most of the countries' people.

[c] The percentage of the population living below the poverty line deemed appropriate for the country by its authorities.

[d] The difference between the countries is exaggerated because average monetary income was used for Russia and average salary was used for Kyrgyzstan. Comparable figures are not available.

Sources: All data except for urbanization and agricultural employment are from The World Bank, *2001 World Development Indicators* (CD-ROM), The World Bank, November 1, 2001. Figures for urbanization and agricultural employment are from The World Bank, Gonca Okur (e-mail correspondence), Development Data Group, The World Bank, November 8–15, 2002.

contemporary Kyrgyz were nomads who migrated from the upper Yenisei River in present-day Russia in the late 900s and early 1700s. They found new pastures in the western Tien Shan Mountains in territory that is now part of Kyrgyzstan. The nomads herded horses and camels and traveled in an *aul,* a group of 100 or more yurts. Each yurt housed a nuclear family, and each *aul* was largely economically self-sufficient and self-governing. Periodically *auls* engaged in battle with each other. The Kyrgyz had no literary language and were mostly illiterate until they came under Russian influence in the 1860s. The nomads began to settle only in the late 1920s during the Soviet sedentarization campaign. In the 1960s, Moscow recognized the importance of nomadic products, such as hides and dairy goods, and reversed policy, encouraging the remaining nomads to continue their way of life.[30] To this day, a small number of Kyrgyz continue to live as nomads.

By contrast, in the early 20th century, the territory of contemporary Russia was home to peasant villages, provincial towns, and industrial centers. Most Russians were peasants, although by the early 1900s many spent part or all of the year working as industrial laborers in cities. Provincial towns had local administrations, merchants, schools, a market, and in some cases a railroad stop. Major cities included St. Petersburg, Moscow, and Rostov, where steel plants and machine-building factories employed hundreds or thousands of workers. At this time, the government extended over a vast territory and performed numerous functions. It supported a currency and a banking system, oversaw a complex tax structure, directed foreign capital, funded a multiforce military, administered a draft, provided for a police force, and educated children in primary schools. Although literacy was not widespread among the peasantry, elites and urban residents enjoyed a strong literary tradition, thousands of periodicals, and a university system.[31]

Soviet social and economic policies narrowed the development gap between the two territories, although Kyrgyzstan still lags behind. Contemporary Kyrgyzstan has the features of a modern country: a sedentary population, a major city, multiple towns, factories, railroads, a military, a currency, a banking system, primary and secondary education, and universities. However, different natural resource endowments help maintain the development divide. With 49 billion barrels in proven oil reserves and 48 billion barrels in proven natural gas reserves, Russia is rich in natural resources.[32] Exports of these commodities have helped the Russian government fill its coffers. By contrast,

[30] Elizabeth E. Bacon, *Central Asians under Russian Rule: A Study in Culture Change* (Ithaca, NY: Cornell University Press, 1966), 123–124.
[31] Sheila Fitzpatrick, *The Russian Revolution*, 2nd ed. (Oxford: Oxford University Press, 1994), 16–19.
[32] Jan H. Kalicki, "Caspian Energy at the Crossroads," *Foreign Affairs* 80 (September–October, 2001), 123.

Kyrgyzstan has only small amounts of gold, mercury, and uranium, forcing the government to rely solely on foreign aid for large infusions of capital.

Cultural Differences. Conventional wisdom is that democracy faces greater cultural obstacles in Kyrgyzstan than in Russia, further making the inclusion of these two countries in the study useful. Outsiders view Kyrgyz, as well as other Central Asians, as primitive, passive, and traditional. Kyrgyz seem primitive because their recent ancestors were nomadic and their country is not economically advanced. They appear passive because they did not mount large protests against incorporation into the Russian Empire or in pursuit of greater autonomy from the Soviet Union. Finally, Kyrgyz seem traditional because they respect *aksakals* ("white beards," or elderly men), maintain kinship-based allegiances, and identify themselves as Muslims. By contrast, Russia is seen as a more advanced, aggressive, and modern country.

According to observers of the region, Kyrgyz and Central Asian culture more broadly hinder democratic development.[33] Abdummanob Polat, Chairman of the Human Rights Society of Uzbekistan, argues that tradition, such as respect for authority, poses an obstacle to the emergence of civil society in the Western sense.[34] Eugene Huskey, writing about Kyrgyzstan, notes that "[a]mid the strains of the transition from communism, civic traditions have shown little evidence of taking root in a society dominated by a mixture of family, clan, regional, and ethnic loyalties."[35] Kathleen Collins argues that "the fledgling civil and political society [in Kyrgyzstan] has been crowded out by wider support for clan networks."[36] Some scholars have argued that democracy is

---

[33] Karen Dawisha and Bruce Parrott, *Russia and the New States of Eurasia: The Politics of Upheaval* (Cambridge: Cambridge University Press, 1994), 147–148; Gregory Gleason, *The Central Asian States: Discovering Independence* (Boulder, CO: Westview Press, 1997), 37–39, 176–177.

[34] Abdumannob Polat, "Can Uzbekistan Build Democracy and Civil Society?" in *Civil Society in Central Asia*, ed. M. Holt Ruffin and Daniel Clarke Waugh (Seattle: University of Washington Press, 1999), 153.

[35] Eugene Huskey, "Kyrgyzstan: The Fate of Political Liberalization," in *Conflict, Cleavage, and Change in Central Asia and the Caucasus*, ed. Karen Dawisha and Bruce Parrott (Cambridge: Cambridge University Press, 1997), 267.

[36] Kathleen Collins, "The Logic of Clan Politics: Evidence from Central Asian Trajectories," *World Politics* 56 (January, 2004), 249.

less compatible with Islam than with Judeo–Christian culture.[37] These conclusions bode poorly for democracy in Kyrgyzstan.

Four Regions

Within each country, my study focuses on two regions – a more democratic oblast (province) and a less democratic oblast. Because some aspects of democracy can exist without others – for example, elections without a free press – the investigation evaluates multiple components of democracy.[38] The study avoids using proxy measures, such as public

---

[37] M. Steven Fish, "Islam and Authoritarianism," *World Politics* 55 (October, 2002), 4–37; Samuel P. Huntington, *The Clash of Civilizations and the Remaking of World Order* (New York: Simon and Schuster, 1996), 29; Lipset, "The Social Requisites of Democracy Revisited," 5; Daniel Pipes, *In the Path of God: Islam and Political Power* (New York: Basic Books, 1983), 145–146, 188.

[38] Numerous studies of the former Soviet Union have illuminated our understanding of democracy by focusing on individual components, including elections, voting, civic and political groups, media, or formal institutions. For example, on elections, see Colton and Hough, *Growing Pains*; Timothy J. Colton and Michael McFaul, *Popular Choice and Managed Democracy: The Russian Elections of 1999 and 2000* (Washington, DC: Brookings Institution Press, 2003); Timothy Frye, "Markets, Democracy, and New Private Business in Russia," *Post-Soviet Affairs* 19 (January–March, 2003), 24–45; Hale, "Explaining Machine Politics"; Stephen White, Richard Rose, and Ian McAllister, *How Russia Votes* (Chatham, NJ: Chatham House Publishers, 1997). As examples of studies of voting, consider the numerous articles by Richard Rose and Stephen White, as well as Timothy J. Colton, *Transitional Citizens: Voters and What Influences Them in the New Russia* (Cambridge, MA: Harvard University Press, 2000); Ted Brader and Joshua A. Tucker, "The Emergence of Mass Partisanship in Russia, 1993–1996," *American Journal of Political Science* 45 (January, 2001), 69–83. The following works concentrate on civic and political groups: M. Holt Ruffin and Daniel Clarke Waugh, *Civil Society in Central Asia* (Seattle: University of Washington Press, 1999); Fish, *Democracy from Scratch*; Henry E. Hale, "Why Not Parties? Electoral Markets, Party Substitutes, and Stalled Democratization in Russia," *Comparative Politics* 37 (January, 2005), 147–166; Marc Morjé Howard, *The Weakness of Civil Society in Post–Communist Europe* (Cambridge: Cambridge University Press, 2003); Valerie Sperling, *Organizing Women in Contemporary Russia: Engendering Transition* (Cambridge: Cambridge University Press, 1999). Also consider Robert G. Moser's numerous works on political parties. Multiple studies of the media have been conducted by Ellen Mickiewicz. Works that focus on formal institutions include: Pauline Jones Luong, *Institutional Change and Political Continuity in Post-Soviet Central Asia: Power, Perceptions, and Pacts* (Cambridge: Cambridge University Press, 2002); Steven S. Smith and Thomas F. Remington, *The Politics of Institutional Choice: The Formation of the Russian State Duma* (Princeton, NJ: Princeton University Press, 2001); Stoner-Weiss, *Local Heroes*.

opinion and incumbent turnover rates.[39] People may support democratic rights but not be able to exercise them. Similarly, low turnover
rates may suggest weak contestation in a region, but alternatively they
could indicate that residents are satisfied with their leaders. Instead,
using Dahl's definition of democracy, I directly measure the degree to
which the following eight components of democracy exist: alternative sources of information, freedom to form and join organizations,
eligibility for public office, the right of political leaders to compete
for support, freedom of expression, the right to vote, free and fair
elections, and institutions for making government policies depend on
voters' preferences.[40]

To select the four regions, I conducted a survey of experts of regional
politics in each country, in which these individuals ranked levels of
democracy in the regions based on Dahl's definition.[41] Besides assisting in case selection, these surveys depict the uneven development of
democracy within these countries. Prior to these surveys, no ranking
of democracy in Russian and Kyrgyzstani regions existed.[42] Appendix
A describes the surveys and their results in-depth.

[39] Other common proxy measures include voter turnout and the percentage of votes
cast for winning candidates. See, for example, Christopher Marsh, "Measuring and
Explaining Variations in Russian Regional Democratisation," in *Russian Politics
under Putin*, ed. Cameron Ross (Manchester: Manchester University Press, 2004),
176–197.

[40] Dahl, *Polyarchy*, 2–3.

[41] Had I selected provinces randomly, it is likely that I would not have had any more
democratic regions because these are the exception rather than the rule. Moreover, matching regions was preferable to random selection because there are few
provinces in Kyrgyzstan. Choosing regions based on hypotheses about uneven development was also ill-advised because there are no existing theories about subnational
democracy. Hypotheses could have been grossly inaccurate and could have mis-
guided the research. See Gary King, Robert O. Keohane, and Sidney Verba, *Designing
Social Inquiry: Scientific Inference in Qualitative Research* (Princeton, NJ: Princeton
University Press, 1994), 126.

[42] Freedom House measures democracy across countries, not within countries. In Russia
foreign democracy-promoting organizations either just evaluate the effectiveness of
their own programs or assess regional politics based only on personal experience,
advice from the Russian government, and word-of-mouth. The National Democratic
Institute and the United States Agency for International Development take the first
approach, and the United States Peace Corps and the European Union program Technical Assistance to the Commonwealth of Independent States (TACIS) take the second approach. Banks and credit agencies have begun to rate regions of Russia, but
these organizations are more interested in political stability than democracy. Since
conducting the Russian survey with me, Nikolai Petrov has continued to evaluate

The regions I chose from the experts' rankings were clearly identified as more democratic or less democratic, and they share borders and
socioeconomic characteristics. Choosing provinces with undisputed
ratings helped ensure that levels of democracy really did differ between
the two regions in each country, whereas matching socioeconomic characteristics controlled some possible influences on democracy. There is
no doubt that a region's wealth or level of modernity can affect its political system; however, democratization in Latin America and Southern
Europe has shown that these basic characteristics do not determine
democratization. Explanations like "poverty precludes democracy and
wealth sustains it"[43] are not very helpful because intervening factors,
such as citizens' individual decisions, connect these socioeconomic conditions and democratic or nondemocratic outcomes.[44]

I conducted fieldwork in the four regions in 1997 and 1998, measuring democracy in order to confirm that the experts' evaluations were
correct and gathering information to determine why one region was
more democratic than the other in each country. I conducted interviews,
observed regional legislatures, analyzed the content of media reports,

democracy in Russia's regions using a different approach. He includes economic
liberalization as one indicator, which does not reflect Dahl's definition of democracy. See Freedom House, *Freedom in the World*, Freedom in the World Series (New
York: Freedom House, 1978–2002); Author's interview (251) with Boris Iarochevitch,
First Secretary, Delegation of the European Commission in Russia, European Union,
Moscow, March 11, 1998; Author's interview (250) with Andrei Melnikov, Director of Programs, Western Russia, Peace Corps, Moscow, March 10, 1998. Tom
Melia of the National Democratic Institute's Washington office provided informa-
tion about his organization in a phone conversation with me in the winter of 1997.
See also *Predprinimatel'skii klimat regionov Rossii: geografiia Rossii dlia investorov
i predprinimatelei* (Moscow: Nachala-Press, 1997); Nikolai Petrov, "Regional Models of Democratic Development," in *Between Dictatorship and Democracy: Russian
Post-communist Political Reform*, ed. Michael McFaul, Nikolai Petrov, and Andrei
Ryabov (Washington, DC: Carnegie Endowment for International Peace, 2004),
239–267.

43 This idea is paraphrased from Lipset, "Some Social Requisites of Democracy." Lipset
amended his conclusions in "The Social Requisites of Democracy Revisited."

44 The debate between Adam Przeworski et al. and Carles Boix and Susan Stokes
emphasizes the complexity of the relationship between economic development and
democracy. See Boix and Stokes, "Endogenous Democratization"; Adam Przeworski,
Michael E. Alvarez, Jose Antonio Cheibub, and Fernando Limongi, *Democracy
and Development: Political Institutions and Material Well-Being in the World,
1950–1990* (New York: Cambridge University Press, 2000); Adam Przeworski and
Fernando Limongi, "Modernization: Theories and Facts," *World Politics* 49 (1997),
155–183.

gathered socioeconomic and electoral statistics, and conversed with average citizens while I lived in each province.

Samara and Ul'ianovsk. From Russia, I selected Samara oblast as the more democratic region and Ul'ianovsk oblast as the less democratic region. The two regions share geographical features, historical memories, and socioeconomic conditions. Located along the Volga River in the European part of Russia, Samara and Ul'ianovsk were once joined together in Kuibyshev oblast (see Map 1 on p. 23). Both are home to large Russian majorities as well as various ethnic minorities, including Tatars, Chuvashes, Mordvins, and Ukrainians. The average income in both oblasts is lower than the average for the entire country (487,300 rubles),[45] and levels of unemployment and urbanization are similar in the two oblasts, as noted in Table 1.2.

Of course, it is impossible to match provinces completely. Samara and Ul'ianovsk differ most dramatically in population size and population density, with Samara having twice as many people as Ul'ianovsk and almost twice as many people per square kilometer. Also, the average income and the cost of living are slightly higher in Samara.[46] Statistics provide only a partial picture of these provinces, so to better understand life in these regions, I spent time in both Samara and Ul'ianovsk.

After a 17-hour overnight train ride from Moscow, I arrived in Samara oblast's provincial capital of the same name in the dead of winter. Old wooden buildings with the traditional Russian "gingerbread," classical pastel structures, and a few new, fashionable brick apartment complexes fill the city center. Factories and enormous Soviet-style apartment buildings surround the city. During World War II, much of Russia's industry and government, including underground offices

---

[45] Michael McFaul and Nikolai Petrov, eds., *Politicheskii al'manakh Rossii 1997: sotsial'no-politicheskie portrety regionov*, vol. 2 (Moscow: Tsentr Karnegi, 1997).

[46] The higher population density in Samara likely does not account for the greater ease of practicing democracy in the region even though it might increase anonymity. As Chapter 6 elaborates, activists cannot be both anonymous and effective. Relative to the rest of the regions of Russia, Samara and Ul'ianovsk are very similar. Of Russia's 57 oblasts, *krais*, and federal cities, Samara and Ul'ianovsk fall within seven places of one another in a ranking of regions by their income–subsistence ratio. In terms of the percentage of Russians living in each region, Samara and Ul'ianovsk are within nine places of one another. Samara and Ul'ianovsk fall in the 36th and 43rd places, respectively, in a ranking of territory in descending order. These calculations are based on data from *Predprinimatel'skii klimat regionov Rossii: geografiia Rossii dlia investorov i predprinimatelei.*

TABLE 1.2. *Characteristics of the Russian Regions*

	Samara	Ul'ianovsk
Economic Characteristics		
Average income, 1995 (rubles)	394,400	276,300
Minimum consumer budget, 1995 (rubles)	243,900	131,800
Budget as a percentage of income, 1995 (percentage)	61.8	47.7
Industrial gross regional product, 1998 (percentage of total)	39.2	35.8
Employment in industry, 1998 (percentage of total)	29.8	29.0
Unemployment, 1997 (percentage)[a]	4.5	4.6
Social Characteristics		
Population, 1995 (persons)	3,305,000	1,492,300
Population density, 1995 (persons per 100 square kilometers)	6,166	4,001
Urban residents, 1995 (percentage)	80.4	72.6
Ethnic Composition, 1995 (percentage)		
Russian	83.4	72.8
Chuvash	3.6	8.4
Mordvin	3.6	4.4
Tatar	3.5	11.4
Ukrainian	2.5	1.3
Geographic Characteristics		
Territory, 1995 (square kilometers)	53,600	37,300
Region of Russia	Volga region	Volga region

Note: This table provides data from 1997 and 1998 unless they were unavailable at the time that I conducted research in the regions. In that case, I use data from earlier years.

[a] Official unemployment statistics tend to be based on those who have registered as unemployed and thus they underestimate unemployment.

Sources: Data for employment in industry and unemployment are from *Regiony Rossii, 1999: statisticheskii sbornik*, vol. 2 (Moscow: Goskomstat Rossii, 1999), 32, 80, 88. Data for industrial gross regional product are from *Regiony Rossii, 1999: statisticheskii sbornik*, vol. 1 (Moscow: Goskomstat Rossii, 1999), 233, 245. Remaining data are from *Politicheskii al'manakh Rossii 1995*, eds. Michael McFaul and Nikolai Petrov (Moscow: Carnegie Moscow Center, Carnegie Endowment for International Peace, 1995), 512, 590.

for Joseph Stalin, were evacuated to Samara, then called Kuibyshev, and the city became the temporary capital of the Soviet Union. As the Germans invaded western towns, Soviet people, including my host family's Jewish relatives, also evacuated to Samara. Building upon the evacuated industries, the provincial capital became a center for defense production and research and a "closed city" from 1935 to 1991. Despite its prestige as a technological center, the city was known in the Soviet era for its consumer product shortages. Seventy kilometers north, beyond a bend in the Volga, Samara oblast's second city, Tol'iatti, enjoyed a very different existence. In 1964, an automobile plant was completed as a joint venture with the Italian firm Fiat, and the city was renamed to honor the Italian communist leader. The province of Samara today is home to this Volga Automobile Factory (Volzhskii avtomobil'nyi zavod, or AvtoVAZ) as well as defense, oil-processing, and chemical plants. As in much of Russia, these factories have faced economic challenges in the independence period.

Months earlier, I took a similar train ride to Ul'ianovsk city, the capital of Ul'ianovsk oblast. The Volga River divides the city of Ul'ianovsk into two parts. The Old City, on the west bank, houses government, shopping districts, media firms, some of the population, and a few factories in gingerbread, classical, and Soviet-era buildings. The New City consists largely of the airplane factory Aviastar and blocks of colossal Soviet-style apartment complexes and shops built for Aviastar employees. My hostess was once part of this massive industry, having worked on an assembly line preparing airplane parts. Like Samara, Ul'ianovsk, earlier called Simbirsk, is built upon the evacuated factories of World War II. Ul'ianovsk also became a military-industrial center, although never a closed city, and it is home to the Ul'ianovsk Automobile Factory (Ul'ianovskii avtomobil'nyi zavod, or UAZ). Since the collapse of the Soviet Union, all these heavy industries have faced economic difficulties. Recognized not only as the home of Aviastar and the UAZ, Ul'ianovsk is also known for being V. I. Lenin's birthplace and namesake.[47]

Osh and Naryn. From Kyrgyzstan, I selected Osh oblast as the more democratic region and Naryn oblast as the less democratic region.

---

[47] Lenin's family name was originally Ul'ianov.

MAP 1. The four regions, 1998. Map drawn by Jacquline Johnson.

Osh and Naryn share a border as well as economic characteristics. Although wages are higher in Naryn, expenses are also greater in this mountainous region so that in Osh and Naryn expenses represent almost identical percentages of income. The level of unemployment in

TABLE 1.3. *Characteristics of the Kyrgyzstani Regions*

	Osh	Naryn
Economic Characteristics		
Average wage, 1997 (soms)	498.8	630.8
Minimum consumer budget, 1997 (soms)	492.2	593.5
Budget as a percentage of wages, 1997 (percentage)	98.6	94.1
Industrial gross regional product, 1997 (percentage of total)	3.0	1.8
Unemployment, 1996 (percentage)[a]	8.4	8.2
Social Characteristics		
Population, 1997 (persons)	1,472,100	263,100
Population density, 1997 (persons per 100 square kilometers)	3,186	582
Urban residents, 1995 (percentage)	25.3	21.3
Ethnic composition, 1997 (percentage)		
Kyrgyz	63.6	98.0
Uzbek	28.1	0.5
Russian	2.5	0.6
Geographic Characteristics		
Territory, 1997 (square kilometers)	46,200	45,200
Region of Kyrgyzstan	south	"north"[b]

Note: This table primarily provides data from 1997 and 1998, when I conducted research in the regions; however, in some cases, statistics for those years were not available.

[a] Official counts show 2.3 percent unemployed in Osh oblast and 7.1 percent unemployed in Naryn oblast.

[b] For the purposes of this study, I labeled Naryn as northern because neither those living in the north nor those in the south consider it a southern province.

Sources: Average wage and minimum consumer budget data are from *Bulletin of the National Bank of the Kyrgyz Republic* 1, no. 13 (1997). I obtained unemployment, population, urban residency, ethnic, and territory data directly from the National Statistics Committee. Industrial gross regional product numbers are from "Chapter V: Regions," *National Human Development Report for the Kyrgyz Republic 1999*, The United Nations Human Development Programme in Kyrgyzstan, http://www.undp.bishkek.su/english/publications/nhdr1999/chapter 5.html.

the two regions is also nearly identical. Table 1.3 provides the specific figures.

Like the Russian provinces, Osh and Naryn exhibit differences, particularly in terms of their populations. Nearly one-third of the population in Osh is Uzbek, and only 64 percent is Kyrgyz, whereas the population of Naryn is 98 percent Kyrgyz. Furthermore, the population size and density of Osh are each approximately five times greater than in Naryn.

Although they are neighbors, Osh and Naryn are considered to be in different parts of Kyrgyzstan. Citizens of Kyrgyzstan have tended to view their country as having a southern part composed of the provinces of Osh and Dzhalal-Abad and a northern part composed of the capital city Bishkek and the provinces of Chui, Issik-Kul', and Talas.[48] Northerners tend to characterize the south as more Muslim, more Uzbek, and as culturally and economically underdeveloped, whereas they consider the north as more developed, in part because of the Russian influence. In referring to the north, residents of Kyrgyzstan do not usually list Naryn as a northern province. Geographically, it is directly east of the southern province of Dzhalal-Abad. Moreover, Naryn is almost devoid of Russians and is considered economically underdeveloped. It is often referred to as the true, pristine Kyrgyzstan. Regardless, the regional label is moot because citizens of Kyrgyzstan rate Osh, a province of the "backward" south, as more democratic than Naryn, a province clearly not a member of the "backward" south.

To obtain more complete pictures of Osh and Naryn, I lived in each of the regions. After a 45-minute plane ride from Bishkek on the national airline, Kyrgyzstan Aba Zholdoru, I arrived in the provincial capital of Osh oblast, also called Osh, during the first days of summer. An enormous outdoor bazaar dominates the city center, where I lived with a Kyrgyz family. On the blocks surrounding the bazaar, vendors sell produce and preserved vegetables, and kiosks offer haircuts and the latest Western videos. Cafés and teahouses spill out of the bazaar area onto adjacent streets, which end in quiet neighborhoods of Soviet-built apartment buildings, businesses, and government offices. In the busier districts, Russian, American, Kyrgyz, and Uzbek music blares, and dust and the buttery smell of *nan* (flatbread) fill the air. Located in the Ferghana Valley and bordering China, Tajikistan, and Uzbekistan, the province is the southernmost oblast of Kyrgyzstan.[49] Once a trading post on the ancient Silk Road, the region is now home to agriculture and

---

[48] Since I conducted this study, Batken oblast has been formed from part of Osh oblast.
[49] This distinction is now shared with Batken oblast.

a variety of industries, including cotton and food processing, machine building, and mining. As in Russia, most of these economic sectors face difficulties.

The previous summer, I had decided against air travel in favor of a bus from Bishkek to Naryn oblast. After five breakdowns and numerous stops for hitchhikers, the bus delivered me and my fellow passengers through the mountains to the small town of Naryn, the provincial capital. The town consists of a main street from which roads run for a few blocks until they abut brush-dotted, tree-covered, or snow-capped mountains. Along the main street, a couple of kiosks offer newspapers, and a few middle-aged women sell candy bars or packages of cookies from small tables. Ubiquitous miniature picket fences painted a brilliant blue divide parks from squares and government buildings from small apartment complexes. Off the main street, asphalt and dirt roads lead to clusters of single-family homes, including the one where I lived with a Kyrgyz family. High walls surrounding each home keep the dust from the roads out of the courtyards, gardens, and animal pens. The province borders China and boasts agricultural concerns, food processing, construction-material manufacturing, and mining, although few industries work at full capacity.

Outside the Former Soviet Union

A comparison of these four post-Soviet provinces will illustrate the importance of economic autonomy to democracy. The influence of economic autonomy is also apparent in other regions of the world where the state has an economic monopoly. To demonstrate this by replicating my investigation in other parts of the world would be a time-consuming and expensive endeavor. Using a proxy for economic autonomy to analyze a large number of countries might lead to skewed results, as the sources of economic autonomy depend on the institutional, cultural, and broader economic contexts of a territory. This is not to suggest that creating a cross-national measure of economic autonomy is impossible, but merely that it is a task for another investigation. Instead, for the purposes of this book, I rely on the research of other scholars who offer clues about economic autonomy in China, Africa, the Middle East, the Americas, and Europe.

OUTLINE OF THE BOOK

The concept of economic autonomy is described thoroughly in Chapter 2. Before moving on to the puzzle of variation in democratic development, we pause in Chapter 3 to consider two methodological issues. Specifically, Chapter 3 lays out a model of how components of democracy interact and a plan for operationalizing Dahl's definition of democracy. In Chapter 4, I present the puzzle of the four provinces, confirming with extensive evidence from the field that democracy is, in fact, weaker in Ul'ianovsk and Naryn relative to Samara and Osh, respectively. Chapter 5 applies the concept of economic autonomy to the puzzle of the four provinces and to other regions of the world. In Chapter 6, I explore how the concept of economic autonomy and the model of interaction among components of democracy shed light on the global proliferation of hybrid regimes.

2

The Concept of Economic Autonomy

Economic autonomy, the ability to earn a living independent of the state, operates at both the individual and regional levels. The degree of *personal* economic autonomy determines a citizen's willingness to challenge local authorities or, alternatively, to practice self-censorship.[1] In hybrid regimes, the risk to citizens is that they will lose their jobs or businesses if they oppose state authorities. To punish those who challenge them, officials fire activists or interfere with their companies by disconnecting utilities, ending leases, denying access to equipment, and conducting bogus fire, sanitation, or tax inspections.[2] More severe punishments, such as jail time or death, are less common since government

---

[1] Which government officials pose a risk depends on the target of an individual's activism. For instance, members of a political group formed to expose city officials' corrupt practices need economic autonomy from the city government. Because this book investigates uneven democratic development at the regional level, the focus is on provincial officials.

[2] Some of these livelihood punishments are similar to violations that occur in advanced democracies. Periodic cases of authorities threatening the livelihoods of activists in advanced democracies are not surprising because these countries, despite their label, only approximate the democratic ideals. For example, in the 2002 mayoral race in Newark, New Jersey, city employees were threatened with dismissal for their support of the opponent. A business owner, a supporter of the opposition, had his company shut down by city officials under questionable circumstances, and firefighters faced reprisals when their union came out in support of the opponent. The key differences between government violations in democracies and those in hybrid regimes are the frequency of the punishments and the possibilities for avoiding and eliminating them. See Andrew Jacobs, "Newark Relives Day of Machine in Mayor's Race," *New York Times*, April 9, 2002, 1, 28.

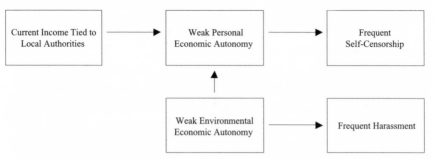

FIGURE 2.1. Economic autonomy and political activism

officials have made some commitment – genuine or insincere – to democratic liberties. Fearing sanctions against their livelihood, citizens with little economic autonomy will self-censor, meaning they will avoid oppositional activity. Either they will not engage in the civic sphere at all or they will engage but they will not challenge authority. For example, an individual may establish a newspaper but never print any criticism of local officials. Current activists whose economic autonomy declines or who initially miscalculated their economic autonomy may self-censor by abandoning their civic pursuits or making them less oppositional. In aggregate, these individual decisions about the risks of activism shape the practice of democracy in a region.

The extent of *environmental* economic autonomy, or opportunities in a province for earning income beyond the reach of local authorities, informs individual decision making and helps account for the frequency of workplace harassment. Namely, in regions providing little economic autonomy, only those few individuals with *personal* economic autonomy will risk civic pursuits. Also, in these regions, government punishments are more effective, and thus officials have a greater incentive to employ them. Because the degree of economic autonomy can vary among territories, democracy is stronger in some regions than in others. Figure 2.1 depicts these relationships.

PERSONAL ECONOMIC AUTONOMY

Individuals calculate their *personal* economic autonomy based on their current means of earning income and their possibilities for finding a different job. Employment at an enterprise directed or owned by the provincial government, entrepreneurship limited to one's home region, and a deficit of skills critical to the government all reduce an individual's economic autonomy.

Workplaces under the influence of the provincial government may include regional government organs, schools, hospitals, enterprises, and privatized businesses in which the provincial government holds a controlling number of shares. Provincial government officials may also have significant control over county, city, and village organs by appointing their leaders. Provincial authorities may try to influence local branches of national institutions by denying office space, utilities, and employee housing. However, activists who head divisions of national institutions can avoid or combat local harassment by requesting support from officials in their country's capital.

Private businesspeople who do not earn sufficient profits from outside their region can easily be deterred from activism by groundless fines levied by government tax, fire, and sanitation inspectors. Other forms of government pressure, such as tampering with utilities and denial of office space and equipment, are also more difficult to combat without cash and allies from outside the region. Media entrepreneurs face an additional set of informal government restrictions, including bogus libel lawsuits, pressure on advertisers, and information unnecessarily withheld from reporters.

Most people do not have skills that are in such great demand that they can withstand government harassment. In the former Soviet Union, doctors are an exception to this rule. As a result of the health and education crises in post-Soviet countries, doctors' years of training protect them from government punishments. If local authorities harass a doctor, even one who works at a provincial clinic, she may take her services to a more welcoming region. This bargaining power allays doctors' fears of engaging in political activity. Other professions, such as teaching, management, and engineering, do not afford this protection because these fields do not require as extensive training. Moreover, these professions are not as immediately essential to the population.

In the former Soviet Union, most individuals who do not earn income have little economic autonomy. Three groups of adults do not earn income – the unemployed, retirees, and unpaid workers. The unemployed and retired typically receive small benefits from the national government. Provincial authorities have been able to post-pone payments,[3] thus weakening the economic autonomy of these individuals. The nonpayment of wages has been a common problem in postcommunist states; people continue to work, but they receive their salaries months late, if at all. Those unpaid employees who work at an enterprise directed or owned by the provincial government or who lack critical skills also have little economic autonomy. If they hope to someday receive their salaries, they may not risk engaging in politi-cal activism. However, many unpaid workers engage in petty trade or some other business in order to survive. If their entrepreneurial ven-tures earn sufficient income from outside their region, the individuals increase their economic autonomy.[4]

Among individuals with paying jobs, some people with little auton-omy from local authorities will engage in political activity. For this to occur, these individuals must believe that they could find employ-ment outside the influence of local officials were they to lose their current positions. Opportunities for jobs beyond the reach of local government are determined by an individual's skills, as in the case of doctors, but also by the extent of *environmental* economic autonomy.

ENVIRONMENTAL ECONOMIC AUTONOMY

Environmental economic autonomy exists when the characteristics of a province enable businesses to be profitable and earn income from out-side the borders of the region. Territories that attract foreign capital and produce goods and services that are coveted and transportable out-side of the area offer greater economic autonomy. Measures of foreign direct investment and exports can reflect the degree of *environmental*

---

[3] Jerry F. Hough, *The Logic of Economic Reform in Russia* (Washington, DC: Brookings Institution Press, 2001).

[4] Even unpaid workers, unemployed people, and retirees with economic autonomy rarely engage in long-term activism. Unemployed and unpaid workers spend their time seeking income and therefore typically are not politically active. Among the retired, there are some middle-aged activists who previously worked in the military and now live primarily off their retirement benefits. Most retired people, however, are senior cit-izens. Seniors do engage in street protests, a form of civic involvement that requires no commitment or adaptation to the new economic and political orders. But, because of their age, they rarely engage in long-term activism, such as running a nongovernmental organization (NGO).

economic autonomy. However, broader economic, cultural, and institutional contexts, such as level of development, commercial traditions, and center–periphery relations in a country, also shape the sources of autonomy in a particular territory.

In the former Soviet Union, financial success through outside contacts is the best guarantee of economic autonomy. Soviet economic legacies make government interference in this type of commerce the most difficult and therefore the least likely. Businesses earning profits outside their regions tend to be newly established, under new ownership, or experienced operating illegally in the Soviet period. As a result, local officials cannot draw on tried and true Soviet-era patterns of interference. Instead, to harass businesses with outside contacts authorities have to learn the dynamics of the new market economy and expend the resources to create new institutions for interference, such as marketing boards and border posts. Organs of local government and companies in which local officials hold significant shares are easier targets. To punish individuals in these organs and firms, local authorities can revert to techniques of workplace harassment from the Soviet era,[5] when the state owned all places of employment. Citizens are aware that government reprisals are most likely in the old economy. They know that success in the new market economy, coupled with the inertia of Soviet patterns of interference, will afford them protection from local authorities.

It would be easy to dilute the idea of economic autonomy to one of private ownership. However, this would be inaccurate. The term "private" has meant little in the postcommunist world in particular. Here government organs, individual officials, and their friends and family often own controlling numbers of shares in private firms,[6] and authorities manipulate state inspections, credit, and leasing to

---

[5] In the Soviet era, the Communist Party would punish dissidents by refusing to let them work in their professions. A leading scientist would be reassigned as a boiler operator, for example. See Stephen Crowley, *Hot Coal, Cold Steel: Russian and Ukrainian Workers from the End of the Soviet Union to the Post-communist Transformations* (Ann Arbor: University of Michigan Press, 1997), 51, 82–91; M. Steven Fish, *Democracy from Scratch*, 162–165.

[6] Andrew Barnes, "Russia's New Business Groups and State Power," *Post-Soviet Affairs* 19 (2003), 176.

dominate businesses owned by their adversaries.[7] Successful firms with outside contacts are the truly independent enterprises. They are able to pay repeated groundless fines with profits earned beyond the provincial borders, and they can obtain financing, lease equipment, and rent space outside the region.

Similarly, it would be a mistake to equate economic autonomy with high employment levels. Only certain jobs provide protection from the punishments of local authorities. It is possible for there to be an abundance of jobs but few that offer economic autonomy. Or, there could be limited employment opportunities in a region, but residents may be able to devise new ways to earn income and to earn it independently of local authorities.

In provinces that offer greater economic autonomy, citizens calculate that civic activity is not risky, and thus they do not avoid the public sphere or censor their political actions. By contrast, people in regions that provide little economic autonomy fear that engaging in oppositional activity could undermine their economic survival. This anxiety deters potential activists. Authorities do not have to punish behaviors in order for activists to fear engaging in them; weak economic autonomy is sufficient. Moreover, weak economic autonomy forces individuals who take a chance with activism to either abandon their pursuits or practice self-censorship. In provinces that offer limited autonomy, only those few individuals with jobs or skills that enable them to withstand harassment will engage in oppositional activity.

Besides influencing citizens' decisions about activism, the extent of *environmental* economic autonomy also seems to affect the frequency of punishments in a province. In regions where people have greater economic autonomy, government harassment is less effective. More jobs are beyond the reach of authorities, so citizens are less apprehensive about finding such employment. When punishments are ineffective, officials are less likely to employ them. Where economic autonomy is limited, government reprisals are more successful. Local leaders can

---

7 Virginie Coulloudon, "Crime and Corruption after Communism: The Criminalization of Russia's Political Elite," *East European Constitutional Review* 6 (1997); Jadwiga Staniszkis, "Political Capitalism in Poland," *East European Politics and Societies* 5 (Winter, 1991), 127–141; David Stark, "Recombinant Property in East European Capitalism," *American Journal of Sociology* 101 (January, 1996), 993–1027.

interfere in a greater number of workplaces, and citizens are more fearful of losing their current jobs. Consequently, workplace harassment is more attractive to authorities.

In sum, economic autonomy reduces self-censorship and seems to decrease punishments, resulting in a richer civic environment. The aggregate of individuals' calculations about the risks of political involvement shapes the breadth and depth of oppositional activity in a region, and *personal* economic autonomy accounts for the behavior of the few activists in provinces that provide little economic autonomy. The extent of *environmental* economic autonomy helps define possibilities for personal economic independence and seems to influence the frequency of harassment.

ECONOMIC AUTONOMY AS A THEORETICAL FRAMEWORK

The concept of economic autonomy illuminates why some democratic transitions are completed and consolidated, whereas others falter or fail. In individuals' decisions to become and remain politically active, economic autonomy outweighs other factors, including interests, resources, and organizational capacity, each of which I consider in this section. In Appendix B, I explore additional alternative explanations – political opportunity structures, political institutions, leadership, and the international promotion of democracy. The concept of economic autonomy also helps us open the black box between stages of democratization by adding a territorial dimension to our understanding of these processes. A final theoretical advantage of the idea of economic autonomy is that it bridges competing approaches to explaining democratization and participation and therefore offers a more complete picture of these phenomena.

The Foremost Factor

Economic autonomy is necessary, but not sufficient, to the completion of democratic transition and consolidation. Democratic transition includes the extraction from the nondemocratic regime, the establishment of democratic institutions and liberties, and the observance of these new rules. Democratic consolidation is "a matter of the durability of rules that are the outcome of the transition process."[8] Economic autonomy is necessary to the completion of transition and to consolidation because it provides citizens with the capacity to use democratic institutions and exercise democratic rights. Citizens' activism, in turn, encourages government officials to abide by democratic procedures.

Economic autonomy is not, however, necessary for the onset of transition – the extraction from a nondemocratic regime and the establishment of democratic rules. Acute crises, such as military defeats or environmental tragedies, often spark transitions. When leading a normal existence is precluded by events or outweighed by a grander purpose, citizens are willing to risk their economic survival for civic purposes. For example, in the early 1990s, during the dismantling of the Soviet Union, street protests and political meetings were common in all four of the provinces. However, as in other parts of the world, the fervor of transition has since faded. Most people are unwilling to sacrifice their means of economic survival for long-term, more conventional engagement in public life.[9]

Economic autonomy is also not sufficient for either transition or consolidation. Other factors, including interests, resources, and organizational capacity, play a role in democratic activism as well. However, economic autonomy is more important than other influences because it is individuals' first consideration in their decisions to become and remain civically engaged.

Interests. Even people who have the passion to pursue a cause will cease civic activity if it threatens their economic survival. Participation

---

[8] I use these definitions in order to overcome a problem highlighted by Gerardo Munck. Traditionally, only the creation of democratic rules has been considered transition, whereas actors' attitudes and behaviors in relation to these rules are counted as consolidation. So, strangely, a regime with democratic rules on paper but not in practice would be considered to have completed a transition to democracy. See Gerardo L. Munck, "The Regime Question: Theory Building in Democracy Studies," *World Politics* 54 (October, 2001), 127–128.

[9] The distinction between short-term and long-term political engagement is an important one. Grzegorz Ekiert and Jan Kubik found that in Poland state workers were common among strikers. However, these strikes represented a short-term protest against national officials, not long-term oppositional activity against local officials. See Grzegorz Ekiert and Jan Kubik, *Rebellious Civil Society: Popular Protest and Democratic Consolidation in Poland, 1989–1993* (Ann Arbor: University of Michigan Press, 2001).

theories that emphasize interests argue that for people to engage collectively in the political sphere, they must share grievances.[10] This is likely true; however, disgruntled individuals will avoid oppositional activity if they cannot withstand the risks to their livelihoods. Furthermore, those who have already begun to act on their interests, by engaging in the civic sphere, will abandon their efforts if they find they have miscalculated their economic autonomy. Accounts of former activists in Ul'ianovsk and Naryn will illustrate this idea in Chapter 5.

Similar to participation theories, democratization theories have contended that capitalist development encourages those with democratic interests to mobilize.[11] However, people need not be primarily interested in democracy in order for them to sustain democratic institutions through their civic activity. Civic involvement is the means through which people express their preferences – regardless of the nature of these preferences – and this expression of desires is the foundation on which democracy rests. The interests of those who can afford to engage in the public sphere, such as successful entrepreneurs and doctors, may not reflect the "common good." Some of the most energetic civic activists in Russia, for example, are members of the Communist Party of the Russian Federation (Kommunisticheskaia Partiia Rossiiskoi Federatsii, or KPRF) and the Liberal Democratic Party of Russia (Liberal'naia Demokraticheskaia Partiia Rossii, or LDPR) – organizations less supportive of democracy, at least its Western variant.[12]

Resources. Scholars of democratization argue that wealth promotes democracy, and students of activism assert that resources, especially

---

[10] Ted R. Gurr, *Why Men Rebel* (Princeton, NJ: Princeton University Press, 1970); Chalmers A. Johnson, *Revolutionary Change* (Boston: Little Brown, 1966); Neil J. Smelser, *Theory of Collective Behavior* (New York: Free Press of Glencoe, 1963).

[11] Barrington Moore, *Social Origins of Dictatorship and Democracy*; Rueschemeyer et al., *Capitalist Development and Democracy*; Bellin, "Contingent Democrats"; Bellin, *Stalled Democracy*.

[12] However, all the activists I interviewed expressed support for the democratic rules of the game, even if they disdained certain features of advanced Western democracies, such as American individualism. Michael McFaul also argues that in Russia major political actors have abided by the rules of the game since 1993. From his survey research, James Gibson has concluded that Russians tend to support democratic rules of the game. See James L. Gibson, "The Russian Dance with Democracy," *Post-Soviet Affairs* 17 (April–June, 2001), 101–128; Michael McFaul, *Russia's Unfinished Revolution: Political Change from Gorbachev to Putin* (Ithaca, NY: Cornell University Press, 2001), 3.

money, encourage political engagement. In particular, students of activism contend that individuals become activists when there are funds to support political pursuits,[13] or the promise of personal gain encourages individuals to become involved in the civic sphere.[14] Yet, evidence from the four post-Soviet regions and other parts of the world demonstrates that the impoverished and those with little hope of personal financial gain can be politically involved. One poignant story from the province of Naryn illustrates this point. In a race for a regional parliamentary seat, a position that offers no financial benefit, three opposition candidates collaborated to overcome their lack of resources relative to the fourth candidate, a "first deputy *akim* [a leader, who] had his own means, such as a car."[15] The three candidates met together with voters in events throughout the oblast in order to conserve costs, particularly the expense of gasoline. One of them, a doctor,[16] won the race. There is no doubt that resources facilitate activism and that money is an advantage in politics, but poverty does not preclude the practice of democracy.

Money can contribute to economic autonomy by making it easier for harassed activists to pay illegal government fees and fight government suits in court. However, it is no guarantee of economic autonomy. The source of income is more important than the amount. Moreover, resources for activism, or even personal profit, may not be sufficient to compensate for the livelihood losses individuals incur because of their activism.

Organizational Capacity. Theories of social capital, mobilizing structures, and social networks all incorporate the idea that links among citizens can promote activism by increasing people's organizational capacity.[17] For example, bonds people form by playing soccer together

---

[13] John D. McCarthy and Mayer Zald, "Resource Mobilization and Social Movements: A Partial Theory," *American Journal of Sociology* 82 (1977), 1212–1241.

[14] Mancur Olson, *The Logic of Collective Action: Public Goods and the Theory of Groups* (Cambridge, MA: Harvard University Press, 1971); Robert Salisbury, "An Exchange Theory of Interest Groups," *Midwest Journal of Political Science* 13 (February, 1969), 1–32.

[15] Author's interview (29) with a deputy in the oblast parliament, Naryn oblast, July 8, 1997.

[16] Doctors were not well-paid during the Soviet era, and they have not grown rich in the post-Soviet era.

[17] Dennis Chong, *Collective Action and the Civil Rights Movement* (Chicago: University of Chicago Press, 1991); Ekiert and Kubik, *Rebellious Civil Societies*; Howard,

weekly would help them mobilize more easily for political action. This is a plausible idea, thus meriting a test in the four provinces. The difficulty of creating and maintaining independent media and political groups and running as an opposition candidate distinguishes the provinces in each country, as Chapter 4 describes. However, organizational capacity cannot explain the variation because the networks for these forms of activism in each country are quite similar.

In the four provinces, state media served as the network for creating independent media firms in the 1990s. In some cases, an employee or group of employees at a state media outlet left to establish an independent media group. In other cases, employees at a state media outlet opted to transform the enterprise into an independent company. As Chapter 4 will demonstrate, independent media do not exist in Naryn, and they self-censor to a greater degree in Ul'ianovsk than in Samara. Yet, state media exist in Naryn, so there is no reason why these entities could not support the growth of independent media in this province as they have in the other regions. Moreover, the fact that independent media in Samara and Ul'ianovsk draw on the same types of networks suggests that this explanation cannot explain the greater degree of self-censorship in Ul'ianovsk.

Similarly, in the four provinces, the same three types of networks have proved important to the development of political organizations: Soviet-era political ties, workplace relationships, and national groups. In Samara and Ul'ianovsk in the late 1980s and early 1990s, people formed clubs and held large public meetings to discuss political reforms and elections to Soviet and Russian legislative bodies. Later in the 1990s, individuals and clubs in Samara and Ul'ianovsk drew on these earlier networks to form oblast divisions of national political parties. In Osh and Naryn, residents held protests and meetings in the early 1990s, and this activity created a network for the establishment

The Weakness of Civil Society; John D. McCarthy, "Constraints and Opportunities in Adopting, Adapting, and Inventing," in *Comparative Perspectives on Social Movements: Political Opportunities, Mobilizing Structures, and Cultural Framings*, ed. Doug McAdam, John D. McCarthy, and Mayer N. Zald (Cambridge: Cambridge University Press, 1996), 141–151; Robert D. Putnam et al., *Making Democracy Work*; Robert D. Putnam, *Bowling Alone: The Collapse and Revival of American Community* (New York: Simon and Schuster, 2000); Sidney G. Tarrow, *Power in Movement: Social Movements, Collective Action, and Politics* (New York: Cambridge University Press, 1994).

of future political groups. In Osh, civic organizations formed after the summer of 1990 when violence erupted between the Uzbeks and Kyrgyz in the region over Uzbeks' lack of political representation and their threats of secession to Uzbekistan. The organizations aimed to promote the interests of Uzbeks in local and national government but also to seek reconciliation between the different ethnic groups. Current political organizations in Osh developed from these groups as well as from the Soviet Communist Party. In Naryn, the status of the oblast motivated people in the region to become involved in politics in the early 1990s. At that time, Naryn oblast was united with its neighbor Issik-Kul' oblast. Residents of Naryn were disgruntled that the national government was constructing buildings in Issik-Kul', which was home to the new provincial capital. People felt as if Naryn was suffering economically. Coworkers and neighbors began to hold meetings about this issue. They sent a letter with their complaints to national leaders, and in 1991 the oblasts were divided. In 1993, local activists held a demonstration and hunger strike over the difficulties of living at a high altitude, poor provision of electricity, and dissatisfaction over the progress of privatization. The protestors made demands of local and national authorities and eventually united to form an oblast division of a national political party.

To maintain their organizations in the post-Soviet era, activists in the provinces have relied on similar networks. In Samara and Ul'ianovsk, leaders of political NGOs have used money from national affiliates and local businesspeople, as well as membership dues and leaders' own resources, to fund their activities. In Kyrgyzstan, national parties provide little support for the oblast divisions of their organizations, so political groups in Osh seek support from business sponsors as well as their own leaders and members. Although there are no active political groups in Naryn, as elaborated on in Chapter 4, potential sponsors do exist.

Support networks for electoral candidates also differ little between the provinces in each country. In the four regions, groups of coworkers, friends, and neighbors nominated most candidates for office. During the campaign period, these individuals served as campaign managers, distributed literature, and talked to voters on behalf of their candidates. For the small number of candidates affiliated with a party – less than one-fifth in the Russian regions – party members also assisted with the campaigns. In Samara and Ul'ianovsk, a few candidates drew on party and commercial networks for campaign contributions. Candidates in Osh and Naryn tended to spend little money and not seek donations.

Interestingly, clan and ethnic networks cannot account for the lack of self-censorship in Osh oblast. People I spoke with in Osh as well as in Naryn were aware of their clan identity, and clan, in the sense of extended family, does play a role in everyday survival. Yet, these activist networks are not kin-based, and members do not describe them using kinship terms.[18] As evidence in Chapter 4 suggests, clan also does not provide an advantage in regional political activities, such as entering or winning a race for oblast *kenesh*.

Ethnicity is a more salient issue in Osh, where 28 percent of the population is Uzbek, relative to Naryn, which is 98 percent Kyrgyz; however, ethnic networks do not seem to reduce the risk of activism.[19] Networks may, of course, assist people in any of the regions in finding

---

[18] In her work on Central Asia, Kathleen Collins defines clans as "informal social organizations in which kinship or 'fictive' kinship is the core, unifying bond among group members." This definition includes extended family and conceivably networks based on one's village or hometown, alma mater, or workplace, if members view them in terms of kinship. However, activists and others I interviewed did not describe the latter three networks, in terms of kinship or even in terms of marital ties. The definition appears in Kathleen Collins, "The Political Role of Clans in Central Asia," *Comparative Politics* 35 (January, 2003), 173. A similar definition appears in Collins, "The Logic of Clan Politics," 224, 231.

[19] Although there is no direct connection between the relative ease of engaging in political activity in Osh and the region's multiethnic character, the presence of ethnic minorities likely contributes to the number of civic endeavors. In comparison with Naryn, which has no ethnic or religious organizations, Osh has 12 ethnic organizations, including a nascent Uzbek political party, an Uzbek cultural center, and an organization to assist ethnic Russians and those who speak only the Russian language. Osh is also home to 14 religious organizations, most of which are Islamic schools or other groups connected with mosques. The independent Uzbek-language newspaper *Mezon* was founded in Osh to provide Uzbeks with needed information, and the private television company Osh TV offers many programs in Uzbek to fill a void left by the other broadcasters, who offer only Kyrgyz, Russian, and English programming. Finally, the Uzbek minority may account for the larger number of candidates per district in regional elections as compared with Naryn. On average, four candidates ran in Osh, whereas only two competed per district in Naryn. In Osh, the percentage of Uzbek and Kyrgyz candidates approximated the ethnic composition of the region, suggesting that perhaps concern for Uzbek interests does expand the candidate pool. Although ethnicity is important in Osh, it cannot explain why activists there are less likely to engage in self-censorship than activists in Naryn. Moreover, ethnicity offers no insight into the differences between Samara and Ul'ianovsk, which have similar ethnic compositions.

jobs were they to lose their current employment because of civic pursuits. However, it is economic autonomy, not networks, that ensures the availability of jobs independent of the state. Networks themselves do not eliminate the risk of government harassment at the workplace.

Although interests, resources, and organizational capacity influence democratic activism, they cannot account for the puzzle of subnational variation in democratic development in Russia and Kyrgyzstan. In post-Soviet countries and worldwide, these factors likely play a role only after individuals decide they have sufficient economic autonomy to become activists.

A Territorial Dimension

Besides helping to account for activism, the concept of economic autonomy adds a territorial component to our understanding of democratization. That is, it suggests that the extraction from a nondemocratic regime and the establishment of formal democratic institutions are largely national processes, whereas the enforcement of rules is predominantly a local process.

The national capital is home to the regime, and thus extraction from the nondemocratic government must take place there. A subnational civic movement may initiate demands for regime change, but ultimately national elites must be involved in the process. Moreover, it is unlikely that subnational leaders will establish formal democratic institutions without reformers in national offices. If the national regime were nondemocratic, its leaders would likely destroy local democratic institutions so that their own rule would not look comparatively worse to citizens. In addition, the national government would likely have the legal right to change the political character of a subnational democratic government.[20]

By contrast, people throughout a country must engage in civic activities to ensure that leaders abide by the rules of the game. It is not sufficient for national leaders to demand that local authorities follow the new democratic procedures: Without economic autonomy, citizens will still be wary of engaging in the civic activities essential to democracy.

[20] Juan J. Linz and Alfred C. Stepan, *Problems of Democratic Transition and Consolidation*, 19.

Although environmental economic autonomy likely affects the degree of democracy in an entire country, the direct impact of economic autonomy is on citizens' and local authorities' decisions. Unlike existing theories, the concept of economic autonomy does not assume the even development of democracy throughout a country but instead illuminates local processes and explains subnational variation.

A Bridge between Approaches

The idea of economic autonomy also combines different theoretical approaches to democratization and political participation. Existing theories tend to focus on structure *or* agency, elites *or* masses, state *or* society. By bridging these approaches, the concept of economic autonomy provides a fuller account of these phenomena, clarifying the role of the state in particular.

Economic autonomy combines structural socioeconomic theories and agent-oriented crafting theories of democratization by demonstrating how a socioeconomic condition – environmental economic autonomy – delimits the effectiveness of government elites' punishments and shapes individuals' decisions about democratic engagement. At the same time, government elites can influence the degree of economic independence in their regions by closing borders or refusing foreign investment, for instance.

Similarly, theories of participation and activism tend to focus on structural factors, such as resources, mobilizing structures, and political opportunities, or agency, the behavior of individuals with specific traits, such as advanced education.[21] Economic autonomy links the two schools by demonstrating that personal economic autonomy is an individual trait that determines whether a person will take advantage of structural factors, such as mobilizing structures, resources, and political opportunities, for the purpose of political engagement.

By highlighting the role of activists, the concept of economic autonomy bridges elite and mass approaches to explaining democratization. Many studies of the practice of democracy focus exclusively on elites,

---

[21] For example, see Putnam, *Bowling Alone*; Sidney Verba, Kay Lehman Schlozman, and Henry E. Brady, *Voice and Equality: Civic Voluntarism in American Politics* (Cambridge, MA: Harvard University Press, 1995).

such as their behavior in legislatures, or masses, such as their choices at the polls.[22] Yet, it is the activists who create nongovernmental organizations (NGOs), establish alternative media, and campaign for public office, all of which provide elites with information about the masses' preferences, enabling them to create responsive policies.[23]

Finally, economic autonomy marries societal and state approaches to political participation. Specifically, it demonstrates how characteristics of society, such as environmental economic autonomy, and behaviors of the state, such as harassment, factor into personal decisions concerning civic engagement.

In sum, economic autonomy can be considered a general, but not "thick," theory that offers numerous theoretical advantages.[24] The concept is general in the sense that the relationship between economic autonomy and activism should hold in any region of the world. Economic autonomy is not a "thick" theory because it is only the first link in a long chain of causes of activism.

Before putting the idea of economic autonomy to work explaining variation within Russia and Kyrgyzstan and across regions of the world, the next two chapters tackle necessarily prior tasks. Chapter 3 outlines a plan to measure democracy, and Chapter 4 describes the results of executing this plan in the four provinces.

---

[22] Some attitudinal studies have concentrated on both the mass and elite levels, but they consider attitudes toward democracy more than the practice of democracy. For example, see Judith Kullberg and William Zimmerman, "Liberal Elites, Socialist Masses, and Problems of Russian Democracy," *World Politics* 51, (April, 1999), 323–358; Arthur H. Miller, "Comparing Citizen and Elite Belief Systems in Post-Soviet Russia and Ukraine," *Public Opinion Quarterly* 59 (1995), 1–40.

[23] Ekiert and Kubik's *Rebellious Civil Society* considers the impact of activism on democratization, and they also note that few studies of democratic development have focused on activists.

[24] Munck, "The Regime Question," 132.

3

Measurement of Democracy

To measure democracy in the four provinces, two hurdles had to be overcome. First, although Dahl's definition of democracy offers numerous advantages, it does not describe how different components of democracy interact. Understanding the interaction among components is important in providing a comprehensive assessment of the practice of democracy and, more specifically, in evaluating the cumulative effects of workplace harassment. Does the absence of some components weaken others? Are some components prerequisites for the realization of others? Second, Dahl offers little guidance about how to use his abstract description to measure the actual practice of democracy. This chapter offers a model of the interaction among components of democracy and a description of how to operationalize Dahl's definition – two products that should assist others in their evaluations of democracy elsewhere.

A DEFINITION OF DEMOCRACY

Unlike other definitions, Dahl's characterization of democracy is theoretical and relatively easy to use in research. Most definitions of democracy focus on theory, with no hint as to how to measure the ideas, or they emphasize measurement, with no underlying theory.[1]

---

[1] Kenneth Bollen, "Political Democracy: Conceptual and Measurement Traps," *Studies in Comparative International Development* 25 (Spring, 1990), 8.

TABLE 3.1. *Dahl's Eight Guarantees*

Alternative sources of information
Freedom to form and join organizations
Eligibility for public office
Right of political leaders to compete for support
Freedom of expression
Right to vote
Free and fair elections
Institutions for making government policies depend on voters' preferences

---

Source: Robert Dahl, *Polyarchy: Participation and Opposition* (New Haven, CT: Yale University Press, 1971), 2–3.

Moreover, Dahl's definition includes normative and societal elements, and it reflects a common understanding of democracy.

Dahl defines democracy as "a political system one of the characteristics of which is the quality of being completely or almost completely responsive to all its citizens." Dahl theorizes that in order for a government to be responsive, citizens must be able to "formulate" and "signify" their preferences and have them "weighed equally in the conduct of the government." For these opportunities to exist, eight guarantees must be present: alternative sources of information, the freedom to form and join organizations, eligibility for public office, the right of political leaders to compete for support, freedom of expression, the right to vote, free and fair elections, and institutions for making government policies depend on voters' preferences. (These also appear in Table 3.1.) Together, these eight guarantees reflect two dimensions of democracy: contestation and participation. Contestation refers to the amount of opposition permissible in a political system, and participation denotes the number of people granted the right to contest.[2] In total, the eight guarantees can provide a picture of how democratic a society is.

In identifying responsive government as the goal of democracy, Dahl includes a normative element in his definition. He explains why democracy is important instead of just describing the process. Other conceptualizations, such as Joseph Schumpeter's competitive elitist definition,

[2] Robert Dahl, *Polyarchy*, 2–4, 235–236.

depict only the procedures of democracy and ignore the purpose.[3] The normative component justifies why domestic elites and international actors are interested in promoting this model and why scholars seek to better understand it.

Dahl's definition is also attractive because he incorporates society into his model of democracy. Unlike the scholars of the competitive elitist school, Dahl acknowledges the importance not only of leaders and political structures but also nonstate actors and institutions. If democracy is to benefit the general population, then any model of democracy must explain how citizens' desires become policy. For governmental processes, such as elections or policy making, to work in a democratic manner, citizens must have civil liberties such as the freedom of expression. If citizens cannot freely express their desires, for example, leaders cannot create policies that incorporate citizens' wishes. By including civil liberties, Dahl's model offers a more complete picture of the dynamics of democracy.

The idea that society together with government institutions compose a political system reflects a common understanding of democracy. In their descriptions of democracy, domestic elites, leaders of international groups, and scholars tend to portray democracy as a political system that acts on the wishes of most of the population, in part because the people select their leaders. Local leaders and representatives of foreign groups that promote democracy in Russia and Kyrgyzstan typically mention the rights and role of citizens as well as government structures when they describe the democratic ideal.[4] Scholars accept not only this general idea but also Dahl's elaboration of it. Dahl's definition has become a standard among academics.[5]

Using a common conceptualization of democracy is important because an examination of democratic development should rest on the understanding of those promoting it as well as the definitions of

---

[3] David Held, *Models of Democracy*, 2nd ed. (Stanford, CA: Stanford University Press, 1996), 196; Joseph Schumpeter, *Capitalism, Socialism, and Democracy* (New York: Harper and Brothers, 1942), 269.

[4] I base this assessment on definitions provided by Russian and Kyrgyzstani elites and representatives of foreign NGOs in the course of my interviews with them. "Leadership" in Appendix B provides a brief account of local officials' views.

[5] Larry Diamond, "Is the Third Wave Over?" *Journal of Democracy* 7 (July, 1996), 21; David Collier and Steven Levitsky, "Democracy with Adjectives: Conceptual Innovation in Comparative Research," *World Politics* 49 (April, 1997), 431.

scholars. It makes little sense to look through Dahl's lens of democracy if his definition does not resonate with the definitions used by international organizations and domestic actors. Furthermore, in order for scholars of other regions of the world to readily interpret and apply my conclusions about economic autonomy, it is essential to employ a common definition of democracy. Although newer definitions of democracy, such as legal and participatory ones, exist, they have not become standard.

Dahl's description of democracy offers many advantages, but it suffers from one notable weakness. Like other definitions, Dahl's model does not explain how different components of democracy interact.[6] Dahl has stressed their significance, but he has not clarified how they relate to one another: "Because certain rights, liberties, and opportunities are essential to the democratic process itself, as long as that process exists then these rights, freedoms, and opportunities must necessarily also exist. These include rights to free expression, political organization, opposition, fair and free elections, and so on."[7]

Empirical studies of democracy offer few clues about how Dahl's eight institutional guarantees influence one another. In his own conceptualization of democracy, Samuel Huntington includes "the existence of those civil and political freedoms to speak, publish, assemble, and organize that are necessary to political debate and the conduct of electoral campaigns," but he does not elaborate.[8] Similarly, Guillermo O'Donnell argues that "for this [democratic] electoral process to exist, freedom of opinion and of association (including the freedom to form political parties) and an uncensored media must also exist,"[9] but he does not clarify how the latter contributes to the former. Likewise, Fareed Zakaria notes that "elections must be open and fair, and this requires some protections for freedom of speech and assembly" without further explanation of how these liberties promote free and

---

[6] Dahl, *Polyarchy*, 237; Dahl, *A Preface to Economic Democracy*, 73.

[7] Dahl, *Democracy and Its Critics*, 88–89.

[8] Samuel P. Huntington, *The Third Wave: Democratization in the Late Twentieth Century*, vol. 4, The Julian J. Rothbaum Distinguished Lecture Series (Norman: University of Oklahoma Press, 1991), 7.

[9] Guillermo O'Donnell, "Illusions About Consolidation," in *Consolidating the Third Wave Democracies*, ed. Larry Diamond (Baltimore: Johns Hopkins University Press, 1997), 43.

fair elections.[10] In differentiating between "hollowed out," electoral democracies and complete, liberal democracies, Larry Diamond highlights the importance of liberties to elections; however, he does not trace the connections between the two.[11]

Investigations of how to measure democracy have also paid little attention to the interactions among democratic guarantees. These studies combine components into indices, yet rules indicating the relative importance of the components tend to be arbitrary, lacking theoretical justification.[12] Even one of the more theoretically informed studies, by Axel Hadenius, carefully explores the links among only three components of democracy. Hadenius uses logic to demonstrate that eligibility for office, free and fair elections, and institutions have an impact on one another.[13]

A MODEL OF INTERACTION

In contrast to studies of measurement by Hadenius and others, investigations of individual components explain how the guarantees interact. Together, these theories demonstrate that there are 24 relationships among the eight guarantees. From these relationships, we can discern that some guarantees are prerequisites for others. Namely, the liberal components – freedom to form and join organizations, alternative sources of information, and to a lesser extent freedom of expression – are essential in order for the remaining guarantees to work. Let us

---

[10] Fareed Zakaria, "The Rise of Illiberal Democracy," *Foreign Affairs* 76 (November–December, 1997), 25.

[11] Diamond, "Is the Third Wave Over?"

[12] Gerardo L. Munck and Jay Verkuilen, "Conceptualizing and Measuring Democracy: Evaluating Alternative Indices," *Comparative Political Studies* 35 (February, 2002), 22–27. As examples, see Mark Gasiorowski, "The Political Regimes Project," in *On Measuring Democracy: Its Consequences and Concomitants*, ed. Alex Inkeles (New Brunswick, NJ: Transaction Publishers, 1991), 105–122; Michael Coppedge and Wolfgang Reinicke, "Measuring Polyarchy," *Studies in Comparative International Development* 25 (Spring, 1990), 56; Bollen, "Political Democracy," 14, 20. Kenneth Bollen, "Issues in the Comparative Measurement of Political Democracy," *American Sociological Review* 45 (1980), 375–379, 380.

[13] Hadenius uses the terms open, correct, and effective elections to capture these ideas. See Axel Hadenius, *Democracy and Development* (Cambridge: Cambridge University Press, 1992), 51.

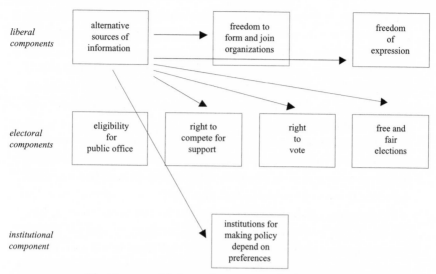

FIGURE 3.1. Ideal impact of "alternative sources of information"

examine the 24 relationships first and then explore these implications in greater detail.

The guarantee *alternative sources of information* has an impact on six of the other components of democracy, as depicted in Figure 3.1. Press freedom bolsters electoral processes because newspapers and broadcasts inform voters about candidates and encourage public debate.[14] By receiving and discussing information, citizens can better evaluate issues, form opinions about topics, and thus make wiser decisions at the polls. Informed voters can improve their chances for representation by selecting officials who share their views and will likely advance their interests in the halls of government.[15] According to one scholar, "without [press freedom] elections could not be considered free

[14] Samuel L. Popkin, *The Reasoning Voter: Communication and Persuasion in Presidential Campaigns* (Chicago: University of Chicago Press, 1991), 8; David Kelley and Roger Donway, "Liberalism and Free Speech," in *Democracy and the Mass Media: A Collection of Essays*, ed. Judith Lichtenberg (Cambridge: Cambridge University Press, 1990), 70; Pippa Norris, *A Virtuous Circle: Political Communications in Postindustrial Societies* (Cambridge: Cambridge University Press, 2000), 17–18.

[15] Judith Lichtenberg, "Introduction," in *Democracy and the Mass Media: A Collection of Essays*, ed. Judith Lichtenberg (Cambridge: Cambridge University Press, 1990), 11–15.

and effective expressions of the voters' wishers. . . . Periodic elections without continuous press freedom would resemble a farm on which 'for eight months in the year, all sheep dogs were to be kept locked up, and the sheep committed during that time to the guardianship of the wolves.'"[16] At the polls, independent journalists observe balloting, increasing the likelihood that the right to vote will be protected and that elections will be free and fair.

Between elections, independent media keep incumbents abreast of societal problems, and they reveal when officials are not being responsive. In these ways, press freedom helps ensure that institutions, like legislatures, act in the voters' interests.

Independent media are also important to free speech and assembly. By serving as forums for advocacy,[17] newspapers and broadcasts strengthen freedom of expression and the right to form and join organizations. Media provide a larger audience to which people and organizations can express their ideas. Furthermore, publications and broadcasts help groups recruit supporters by introducing certain issues and goals to the public consciousness.[18]

More than 150 years ago, Alexis de Tocqueville emphasized the importance to democracy of the *freedom to form and join organizations*. From his study of early America, he concluded that associations help people refine their ideas,[19] and this enables government institutions to better reflect voters' wishes. Political parties, in particular, aggregate citizens' preferences and inform government officials of them.[20] Associations also improve institutional performance by protecting

[16] From Jeremy Netham, "On the Liberty of the Press and Public Discussion," London, 1820–1, page 18, as quoted in John Keane, *The Media and Democracy* (Cambridge: Polity Press, 1991), 16.

[17] M. Gurevitch and J. Blumler, "Political Communications Systems and Democratic Values," in *Democracy and the Mass Media: A Collection of Essays*, ed. Judith Lichtenberg (Cambridge: Cambridge University Press, 1990), 270.

[18] Alexis de Tocqueville, *Democracy in America*, Vols. 1, 2, Vintage Classics (New York: Vintage Books, 1990).

[19] Ibid.

[20] Joseph LaPalombara and Myron Weiner, eds., *Political Parties and Political Development* (Princeton, NJ: Princeton University Press, 1966), 3; Samuel P. Huntington, *Political Order in Changing Societies* (New Haven, CT: Yale University Press, 1968), 24–25; Seymour M. Lipset and Stein Rokkan, *Party Systems and Voter Alignments: Cross-National Perspectives*, International Yearbook of Political Behavior Research (New York: Free Press, 1967), 5.

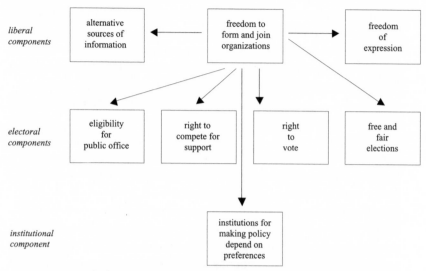

FIGURE 3.2. Ideal impact of "freedom to form and join organizations"

government against the dominance of a single group. In the 20th century, David Truman argued that overlapping associational memberships and the possibility of new associations discourage tyranny.[21]

Beyond their impact on government institutions, associations act as alternative sources of information by disseminating facts, personal accounts, and opinions,[22] as noted in Figure 3.2. Opposition groups, in particular, expose problems in government.[23] Freedom of association

---

[21] Tocqueville, *Democracy in America*, 192, 195; David Truman, *The Governmental Process*, 1st ed. (New York: Knopf, 1951). Associations may also have a negative impact on democracy. Nondemocratic associations are not likely to promote democratic values. There is also the continuing fear that associations will promote political divides. See Amy Gutmann, "Freedom of Association: An Introductory Essay," in *Freedom of Association*, ed. Amy Gutmann (Princeton, NJ: Princeton University Press, 1998), 13–32; Robert D. Putnam, "Bowling Alone: America's Declining Social Capital," *Journal of Democracy* 6 (1995), 340; Yael Tamir, "Revisiting the Civic Sphere," in *Freedom of Association*, ed. Amy Gutmann (Princeton, NJ: Princeton University Press, 1998), 214–238; James Madison, *The Federalist Papers: Alexander Hamilton, James Madison, John Jay*, no. 10 (New York: New American Library, 1961).

[22] Margaret E. Keck and Kathryn Sikkink, *Activists Beyond Borders: Advocacy Networks in International Politics* (Ithaca, NY: Cornell University Press, 1998), 19.

[23] Ian Shapiro, *Democracy's Place* (Ithaca, NY: Cornell University Press, 1996), 234–235.

also makes free speech more effective because there is power in numbers.[24] Nongovernmental organizations facilitate the right to vote and free, fair elections because members of political groups observe elections. Organizations influence eligibility and competition for public office by serving as gatekeepers to elected posts. The ability to receive a nomination from a political party and use its manpower and financial support in a political campaign influences whether a potential candidate will enter a race.

Freedom of expression is the cornerstone of deliberative democracy. This idea that discussion leads to better political outcomes is supported by the work of Immanuel Kant, John Stuart Mill, James Madison, John Rawls, and Jürgen Habermas. By sharing information and opinions, the members of a society reach better individual and collective decisions, in part because the veracity of claims can be explored.[25] Freedom of expression facilitates communication between citizens and leaders and ultimately helps government decisions reflect the public interest.[26]

Besides enabling institutions to make more responsive policies, freedom of expression is essential for alternative sources of information to exist and for political leaders to compete for support, as depicted in Figure 3.3. Free speech enables media outlets to offer perspectives besides the government's, and it allows candidates to share their ideas openly in order to vie for citizens' votes.[27] Freedom of expression also allows people to learn of each other's views, thus facilitating the creation and maintenance of public associations.

In order for government institutions to respond to citizens' needs, citizens must be well represented in these bodies.[28] The guarantee of

---

[24] Gutmann, "Introductory Essay," 3; Tamir, "Revisiting the Civic Sphere," 214–215.

[25] Jon Elster, *Deliberative Democracy* (Cambridge: Cambridge University Press, 1998); Judith Lichtenberg, "Foundations and Limits of Freedom of the Press," in *Democracy and the Mass Media: A Collection of Essays*, ed. Judith Lichtenberg (Cambridge: Cambridge University Press, 1990), 108; Cass R. Sunstein, *Democracy and the Problem of Free Speech* (New York: The Free Press, 1993), 18–19, 243, 248. Mill argues that expression of ideas can help people reach the truth. See John Stuart Mill, *On Liberty with the Subjection of Women and Chapters on Socialism*, ed. Stefan Collini (Cambridge: Cambridge University Press, 1989), 20, 23, 53.

[26] Sunstein, *Democracy and Free Speech*, 19, 244; Lichtenberg, "Foundations and Limits of Freedom of the Press," 111.

[27] Kelley and Donway, "Liberalism and Free Speech," 91.

[28] John Stuart Mill, *Considerations on Representative Government* (New York: Prometheus Books, 1991), 65, 197–198.

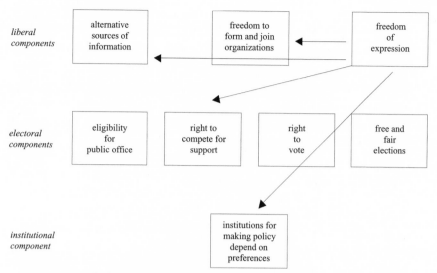

FIGURE 3.3. Ideal impact of "freedom of expression"

eligibility for public office is the first step in this process of representation. This component of democracy affects the right to compete for support, the right to vote, and the performance of institutions, as illustrated in Figure 3.4. If certain groups are denied the right to run for office, then competition and voters' selection will be limited. Without a broad spectrum of candidates from which to choose, voters have difficulty selecting representatives who will respond to their needs once they take office. In other words, limited eligibility distorts representation.

Samuel Popkin wrote that "To arouse public opinion and generate support for their cause, [political leaders]... must defend their old policies, sell new policies, and justify their rule."[29] The *right of political leaders to compete for support* is mostly exercised during electoral campaigns, when incumbents and hopefuls vie for votes. Ideally, a campaign provides information to voters about issues and contenders, making the right to vote more meaningful. Candidates help to aggregate interests by urging voters to ally with them.[30] Ultimately, this

[29] Popkin, *The Reasoning Voter*, 8.
[30] Ibid., 8, 12, 15.

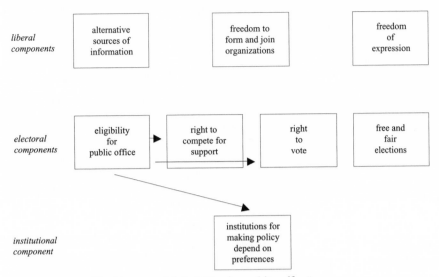

FIGURE 3.4. Ideal impact of "eligibility for public office"

competition among political leaders can result in more responsive policy making,[31] as noted in Figure 3.5.

The *right to vote* is a way to ensure that institutions make policies that reflect citizens' wishes, as depicted in Figure 3.6. Voting is a means of "connecting the actions of government with the preferences of a mass citizenry."[32] The size of modern democracies necessitates voting for representatives instead of serving in government oneself.[33]

Voting will only accurately represent citizens' preferences if it occurs through *free and fair elections*. Without free and fair elections, institutions cannot translate citizens' wishes into policies, as diagramed in Figure 3.7.

The final democratic guarantee, *institutions for making government policies depend on preferences*, is unusual in that it is affected by all the other components yet influences none. The responsiveness of

---

[31] Key and Heard, *Southern Politics.*
[32] Angus Campbell, Philip Converse, E. Miller, and Donald Stokes, *The American Voter* (New York: Wiley, 1960), 3.
[33] Campbell et al., *The American Voter*, 3; Mill, *Considerations on Representative Government*; Stein Rokkan, *Citizens, Elections, Parties: Approaches to the Comparative Study of the Processes of Development* (Oslo: Universitetsforlaget, 1970); Elster, *Deliberative Democracy.*

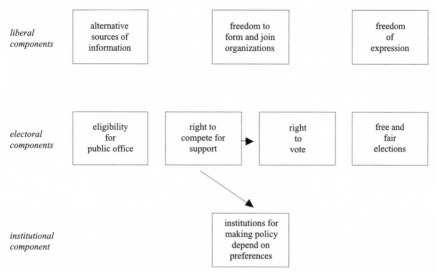

FIGURE 3.5. Ideal impact of the "right to compete for support"

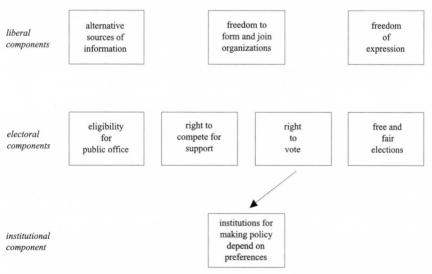

FIGURE 3.6. Ideal impact of the "right to vote"

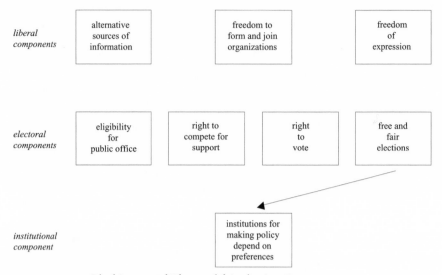

FIGURE 3.7. Ideal impact of "free and fair elections"

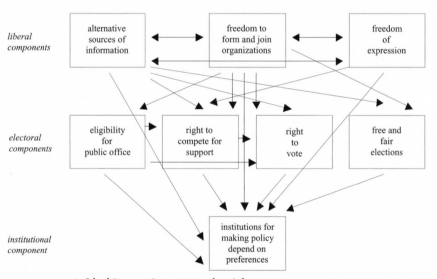

FIGURE 3.8. Ideal interaction among the eight guarantees

governmental institutions is the essence of democracy and the purpose of all the other guarantees.

The 24 relationships among the eight guarantees, depicted in Figure 3.8, suggest that they are all necessary, but some have a greater

TABLE 3.2. *Impact of Individual Components*

Components of Democracy	Number of Other Components Influenced
1. Freedom to form and join organizations	7
2. Alternative sources of information	6
3. Freedom of expression	4
4. Eligibility for public office	3
5. Right of political leaders to compete for support	2
6. Right to vote	1
6. Free and fair elections	1
7. Institutions for making policy depend on preferences	0

Note: The numbers on the left indicate the ranking of components.

impact on democracy. The liberal components – alternative sources of information, freedom to form and join organizations, and freedom of expression – feed into the electoral components, which in turn help institutions respond to voters' preferences. Two of the liberal components – alternative sources of information and freedom to form and join organizations – influence numerous electoral guarantees, whereas none of the electoral guarantees affects the liberal components. From the analysis, it is also clear that the members of each set of components have an influence on one another. Three reciprocal relationships exist among the liberal components, and three unidirectional relationships exist among three of the four electoral components.

The logic behind each guarantee demonstrates that the absence of one would hinder the ability of institutions to make policies based on citizens' preferences. However, the loss of certain components would be more harmful than the loss of others because some components have an impact on more guarantees, as enumerated in Table 3.2. For example, the guarantee of freedom to form and join organizations influences seven other components, whereas that of free and fair elections affects only one.

The varying influence of the components indicates that some are prerequisites for others. It is the liberal guarantees – particularly the freedom to form and join organizations and alternative sources of information – that are highly critical to democracy because they form the foundation on which political institutions can thrive. Freedom of association expands the scale of freedom of expression, provides a party network to support electoral candidates, improves the quality and quantity of electoral observers, and strengthens citizens' connections to government institutions. By contrast, violations of the right to vote weaken only the expression of preferences at the polls and the ability of institutions to base their actions on electoral outcomes.

The liberal components act as government watchdogs and conduits for citizens' preferences. They allow individuals outside of the government to reveal to society violations and weaknesses in the electoral and institutional processes. Ideas such as "the ballot box was stuffed at this poll" or "the incumbent has not acted in the interest of his constituents" can be broadcast and investigated only when independent media, NGOs, and freedom of expression exist. The risk that society will find fault and choose to throw out incumbents serves as a check on government wrongdoing. The liberal guarantees also provide additional channels for citizens' preferences to reach government officials. Independent media report and publish citizens' concerns, nongovernmental organizations link citizens and officials, and freedom of expression enables citizens to voice their preferences directly to government officials.

As institutional watchdogs and alternative channels, the liberal components serve democracy beyond the ballot box. Diamond wrote that "The crucial distinction [between different conceptualizations of democracy] turns on whether political and civil freedoms are seen as relevant mainly to the extent that they ensure meaningful *electoral* competition and participation, or are instead viewed as necessary to ensure a wider range of democratic functions."[34] The elaboration of Dahl's conceptualization indicates that the latter is accurate.

For those interested in measuring democracy across territories, the relationships among the components suggest that weighting of the guarantees is necessary. Specifically, a weighting system would demonstrate that some of the components would be less meaningful if others were absent. Based on the data in Table 3.2, freedom to form and join organizations would carry the greatest weight, followed by alternative sources of information, freedom of expression, eligibility for public

---

[34] Diamond, "Is the Third Wave Over?" 25.

office, and the right of political leaders to compete for support. Then, the right to vote and free and fair elections would be weighted equally, and institutions for making policy depend on preferences would have the least weight. This would represent a weighting scheme driven by theory instead of arbitrary rules.

DEMOCRACY OPERATIONALIZED

For the purposes of this study, I use Dahl's definition to evaluate a process, not outcomes. Democracy is a process designed to maximize government responsiveness to citizens, but other factors, such as state finances, also influence outcomes. Evaluating the process itself is valuable because many people living under hybrid regimes are committed to democratizing their governments, and the international community has devoted considerable financial and human resources to promoting democracy worldwide. Moreover, although democratic systems have their weaknesses, they seem to be the least of all evils. As Winston Churchill said, "No one pretends that democracy is perfect or all-wise. Indeed, it has been said that democracy is the worst form of Government except all those other forms that have been tried from time to time."[35] Although a study of outcomes is possible,[36] it is a different study.

Prior attempts to operationalize Dahl's definition of democracy misrepresented Dahl's underlying theory by disregarding some of his guarantees and by severely restricting the possible values of their indicators. Scholars should avoid aggregating or excluding the guarantees because certain components can be strong while others are not and some components are necessary in order for others to operate. Understandably, the large number of cases these studies examined would have made such an approach difficult. To measure democracy in 117 countries over four decades, Mark Gasiorowski combined Dahl's eight guarantees into three, allowing most of them only two possible

---

[35] Churchill said this in the House of Commons on November 11, 1947. See Antony Jay, *The Oxford Dictionary of Political Quotations* (Oxford: Oxford University Press, 1996), 93.

[36] See, for example, Putnam et al., *Making Democracy Work*; Stoner-Weiss, *Local Heroes*.

values.[37] Similarly, in their ranking of 137 countries for 1985, Michael Coppedge and Wolfgang Reinicke reduced Dahl's eight components to five variables and used only three to four possible values for each variable.[38]

By contrast, my focus on four provinces enabled me to preserve all eight of Dahl's guarantees, making only one minor adjustment. I defined "free and fair elections" as "accurate counting of ballots" because otherwise this component would include three other guarantees – eligibility for public office, the right to compete, and the right to vote.

Measures

For each of Dahl's guarantees, I used multiple measures. I did not rely merely on counts of democratic institutions; this approach can capture the extent of participation but not the degree of contestation. For example, counts of independent media outlets – three in this region, four in that region – are an acceptable first indicator of how many people are exercising their right to alternative sources of information. Yet, what if the independent media outlets self-censor, never challenging the government? Then, they are not serving as an alternative source of information. Or what if the number of outlets is low in one territory because people lack capital but low in another because authorities illegally harass journalists? Then, democracy is weaker in the latter because the state does not enforce the guarantee of alternative sources of information. These questions highlight the importance of contestation. We can measure contestation with the concepts of self-censorship and government harassment.

Measuring self-censorship and government harassment is challenging because these incidents often are not as visible as the democratic institutions themselves. Moreover, self-censorship and government harassment must be considered relative to the number of attempts

---

[37] Gasiorowski used only freedom of organizations and expression, representative process for selecting government officials, and representative state institutions. See Gasiorowski, "The Political Regimes Project," 107, 111–113.

[38] The five were free and fair elections, freedom of organization, freedom of expression, alternative sources of information, and right to vote. See Coppedge and Reinicke, "Measuring Polyarchy," 53.

at exercising a right. I assessed the frequency of self-censorship and harassment in each province based on interviews with all individuals or a sample of individuals who tried to exercise that right. I confirmed their reports by speaking with representatives of the media, human-rights advocates, and appropriate government officials. Estimating the frequency of harassment relative to the exercise of rights distinguishes between few violations of democratic liberties as an indicator of vibrant democracy and few violations as an indicator of the most severe form of self-censorship – not exercising a democratic freedom for fear of negative repercussions.

In sum, I measured Dahl's first seven guarantees in terms of counts of participation, self-censorship, and government harassment. Take, for example, the guarantee freedom to form and join organizations. The number and types of NGOs in the oblast indicated the degree of participation. Self-censorship comes in the form of not creating an organization, dissolving an existing group, or limiting activities to only nonoppositional ones. Therefore, I examined whether a low number of NGOs reflected fears of creating them, and I measured the frequency with which NGOs disband or limit their activities. Possible forms of government harassment include informal obstacles to NGO registration, threats of job loss, firings, state inspections and interference in NGOs leaders' and members' businesses, arrests, and violence.

Dahl's eighth guarantee, institutions for making policies depend on voters' preferences, is different because the seven others feed into it. Therefore, I focused on how the government institutions in each oblast operate instead of measuring participation, self-censorship, and harassment. The measures for each of the eight guarantees appear in Table 3.3. Having multiple measures of each guarantee maximizes the validity of my findings about levels of democracy in the four regions.

Sources of Information

For each of the measures, I relied on multiple sources. These included interviews, printed materials, and observational studies, as indicated in Table 3.3. Using multiple sources increases the reliability of the measures.

TABLE 3.3. *Evaluating Democracy: Measures and Sources*

Measures	Sources
Alternative sources of information	
Participation	
Number of state and independent media outlets	Media representatives; media surveys; kiosk workers; TV guides
Extent of coverage of oblast politics	Newspapers; TV guides and programs; radio broadcasts; media representatives; media surveys; kiosk workers
Geographic availability	Media representatives; media surveys; kiosk workers; citizens
Language accessibility	Newspapers; TV guides and programs; radio broadcasts; media representatives; citizens
Cost of media	Media representatives; media surveys; kiosk workers; citizens
Contestation: Self-censorship	
Independent outlets' coverage of local authorities	Newspapers; TV guides and programs; radio broadcasts; media representatives; media surveys; kiosk workers
State outlets' coverage of local authorities	Newspapers; TV guides and programs; radio broadcasts; media representatives; media surveys; kiosk workers
Contestation: Government Harassment	
Frequency of information withheld	Media representatives; oblast administration officials; human-rights observers
Frequency of refusals to print newspapers	Media representatives; oblast administration officials; human-rights observers
Frequency of harassment of advertisers	Media representatives; oblast administration officials; human-rights observers
Frequency of state inspections	Media representatives; oblast administration officials; human-rights observers
Frequency of lawsuits	Media representatives; oblast administration officials; human-rights observers
Frequency of office leases broken	Media representatives; oblast administration officials; human-rights observers
Frequency of utilities disconnected	Media representatives; oblast administration officials; human-rights observers
Frequency of arrests	Media representatives; oblast administration officials; human-rights observers
Frequency of violence	Media representatives; oblast administration officials; human-rights observers

Measures	Sources
Freedom to Form and Join Organizations	
Participation	
Number of NGOs	State registration lists; NGO resource centers' lists; telephone directories
Number of political NGOs	State registration lists; NGO resource centers' lists; telephone directories; NGO leaders
Contestation: Self-censorship	
Type of NGO activity	NGO leaders and members; citizens; state registration lists; NGO resource centers' lists
Number of NGOs dissolved	Former NGO leaders and members; media representatives; human-rights observers
Contestation: Government Harassment	
Difficulty of registration process	Registration official(s); NGO leaders
Number of NGOs denied registration	Registration official(s); NGO leaders; media representatives; human-rights observers
Types of NGOs denied registration	Registration official(s); NGO leaders; media representatives; human-rights observers
Frequency of threat of job loss	NGO leaders and members; media representatives; human-rights observers
Frequency of firings	NGO leaders and members; media representatives; human-rights observers
Frequency of workplace inspections and interference	NGO leaders and members; tax-inspection official; media representatives; human-rights observers
Frequency of arrests	NGO leaders and members; media representatives; human-rights observers
Frequency of violence	NGO leaders and members; media representatives; human-rights observers
Eligibility for Public Office	
Participation	
Number of candidates for oblast office	Official candidate lists for oblast parliamentary and gubernatorial elections
Characteristics of candidates for oblast office	Biographies of oblast parliamentary and gubernatorial candidates; candidates; citizens
Contestation: Self-censorship	
Number of candidates who abandon races	Election officials; candidates; media representatives; human-rights observers

(continued)

TABLE 3.3 *(continued)*

Measures	Sources
Number of interested individuals who never join races	Potential candidates; media representatives; human-rights observers

Contestation: Government Harassment

Measures	Sources
Difficulty of registration process	Election officials; candidates; media representatives; human-rights observers
Number of candidates denied registration	Election officials; candidates; media representatives; human-rights observers
Characteristics of candidates denied registration	Election officials; candidates; media representatives; human-rights observers
Frequency of pressure to abandon race	Election officials; candidates; media representatives; human-rights observers
Frequency of threats of job loss before race	Election officials; candidates; media representatives; human-rights observers
Frequency of firings before race	Election officials; candidates; media representatives; human-rights observers
Frequency of workplace inspections and interference before race	Election officials; tax official; candidates; media representatives; human-rights observers
Frequency of arrests before race	Election officials; candidates; media representatives; human-rights observers
Frequency of violence before race	Election officials; candidates; media representatives; human-rights observers

Right of Political Leaders to Compete for Support

Participation

Measures	Sources
Number of candidates who campaign	Candidates; election officials; media representatives
Type of campaigning	Candidates; election officials; media representatives

Contestation: Self-censorship

Measures	Sources
Number of candidates who choose not to run again	Candidates; media reports

Contestation: Government Harassment

Measures	Sources
Interference in campaigning	Candidates; election officials; media representatives; human-rights observers
Frequency of threats of job loss during and after race	Candidates; election officials; media representatives; human-rights observers
Frequency of firings during and after race	Candidates; election officials; media representatives; human-rights observers

Measures	Sources
Frequency of workplace inspections/interference during/after race	Candidates; election officials; media representatives; human-rights observers
Frequency of arrests during and after race	Candidates; election officials; media representatives; human-rights observers
Frequency of violence during and after race	Candidates; election officials; media representatives; human-rights observers

Freedom of Expression
Participation

Number of protests	Media reports; media representatives; NGO leaders; citizens
Extent of contact with officials	Oblast deputies; oblast administration officials; media representatives; citizens
Number of letters to the media	Media representatives

Contestation: Self-censorship

Content of citizens' protests	Media reports; human-rights observers; media representatives; citizens
Content of citizens' contact with officials	Oblast deputies; oblast administration officials; media reports; media representatives; citizens
Content of citizens' letters to the media	Media reports; media representatives; citizens

Contestation: Government Harassment

Frequency of arrests	Media reports; human-rights observers; media representatives; citizens
Frequency of fines	Media reports; human-rights observers; media representatives; citizens
Frequency of threats of job loss	Media reports; human-rights observers; media representatives; citizens
Frequency of firings	Media reports; human-rights observers; media representatives; citizens
Frequency of workplace inspections and interference	Media reports; human-rights observers; media representatives; citizens
Frequency of arrests	Media reports; human-rights observers; media representatives; citizens
Frequency of violence	Media reports; human-rights observers; media representatives; citizens

(continued)

TABLE 3.3 *(continued)*

Measures	Sources
Right to Vote	
Participation	
Number of registered voters	Oblast electoral commission documents
Contestation: Self-censorship	
Number of individuals who choose not to vote out of fear	Citizens; oblast electoral officials; media representatives; human-rights observers
Contestation: Government Harassment	
Difficulty of registration	Citizens; oblast electoral officials; media representatives; election observers
Number of individuals denied registration	Citizens; oblast electoral officials; media representatives; election observers
Frequency of pressure at the polls to vote a particular way	Citizens; oblast electoral officials; media representatives; election observers
Frequency of denial of right to vote at the polls	Citizens; oblast electoral officials; media representatives; election observers
Frequency of arrests	Citizens; oblast electoral officials; media representatives; election observers
Frequency of violence	Citizens; oblast electoral officials; media representatives; election observers
Free and Fair Elections	
Participation	
Voter turnout	Oblast electoral commission reports; media reports
Contestation: Self-censorship	
Number of individuals who did not select their preferred candidate	Citizens; media representatives
Contestation: Government Harassment	
Number of oblast election violation complaints	Oblast electoral officials; candidates; media representatives; election observers
Types of oblast election violation complaints	Oblast electoral officials; candidates; media representatives; election observers
Percentages winners received	Oblast electoral documents; media reports
Extent of acceptance of results	Media reports; media representatives; candidates; oblast electoral officials; citizens
Characteristics of winners and losers	Biographies of oblast parliamentary and gubernatorial candidates; electoral results
Frequency of arrests	Oblast electoral officials; candidates; media representatives; election observers

Measures	Sources
Frequency of violence	Oblast electoral officials; candidates; media representatives; election observers
Institutions for Making Government Policies Depend on Voters' Preferences	
Number of oblast officials elected	Oblast government documents; oblast administration officials
Oblast officials' perceived mission	Oblast deputies; oblast administration officials
Oblast officials' activities	Oblast deputies; oblast administration officials; media representatives; observation of parliament
Perception of oblast officials' effectiveness	Citizens; media representatives
Obstacles facing oblast officials	Oblast deputies; oblast administration officials; media representatives; NGO leaders; citizens

In total, I conducted 252 interviews, mostly with people from the provincial capital and outlying districts in each region.[39] A small number of interviews were with people in the national capitals. Schematically, people I interviewed were individuals who try to exercise Dahl's first seven guarantees, representatives in the institutions that are supposed to be responsive to these civic demands (Dahl's eighth component), people who observe the exercise or violation of these freedoms, and individuals who provided background information. If a category of people was large, such as regional parliamentary candidates, I did not interview all the members but instead selected a number of them, in most cases randomly.

More concretely, people I interviewed included media representatives, NGO leaders, oblast administration officials, oblast parliamentary deputies, losing candidates, heads of international organizations, and liaisons between the provinces and national governments. Another set of interviews was with individuals who provided background

[39] In the interviews, I opted not to use a tape recorder in order to put people at ease. This approach was particularly important because individuals were often talking about sensitive topics, such as government harassment. I took notes on paper during the interviews, and I transcribed the notes into computer files at the end of the day. The only drawback of this approach is that I have relatively few long quotations from individuals.

information or spoke on behalf of a government organization. In each region, these people included a human-rights advocate, a tax-inspection official, and a clerk who registers NGOs. To test possible explanations for the uneven development of democracy, I conducted interviews with business leaders, privatization and budget officials, representatives of international organizations engaged in civic work in each region, national parliamentary deputies representing each region, and presidential representatives to each province.[40] A list of interviewees appears in Appendix C, and Appendix D provides additional details about the interviews.

While I lived in each of these regions, I also acquired information from people informally. I confirmed newspaper editors' accounts about the prices and popularity of their publications by speaking with kiosk workers. My conversations with my host families, local colleagues, and new acquaintances provided a window into the opinions, fears, and everyday lives of average citizens.

In total, the printed materials, observational studies, 252 interviews, and informal conversations confirmed the surveyed experts' assessments that Samara is more democratic than Ul'ianovsk and that Osh is more democratic than Naryn. These sources of information also revealed the nature of the differences. Using the measures in Table 3.3 as my guide, in the next chapter I highlight the key distinctions and similarities between the provinces in each country. Appendix D provides additional details about democracy in the four provinces.

---

[40] Yeltsin appointed a representative to each region to observe and report to him. Kyrgyzstan has a similar system, although representatives tend to reside in Bishkek instead of the regions.

4

Activism under the State's Thumb

Democracy on paper is not a measure of democracy in practice, particularly in the former Eastern bloc, where the rule of law has historically been weak. How difficult is it to establish independent media, create political parties, criticize provincial authorities, and run for local offices? Are government institutions designed to incorporate the preferences expressed through these civic activities? This chapter provides a window on the practice of democracy in the former Soviet Union. Specifically, it demonstrates that democracy in Ul'ianovsk and Naryn is weaker than in Samara and Osh, respectively. Unlike their neighbors in Samara and Osh, residents of Ul'ianovsk and Naryn cannot freely operate independent media outlets, run political organizations, enter key electoral races, or campaign against important incumbents. The four other guarantees are comparable between Ul'ianovsk and Samara and between Naryn and Osh, as noted in Table 4.1. However, as the model of interaction indicates, these four guarantees mean little when the four other rights are difficult to exercise.

DISTINGUISHING GUARANTEES

How do we know that independent media, political organizations, and opposition candidates are more vulnerable in Ul'ianovsk and Naryn than in Samara and Osh, respectively? In the case of Ul'ianovsk, the story is not in the number of these institutions and individuals but in the

TABLE 4.1. *Comparison: Extent of Democracy*

Measures	Russia		Kyrgyzstan	
	Samara	Ul'ianovsk	Osh	Naryn
Alternative information	**stronger**	**weaker**	**stronger**	**weaker**
Freedom of organization	**stronger**	**weaker**	**stronger**	**weaker**
Eligibility for public office	**stronger**	**weaker**	**stronger**	**weaker**
Right to compete	**stronger**	**weaker**	**stronger**	**weaker**
Freedom of expression	similar	similar	similar	similar
Right to vote	similar	similar	similar	similar
Free and fair elections	similar	similar	similar	similar
Responsive institutions	similar	similar	similar	similar

Note: Those measures that differ between the regions in a country appear in boldface type.

ubiquity of self-censorship and government harassment. Ul'ianovsk has nonstate media outlets, political groups, and opposition candidates; however, most activists practice self-censorship by limiting the degree to which they oppose local authorities and by dissolving groups that suffer government punishments. In Naryn, the weaknesses of independent media, political organizations, and opposition candidates manifest themselves in both the number of institutions and the pervasiveness of self-censorship. No media outlets that cover provincial news in Naryn are independent, and members of the single independent political group have dispersed, fearing government reprisals. Individuals in Naryn who have run against incumbents and candidates favored by the government have faced government harassment. By contrast, individuals in Samara and Osh rarely suffered punishments and did not practice self-censorship. The distinctive story of these four guarantees in each province unfolds in the next section. The section after that one examines those guarantees that are comparable across the four provinces.

Alternative Sources of Information

When residents of Samara, Ul'ianovsk, Osh, and Naryn turn on their radios, open their newspapers, and switch on their televisions, they find

TABLE 4.2. *Comparison: Alternative Sources of Information (given as the percentage followed by the ratio)*

	Russia		Kyrgyzstan	
Measures	Samara	Ul'ianovsk	Osh	Naryn
Independent media punished	0% (0/3)	80% (4/5)	0% (0/3)	No independent media (0/0)
Independent media that self-censor	0% (0/3)	40% (2/5)	0% (0/3)	No independent media (0/0)

Notes: The ratios are the number of independent media that have been punished or that practice self-censorship relative to the total number of media. The total number represents all the independent media outlets that cover provincial news in a nontabloid fashion: three for Samara, five for Ul'ianovsk, three for Osh, and zero for Naryn. Although the absolute numbers are small, meaningful conclusions can be drawn from the data because they represent the entire populations, not samples. See Appendix D, "Alternative Sources of Information," for further details.

news about the political and economic situations in their provinces.[1] However, citizens in Naryn have greater difficulty obtaining balanced reports because independent newspapers and broadcasting companies have not formed in Naryn, and media outlets in Ul'ianovsk struggle to disseminate objective reports because they face government reprisals and practice self-censorship. In Ul'ianovsk, 80 percent of the independent media outlets have suffered repeated government punishments, including unfounded state inspections and lawsuits, and 40 percent of the private media companies practice self-censorship, such as avoiding criticism of local authorities. These data appear in Table 4.2.

The Independent Media and Government Harassment. In Naryn, all major media outlets that cover provincial politics are state-sponsored, but in Samara, Ul'ianovsk, and Osh, approximately half of the media are "independent," meaning that they are not included in a government

---

[1] Conclusions in this section are drawn primarily from 40 interviews I conducted with editors and journalists of independent and state media outlets and my reviews of their publications and broadcasts. I confirmed the information through interviews with other political activists, government officials, and representatives of international organizations and conversations with informed citizens. Details about data gathering appear in the section on "Alternative Sources of Information" in Appendix D.

budget and no government entity owns controlling shares in them.[2] Instead, independent newspapers and broadcasting stations rely on revenue from advertising, side businesses, and subscriptions or paid programming. Some have also received monetary assistance from local businesspeople or foreign NGOs. Consider, for example, the independent broadcasting station OSH TV. In 1991, a former communications engineer for Kyrgyz state television began to lease airtime in order to broadcast his own programs. Two years later, the founder purchased a channel, and OSH TV now survives on income from advertising, infrequent foreign grants, and paid programming. For a fee, the station creates tributes to family members and coworkers and advertisements for electoral candidates

Financial independence has guaranteed editorial autonomy in Samara and Osh but not in Ul'ianovsk, where private media suffer government interference. In Ul'ianovsk, provincial officials harass the independent media by declining to grant interviews, turning down requests for statistics, refusing to print issues, discouraging businesspeople from placing advertisements, and bringing lawsuits against private media companies. Media outlets have also been subject to unusual state inspections and loss of utilities and offices. The general impression among independent media representatives in Ul'ianovsk is that the provincial government punishes those who criticize the administration. The one independent media outlet in Ul'ianovsk that has not suffered reprisals has intentionally avoided criticism of the oblast government.

The most benign form of punishment in Ul'ianovsk is the "information blockade." The oblast administration gives information to the media that support the governor and restricts information to those that do not. Depending on a media outlet's prior coverage of the governor, "The governor finds or does not find time [for an interview]. It is the style of work here."[3] Typically, the governor grants interviews only to state media outlets, so the independent media must rely on the governor's press service for information. One independent broadcasting

---

[2] The list of the state and independent media outlets appears in Appendix D in the section on "Alternative Sources of Information."

[3] Author's interview (178) with an editor of an independent media outlet, Ul'ianovsk oblast, November 14, 1997.

company has not been able to get statistics about murders in the oblast, whereas state media have access to these data. Another independent media outlet has found it impossible to obtain statistics on the provincial hockey team: The staff suspects that the information is not forthcoming because the governor's son sponsors the team. Besides the outright denial of information, government officials in Ul'ianovsk also make the process of obtaining material more difficult for independent media. One private media outlet threatened to take provincial government officials to court for withholding information, but the officials claimed that they would simply lie and say they had never received the verbal request. After this exchange, the correspondents began to submit written requests for information, but this has not solved the problem because officials do not provide the information in a timely manner, claiming that the request is being reviewed by first one civil servant and then another.

The Ul'ianovsk government also pressures media outlets by making state inspections, breaking leases, and disconnecting utilities. When the private newspaper *Simbirskii kur'er* refused to relinquish ownership to a local government leader in 1993, local officials conducted a month-long inspection of the newspaper. The officials looked through the newspaper's records for signs that it had illegally used government funds during the Soviet era when it had been the newspaper of the oblast soviet (council). The newspaper was fined 20 million rubles, a significant amount for the organization at the time, but the company refused to pay and was in court over the issue for two and a half years. In the end, the paper won the case, but its troubles have continued. In 1994, after unsuccessfully trying to take ownership of the newspaper, the city mayor at the time claimed that the newspaper's lease had ended and the paper had to move. The editor-in-chief argued that the lease could only be terminated if the newspaper had violated the agreement, and she mentioned that the paper had contacts in the international media and threatened to publicize their predicament. In the face of this threat, the paper was allowed to remain in the building. Similarly, another media outlet reported that its telephones were turned off for political reasons.

Because the provincial government in Ul'ianovsk has a near monopoly on printing, restricting access to the government press is another

means of harassing private newspapers.[4] Twice the government printing facility refused to print one independent newspaper, the first
time in reaction to coverage of the 1996 gubernatorial election campaign and the second in 1997 when the media company owed it
money. A staff member at the paper contends that the reasons behind
the second refusal were also political. After all, this newspaper had
already agreed on a payment plan with the printing facility, and issues
of other publications with debts to the printing facility have been
printed.

The Ul'ianovsk government also pressures private media by discouraging businesses from advertising with them. For example, one enterprise director reported to the editor of an independent newspaper that
the oblast administration specifically forbade him to place ads in the
publication. Businesses need to maintain good relations with the governor in order to remain solvent. Many companies are partially owned
by the oblast government, and those that are not fear tax inspections
and difficulties obtaining credit.

Lawsuits brought by government officials in Ul'ianovsk have led
to a "constant trial against journalists," as one media representative
described the situation.[5] Another said he felt as if oblast government
officials read independent newspapers searching for a reason to sue.
When correspondents are found guilty, their companies issue retrac-
tions and pay fines, which can threaten the survival of the firms.

In many of the court cases, provincial authorities sued local independent media outlets merely for publishing or broadcasting information
that the national press already reported. For example, the oblast parliament sued one newspaper for reporting on a television program doc-
umenting the parliament's work. The governor took two newspapers
to court because they published a document the national parliament
issued about its inquiry into the governor's potential use of federal
credit for the benefit of his family and friends. The governor sued the
provincial newspapers because he claimed that they could not prove
the allegations in the federal document. In another case, the governor

---

4 Despite these problems, independent newspapers and businesspeople have not created an independent printing house because they believe the provincial administration
  would continue to harass them with state inspections of the facility.
5 Author's interview (171) with a journalist from an independent newspaper, Ul'ianovsk
  oblast, November 11, 1997.

sued a newspaper for publishing a national news agency announcement that claimed he had not declared his income.

It is not clear that Ul'ianovsk courts can decide cases like these independent of the administration's influence. In one instance, an Ul'ianovsk newspaper and a newspaper from another province both stood trial in their respective regions for the same alleged violations; however, only the latter won. Similarly, a correspondent for a national newspaper won a case in a Moscow court but lost the same case in front of an Ul'ianovsk judge. Even in libel cases where the governor has not been mentioned in an article, he has won in court.

Government pressure on the independent media in Ul'ianovsk does have limits – officials have not closed media companies nor have they jailed or physically harmed correspondents. Nonetheless, the situation is radically worse than in Samara, where private media companies are free from government harassment. All the independent media leaders I interviewed in Samara considered government information and officials accessible. Furthermore, no one had encountered businesspeople who faced threats from the government for advertising in the independent media. Also, provincial government officials have not sued the "serious" independent media. The tabloid press has come under attack a few times, yet even these newspapers have won some of the cases.

As in the Russian provinces, the media environments in Naryn and Osh also differ greatly. In Naryn, the prosecution of a national correspondent and government harassment of civic activists have discouraged state journalists from leaving their jobs to develop local independent media companies as has occurred in the three other regions. On the initiative of a Naryn oblast prosecutor, a journalist with a national opposition newspaper was jailed for alleged dissemination of misleading information about President Askar Akaev during the presidential election campaign of 1995. This incident, coupled with government harassment of electoral candidates, as later described, has contributed to a climate of fear in Naryn.

By contrast, private media have developed in Osh, and none of their representatives recounted any instances of direct government pressure, such as limited access to information or printing facilities, intimidation of advertisers, or lawsuits. In fact, one independent media leader explained that government officials are sometimes eager to work with the private media because these companies can report things the state media cannot. Essentially, government leaders can use the independent media to wage their own battles.

Self-Censorship by the Independent Media. Government harassment of the independent media is detrimental because it can result in the financial ruin of a firm. Furthermore, negative repercussions, as well as the fear of punishment, encourage self-censorship. As in Samara and Osh, the financial independence of private media firms in Ul'ianovsk ensures that the government will not have direct influence over the content of the publications and broadcasts; however, the unrelenting indirect government pressure in Ul'ianovsk has created an environment of self-censorship. In Naryn, it can be said that the lack of independent media is a form of extreme self-censorship.

In Ul'ianovsk, private media companies tread carefully. One independent media leader explained that his firm would be leery of reporting on corruption in the oblast administration, even if clear evidence existed. "People [meaning representatives of the administration] may come and say we are living too comfortably. Our correspondents are not that type [who investigate corruption]. We don't like to do politics. Politics is a dirty business."[6] Another media representative said that his company would not report on corruption in the provincial government because the governor is powerful and the courts are not necessarily independent: "We would have a big problem. This firm could no longer exist."[7]

Individual journalists also practice self-censorship by abandoning their profession or joining the state media. In response to telephone threats, a broadcast journalist in Ul'ianovsk ceased reporting critically and began to work in the oblast information office. He has three children to feed, and he wanted to continue working as a journalist. He met with the governor and agreed to end his opposition activities.

Most media companies that cover political news lack large numbers of subscribers, so only with the backing of wealthy independent

---

[6] Author's interview (175) with the head of an independent media outlet, Ul'ianovsk oblast, November 13, 1997.
[7] Author's interview (178) with an editor of an independent media outlet, Ul'ianovsk oblast, November 14, 1997.

investors can media outlets in Ul'ianovsk risk irritating provincial authorities. Three private media outlets with a solid financial base have come to accept fines and lawsuits and continue to criticize the provincial government regularly. In fact, these firms organized a demonstration with approximately 800 people in January 1998 to protest violations of freedom of speech in the oblast.[8] As described in the next chapter, these three media outlets have a degree of economic autonomy from local authorities that is rare for Ul'ianovsk, and thus they do not need to practice self-censorship.

In Samara, none of the independent media leaders I interviewed feared reporting on corruption in the oblast government, and many had already done so. Members of private media firms in Osh were also willing to cover provincial corruption.

Editorial "Dependence" of State Media. With government harassment in Ul'ianovsk and Naryn, it is considerably more difficult for independent media to develop and survive in these provinces than in Samara and Osh. But, do state media in Ul'ianovsk and Naryn sometimes challenge government authority, thus serving as an alternative source of information, or do these newspapers and broadcasts simply "toe the party line"?

In Ul'ianovsk and Naryn, as well as in Samara and Osh, state media consistently serve as mouthpieces for the provincial authorities. Typically, the provincial administration or parliament owns the newspaper or station, many of which were once media outlets of the Communist Party or provincial soviets. For example, the newspaper *Volzhskaia kommuna* in Ul'ianovsk was the oblast Communist Party newspaper in the Soviet era, and today it continues to receive government support in the form of subsidies from the oblast budget.

As one would expect, financial dependence on provincial authorities limits the objectivity of the state media. In the daily operation of the state media, government officials play a direct role in editorial decisions or at least occasionally influence content. At one state media outlet in Naryn, a representative from the oblast government helps

---

[8] Sergey Gorin, "Protest Rally for Press Freedom Staged in Ulyanovsk," *Russian Regional Report* 3 (January, 1998); L. B., "'Persecution' of Media Decried in Ulyanovsk," *RFE/RL Newsline*, January 29, 1998.

select topics for reporting, and the board that deals with financial and organizational questions includes a senior secretary from the oblast parliament. In Samara, editors at state media outlets speak with a representative from the administration on potentially controversial issues, and in Ul'ianovsk the governor successfully pressured a state broadcasting company not to report a proposal by an NGO to oust him. State media outlets in Ul'ianovsk also had to support the governor in his election campaign. In Osh, representatives of state media recounted that provincial officials periodically make suggestions for news coverage: " 'Do some more economic articles. Show the reform process. Explain more about the market economy.' "[9] When the prime minister visited the oblast, the Osh administration told the editors which photograph of him to print.

Even when provincial authorities do not directly influence state media, the financial dependence of government newspapers and broadcast companies leads to self-censorship. A state media representative in Ul'ianovsk explained, "We have no censor, but we are our own censor. Each person should know the framework."[10] In the four regions, state correspondents will report unfavorably on the activities of city, county, and national officials and even on oblast government decisions, but they will rarely find fault with the governor. One media representative in Ul'ianovsk explained, "We do not criticize the governor directly. And, when we do question him, we do it without insult."[11] Another explained, "We can swear at the president, but we can only question the governor."[12]

State media outlets in the four provinces censor their own reporting out of respect for their employers and for fear of unpleasant consequences. Correspondents at state media concerns believe that they are working on behalf of the oblast government as "an organ of the state administration," according to the description of one government

---

[9] Author's interview (55) with a deputy editor of a state newspaper, Osh oblast, April 28, 1998.

[10] Author's interview (183) with an editor of a state newspaper, Ul'ianovsk oblast, November 19, 1997.

[11] Author's interview (182) with an editor of a state newspaper, Ul'ianovsk oblast, November 19, 1997.

[12] Author's interview (176) with the head of a state media outlet, Ul'ianovsk oblast, November 14, 1997.

media leader in Naryn.[13] Similarly, a state media representative in Osh claimed that the media outlet's first responsibility was to publish decisions of the oblast administration and parliament.

A member of the Osh media characterized editorial freedom for state outlets by saying, "You can write anything but you have to think.... An editor can be a victim, but an akim cannot be."[14] The least dire consequence for an editor is a barrage of complaints. One state media representative in Osh explained that higher-level officials would often call to defend subordinates, asking, "Why did you say this about respected officials?" Or they will call and say, "We will be swimming," meaning that we are unhappy and we will mull this over. So far, the calls have served as warnings and have never led to more serious repercussions for this editor.

The most common serious consequence is job loss. A media correspondent in Ul'ianovsk refused to praise the governor and was demoted. He began looking for new work, but he could not find employment for a year and a half. The former correspondent claimed that working with a foreign news organization on a controversial issue in the oblast may have further reduced his job opportunities; he suspects officials discouraged potential employers from hiring him.

Coverage and Availability. Because state media do not offer an alternative to the government position in any of the four provinces and independent reporting is under attack in Ul'ianovsk and Naryn, it is accurate to say that alternative sources of information thrive only in Samara and Osh. But, how much coverage of provincial politics do independent media in Samara and Osh provide, and are the reports widely available? Private newspapers and broadcasts are not much use to democracy if they neither offer serious coverage nor reach many citizens.

Independent media in Samara and Osh do cover provincial politics and economics, and although the volume of material is quite small, so are the regions. A Samara resident can find about 11 pages of serious

[13] Author's interview (3) with a journalist from a state newspaper, Naryn oblast, June 20, 1997.
[14] Author's interview (56) with an editor of a state newspaper, Osh oblast, April 29, 1998.

news in the independent newspaper *Samarskoe obozrenie* each week. In Osh, the only independent newspaper is *Mezon*, a publication for Uzbeks in Kyrgyzstan, and each week a person can read a few articles on provincial politics. On television and the radio, residents of Samara and Osh can find daily news programs and analytical shows on political and economic issues most days of the week.

Media reports are in-depth and often challenge local officials and the regional status quo. The Samara newspaper *Samarskoe obozrenie* reported on the formation of a new NGO to protest electoral violations in two regional parliamentary races.[15] *Mezon* described a demonstration in Osh in which more than 300 elderly people demanded money from the government as compensation for their losses in an investment scheme.[16] The television station OSH TV opened the analytical program *Pulse* by noting that the deputy governor had praised the former mayor of the city of Osh when the mayor was in office and then criticized him once he was removed. The host of the program explored how the former mayor should be judged, whether such a relationship between the city and oblast leaderships could develop again, and what problems remain unresolved in the city.

These articles and broadcasts are widely available and, with the exception of issues of the newspaper *Mezon*, broadly accessible. Anyone can receive Samara's independent newspaper *Samarskoe obozrenie* or Osh's *Mezon* by purchasing a reasonably priced subscription. Likewise, in Samara, the broadcasts from the independent broadcasting company RIO cover the entire oblast, and SKAT-TV's signal reaches nearly all residents. OSH TV and ALMAZ radio have trouble reaching the southern region of Osh oblast, which is divided from the north by a mountain chain, but residents of most other parts of the province can receive the signal. Cost is not a deterrent because television and radio signals in both provinces are free. Language is also not a significant barrier, even in Osh, where the population is multiethnic. Non-Uzbeks, approximately 70 percent of the population, are less likely to read *Mezon* than state newspapers because it is produced in Uzbek;

[15] "Proigravshie na vyborakh mashut kulakami posle draki," *Samarskoe obozrenie*, January 19, 1998; 7.
[16] "Aldangan va khurlangan otakhonlar onakhonlar," *Mezon*, April 24–May 1, 1998; 3.

however, OSH TV and ALMAZ appeal to a larger audience. The former has programs in Russian, Uzbek, and Kyrgyz, and the latter broadcasts primarily in Russian, a language known by nearly all residents of the oblast from Soviet times. In Samara, Russian dominates the press and airwaves.

Because independent newspapers and broadcasts in Samara and Osh do not suffer from government interference and are widely available, residents of these regions can more easily obtain alternative sources of information than can people in Ul'ianovsk and Naryn. Residents of Ul'ianovsk have access to independent media, but most of these outlets practice self-censorship for fear of government harassment. In Naryn, there are no independent newspapers or broadcasts covering provincial news. In none of the oblasts are state media a source of alternative information. The democratic guarantee of alternative sources of information is stronger in Samara and Osh than in Ul'ianovsk and Naryn, respectively.

Freedom to Form and Join Organizations

Although civic organizations exist in all four regions, political groups, including parties and human-rights organizations, have significantly greater difficulty operating in Naryn and Ul'ianovsk than in Samara and Osh, respectively.[17] In Naryn, fear of government punishment of activists is so great that the single political organization to emerge no longer functions. In Ul'ianovsk, leaders and members of political organizations have faced threats to their livelihoods and practice self-censorship by limiting their activities or disbanding their groups. Table 4.3 provides data supporting these conclusions.

Harassment of Political Groups. None of the NGO leaders interviewed in any of the oblasts claimed that the oblast government tried

---

[17] This section is based on 55 interviews I conducted with members and leaders of all the independent political groups in each region and with representatives of a sample of nonpolitical civic groups in each province. Interviews with representatives of international organizations, members of the media, other political activists, and government officials, in addition to conversations with informed citizens, corroborated the political groups' accounts. Details about the methodology for this section appear in Appendix D under "Freedom to Form and Join Organizations."

TABLE 4.3. *Comparison: Freedom to Form and Join Organizations (given as the percentage followed by the ratio)*

	Russia		Kyrgyzstan	
Measures	Samara	Ul'ianovsk	Osh	Naryn
Independent political groups punished	8% (1/12)	89% (8/9)	0% (0/6)	0% (0/1)
Independent political groups that self-censor	0% (0/12)	22% (2/9)	0% (0/6)	100% (1/1)

Notes: The ratios are the number of independent political groups that have been punished or that practice self-censorship relative to the total number of political groups. The total number represents all the current and former political parties and human-rights organizations that were active at one time: 12 for Samara, 9 for Ul'ianovsk (one of which is defunct), 6 for Osh, and 1 defunct party for Naryn. Although the absolute numbers are small, meaningful conclusions can be drawn from the data because they represent the entire populations, not samples. See Appendix D, "Freedom to Form and Join Organizations," for further details. Percentages are rounded to whole numbers.

to dissuade them from creating an organization. However, leaders and members of most political organizations in Ul'ianovsk experienced government pressure once they had established their groups, and political activists in Naryn feared government harassment. By contrast, such experiences and sentiments were rare in Samara and Osh. Most likely because they pose little challenge to oblast governments, nonpolitical NGOs in all four oblasts reported no government interference. As a leader of a defunct party in Ul'ianovsk characterized the situation, establishing a party is not difficult, but "if the organization is against the governor, then ... there are problems."[18]

In Ul'ianovsk, nearly all of the leaders of political organizations I interviewed described incidents of firings, threats of job loss, or state inspections as a result of NGO activities. Members of one of the two communist parties in the oblast lost work and received job threats as a result of their political activities. A leader of a centrist party claimed that his members, especially those who are heads of enterprises, feel indirect government pressure at their workplaces through state tax, sanitation, and fire inspections, which are repeated every few months with no sound justification. Likewise, a leader of a democratic party

---

[18] Author's interview (190) with the leader of a defunct party, Ul'ianovsk oblast, December 2, 1997.

recounted that unusual incidents have happened to each of his close colleagues in the organization. Businesspeople experienced repeated inspections, and another colleague did not receive an apartment from the state even though he was next in line.

Although political activists in Naryn expressed fears similar to those of their counterparts in Ul'ianovsk, they did not recount instances of actual government threats or punishments. Reprisals against the one political organization in Naryn are unlikely now, as the group has become inactive. A political activist in Ul'ianovsk made the following general observation: "If a party is healthy, then it is a bother to the administration."[19] Thus, organizations that are not actively engaged in political pursuits are unlikely to provoke the government.

In contrast to Ul'ianovsk and Naryn, pressure on political activists is substantially lower and fear is rare in Samara and Osh. In Samara, fewer than one-tenth of the political activists I interviewed reported government punishments. Leaders of one human-rights organization suspect that the oblast government is tapping their phones, opening their mail, and following them, and they claim that three activists lost their jobs because of their political activity. A leader of a nationalist party contended that its members have not lost work, but one party member could not defend his dissertation and another had his teaching load reduced. A member of the Samara branch of the Communist Party of the Russian Federation claims he was not promoted at work because of his party activity. Overall, such pressure appears much less common in Samara than in Ul'ianovsk. In the latter two examples, it is unlikely that the government played a role in punishing party activists. Instead, disgruntled bosses seem to have punished the activists independently.

In Osh, only one political party leader expressed even slight concern about government pressure. He felt there was a risk that individuals would lose their jobs if they joined his party, yet there had been no cases of threats of job loss or firings. On the contrary, a number of NGO leaders, including human-rights activists and a Communist Party leader, stressed that the government did not bother them. A leader of one of the human-rights organizations in Osh recounted that when its members investigate citizen complaints about state officials, "of course

[19] Author's interview (189) with a party leader, Ul'ianovsk oblast, November 29, 1997.

[the officials] get mad, but we explain that we are lawyers and it is our duty," and they do not interfere.[20]

Self-Censorship by Political Groups. A severe form of self-censorship is the dissolution of a group in response to government punishments or fear of punishments – a practice that has occurred in Ul'ianovsk and Naryn but not in Samara or Osh. Individual group members typically react immediately to pressure by deserting the organization or participating only secretively, in some cases compelling leaders to disband the organization. As described in Chapter 1, the head of a now defunct political party in Ul'ianovsk abandoned the organization because he lost his job as a school director three times between 1991 and 1997 due to his political activity. The party disbanded when similar harassment from local authorities forced other members to leave. Members of a centrist party also left their organization because of repeated state inspections of their businesses; later, one individual confirmed to the party's leader that all incidents have ceased since he relinquished his membership. Some of those that have remained have restricted their activities to giving money anonymously. The entire "democratic" bloc in Ul'ianovsk suffered, according to one former activist, when a key leader had to leave politics because his business could not survive pressure from the administration.

In Naryn, fear of government punishments caused the single political party in the oblast to become inactive. The organization ceased to function "because [the national] leader was jailed [by a national court] and others are afraid," according to the head of the defunct party. When the national leader was jailed in 1996, "this had a big influence," the leader continued. Now "people are afraid to say, 'I am a member of [this party]'.... Then it was easier.... If we created [the party] now, we would be jailed. Then it was peaceful and they gave us the right [to create the party]."[21] The leader of the inactive provincial division explained that now members fear voicing their opinions freely and holding meetings. Although the leader of the defunct party attributed

---

[20] Author's interview (88) with the leader of a human-rights organization, Osh oblast, May 7, 1998.

[21] Author's interview (16) with the leader of a defunct party, Naryn oblast, July 11, 1997.

the fear in his region to the imprisonment of the party's national leader, this is not the primary explanation. After all, members of the Osh division of the same party are also aware of the fate of the national leader, yet they are neither fearful nor inactive.

In Ul'ianovsk and Naryn, fear of government harassment also discourages the formation of groups – the most severe form of self-censorship. An attempt to unite the small community of Ul'ianovsk entrepreneurs failed because businesspeople thought "The administration does not bother me. I won't raise questions," even though 80 percent of them are dissatisfied with regional policies, by one small business owner's estimate.[22] Entrepreneurs in Ul'ianovsk fear political involvement because "those who go against the governor, the administration, are punished."[23] By contrast, organizations in Samara and Osh have not avoided or circumscribed political pursuits, and none has dissolved in response to actual or feared government punishments. As illustrated in the next chapter, the extent of economic autonomy in each region accounts for the difference between each country's provinces, and the degree of personal economic autonomy explains how some individuals in Ul'ianovsk and Naryn nevertheless manage to create and maintain political groups.

Interestingly, authorities in Ul'ianovsk and Naryn have not punished groups by making the registration process difficult.[24] In the late 1990s, the period when I conducted fieldwork, neither Russia nor Kyrgyzstan required that an NGO register with the government; however, completion of registration provided groups with tax privileges and the benefits of legal status, such as the rights to maintain property and to go to court. In Samara and Ul'ianovsk, the registration processes were similar and essentially easy,[25] and registration refusal had not

---

[22] Author's interview (223) with a party leader who is also an entrepreneur, Ul'ianovsk oblast, November 29, 1998.

[23] Author's interview (223) with a party leader who is also an entrepreneur, Ul'ianovsk oblast, November 29, 1998.

[24] This paragraph is based on interviews the author conducted with registration specialists in each region. Accounts of leaders of political NGOs corroborated the information.

[25] By the accounts of registration specialists at the justice bureaus in Samara and Ul'ianovsk, a group holds a founding meeting, decides what kind of organization to register as, and submits to the justice bureau minutes from the meeting, a charter, an application, and a small fee. Within a month, the justice bureau makes a decision.

been a problem in either of the oblasts. In Osh and Naryn, registration proceeded differently. All NGOs from Naryn oblast were required to register in Bishkek, whereas only those Osh groups with a foreign component were forced to register in the capital. The Justice Ministry in Bishkek took over registration of NGOs from Naryn because there were many illegal entities operating, according to a high-level official at the Naryn Oblast Justice Bureau.

The national government may also have made the change in reaction to Naryn's refusal to register a group of 43 Baptists in 1996 under a prior law. According to a high-level official in the oblast administration, the refusal occurred "because we were afraid of [Islamic] religious fanatics. . . . [The religious fanatics] said they would do bad things . . . like beat up the Baptists."[26] The official contends that "Muslim religious fanatics" filled his office, claiming they had supporters in the street, and made this threat. In response to the denied registration, a few journalists suspected the government of religious discrimination, suggesting that the head of the registration organ "did not want to corrupt our religion [and] did not want our people to believe in another religion."[27] Bishkek then reassigned the head of the registration organ to a different oblast, and NGO registration began to take place in Bishkek instead of the oblast.

Even though Naryn NGOs must register in Bishkek, in practice it does not put them at a disadvantage relative to organizations in Osh. Most groups in Osh register in the national capital anyway in order to have the status of a national organization and facilitate expansion beyond the oblast.

Number of Political Groups. The extent of self-censorship and harassment in each region indicates that the right to organize is weaker in

---

If a group's application violates the federal law on organizations, the bureau official refuses to register the group but allows its founders to correct and resubmit their documents. A registration specialist in Ul'ianovsk noted that the law instructs officials not to make registration difficult. "It is written in the law that we should not 'correct' what they are doing." Author's interview (215) with a civil servant, Ul'ianovsk oblast, November 12, 1997.

[26] Author's interview (30) with an official in the oblast administration, Naryn oblast, July 4, 1997.

[27] Author's interview (32) with a journalist with independent media outlets, Naryn oblast, July 2, 1997.

Ul'ianovsk and Naryn. This rich account of the practice of political groups is more informative than looking at the number of groups alone – 127 independent political organizations in Samara, 74 in Ul'ianovsk, 15 in Osh, and 3 in Naryn in 1997, according to lists I compiled from state registries, records of NGO support centers, and telephone directories. (See Appendix D, "Freedom to Form and Join Organizations.") Some of the groups identified as autonomous political groups in these sources receive government funds or are defunct. For example, the three "independent, active" political organizations in Naryn oblast include the defunct party described earlier, a party of those in power, and a human-rights organization that has investigated only family problems – not civil-rights violations. Moreover, the numbers do not indicate how easy or difficult it is to form, join, and maintain an organization. Examining how political organizations actually develop, operate, and dissolve demonstrates that this right to organize is weaker in Ul'ianovsk and Naryn relative to Samara and Osh, respectively.

Activities and Characteristics of Political Groups. Taking advantage of the more permissive environment in their oblasts, parties and human-rights organizations in Samara and Osh are actively involved in local politics, suggesting that the greater freedom to organize is meaningful. These groups encourage public debate on political issues, nominate and support candidates for office, and observe elections – functions that are important in order for democratic institutions to reflect the informed opinions of citizens. The parties and human-rights organizations also provide assistance to the public by offering legal advice and resolving disputes with authorities. These services enable political groups to better understand the problems citizens face and demonstrate to the public that the freedom to organize – part of the package of democratic reforms – offers concrete benefits.

GENERATING DEBATE. Political groups in Samara and Osh use the mass media and their own publications to encourage discussion and resolution of local issues – often government violations of the law. One political group in Samara wrote letters and opinion pieces that were published in the independent press to expose the problems of pollution in the Volga River and violations of environmental-protection laws in the oblast. The leader of a legal-rights organization in Osh has appeared twice on television and has written newspaper columns examining proposed court-reform legislation and the criminal code. Similarly, a human-rights organization in Samara regularly makes use of the airwaves and distributes its own monthly bulletin to oblast officials and local and national activists to raise awareness of human-rights violations. One edition of the bulletin addressed the delays in the formation of a government commission on human rights in Samara.[28] The monthly newspaper of another political group has criticized officials in the regional parliament for engaging in nepotism and providing subsidies to corporations.[29]

IMPROVING ELECTIONS. Electoral periods are typically the busiest time for political parties and movements. The political organizations in Samara and Osh, propose candidates, run their campaigns, and provide poll observers and electoral commission members. Nearly all parties nominate members or supporters for local and national posts, although only a small proportion of candidates are party nominees. The organizations provide support to nominees as well as to favored independent candidates. The most common forms of assistance are distribution of fliers on behalf of candidates and financial contributions to candidates. In Samara, the Liberal Democratic Party of Russia supported ten candidates for the national parliament – all of whom lost – by paying for radio, television, and newspaper advertisements. Other means of assisting favored candidates include hanging posters, organizing meetings with voters, holding press conferences, and designing advertisements. In Samara, a well-known activist from a local political movement offered personal testimonials, and members of the oblast branch of the party Iabloko provided informal advice about candidates to coworkers at their different places of work. Support for a candidate occasionally meant negative campaigning as well. As one party leader in Samara described, "We also worked against candidates we did not like. We recalled what these candidates had done in the

---

[28] "Nastoichivoe trebovanie," *Pravozashchita: Samarskii biulleten'* (May 12, 1997); "Pravo na otkaz," *Pravozashchita: Samarskii biulleten'* (May 12, 1997); Oleg Rusanov, "Ia ne khochu voevat'," *Pravozashchita: Samarskii biulleten'* (May 12, 1997).

[29] "O dinastiiakh, svivshikh gnezdyshko na Molodogvardeiskoi, 187," *Grazhdanskaia initsiativa* 15 (November, 1997); "Sarancha," *Grazhdanskaia initsiativa* 15 (November, 1997).

past and we reminded [voters] through fliers we handed out and put in mailboxes."[30]

Campaigning for favored candidates, even those who lose, enables parties to shape the public debate and perhaps change people's opinions during the election period. By serving as election observers and members of electoral commissions, party representatives can help guard against electoral violations. Observers have played an active role in creating free and fair balloting by notifying the press and government authorities of poll violations, many of which were possible to rectify before voting continued.

RESOLVING PROBLEMS. Democratic theory does not recognize assistance to the general public as a function of political parties, although historically they have served this purpose in democracies. Today, in Samara and Osh, political groups assist nonmembers by providing information and resolving everyday problems. At a time when "democracy" is connected in people's minds with reduced economic stability and increased crime and corruption, parties' assistance to the public indicates to people that there are concrete benefits of liberalism.

With new laws being passed and old laws being rescinded, information about individual legal rights is critical to the public. A legal-rights organization in Osh held four roundtables for schoolchildren to teach them about the law and how to use it to defend themselves. As a human-rights activist in Osh explained, "We inform people about the laws. To resolve violations of human rights, people need to know their rights. We need a legal culture so people question and challenge."[31]

To directly resolve problems for citizens, political groups offer advice, contact government officials, and provide representation in court. Individuals often feel civil servants have wronged them. As the leader of a political group in Samara explained, people "usually [need] defense against the state."[32] In that region, a human-rights organization helped people sue the Russian state bank, Sberbank, for money lost to inflation. The leader of the organization described the aid his group

---

[30] Author's interview (121) with the head of a political party, Samara oblast, February 10, 1998.

[31] Author's interview (63) with the head of a human-rights organization, Osh oblast, April 29, 1998.

[32] Author's interview (119) with the head of a political organization, Samara oblast, February 9, 1998.

offers: "The court process can cost one and a half million rubles, so we provide [free] assistance to people by preparing documents, doing inquiries, and representing them in court. [We] also try to teach people how to do these procedures themselves."[33] Moreover, the group has provided legal support to employees who sought better dormitory conditions and to laid-off workers who lost both their jobs and their apartments at the plant. Other cases have addressed unfair firings and delayed wages.

In Osh, a legal-rights organization provides consultations at its offices in the provincial capital and in the town of Nookat. Lawyers advise individuals on issues similar to those in Samara as well as criminal problems and welfare questions, such as benefits for families with many children. The representatives of the organization explain the law, suggest how to resolve the problem, and provide writing samples for documents and letters to authorities. Another legal-rights group in the oblast has helped people who are struggling with financial issues, such as selling a home or fixing soured deals. In addition, this organization offers specific services for NGOs, including dissemination of information on possible donors and associations' legal rights. Party heads in Osh have provided individual assistance in resolving everyday problems. Leaders give money to people in need and share complaints with representatives of state organs and the national parliament. One party head helped veterans of the war in Afghanistan take their case for free apartments and other benefits to the Supreme Court of the Kyrgyz Republic. According to another leader in Osh, government officials listen to him because he knows about their illegal and unethical activities and because he has good connections in the region.

To assist citizens, most political organizations hold regular office hours, typically in the provincial capitals and in many cases in one or two outlying locations. Office hours usually occur one to three times a week, although people seeking assistance stop by at other times as well. Organizations with office hours tend to average 10 to 28 requests for help per week, whereas groups without formal hours, such as parties in Osh, may help only 3 to 15 people per month. Parties typically

---

[33] Author's interview (138) with the head of a human-rights organization, Samara oblast, February 15, 1998.

receive more requests during election campaigns; they hear ultimatums such as "Resolve this or I won't come to the elections," a practice one party leader attributed to Soviet times.[34] Even though there were no multiparty elections in the Soviet era, the Communist Party required local officials to ensure high voter turnout as a symbol of support for the regime. Today, political parties use this tradition to their advantage, telling assistance-seekers "We could solve your problems better if you voted for us," one party leader in Samara revealed.[35]

Besides shaping debates, participating in elections, and assisting citizens, political organizations in Samara and Osh try to influence government policy. In Samara, parties and political movements staged protests and organized petitions about rent hikes in state housing and sent letters to oblast and national officials about nonpayment of wages. Such forms of activism are common among communist, nationalist, and democratic organizations. In response to a Samara city decision to raise apartment rents, the oblast division of the KPRF lobbied for a more gradual escalation and no hike without salary increases and payment of back wages. Moreover, the party organized a petition against any rent hikes made without citizens' input. The campaign contributed to a reversal of the rent hikes under the next mayoral administration. In Osh, a legal-rights organization has tried to influence policy by reviewing republican legislation on court reform and the criminal code and sharing its suggestions with the region's national parliamentary deputies. The leader of a party in the province has tried to convince the regional governor and *akims* at all levels to appoint party supporters to government posts.

Political groups in both Osh and Samara have had little success getting their people into local offices. Other than Our Home is Russia (Nash Dom Rossiia, or NDR), the party of power in the 1990s,[36] only one party in Samara has a representative in the oblast administration. The head of an oblast department chairs the Samara branch

---

[34] Author's interview (122) with the head of a political party, Samara oblast, February 11, 1998.

[35] Author's interview (117) with a political party leader, Samara oblast, February 6, 1998.

[36] At this time, the governor was chair of the oblast division of NDR and held a national leadership position, and 10 oblast deputies were members. *Regional'naia elita: kto est' kto* (Moscow: SNIK Tsentre, 1998), 255.

of the Russian United Industrialists Party (Rossiiskaia Ob"edinennaia Promyshlennaia Partiia, or ROPP) and serves on the council of the national organization. In the 25-member legislature, the KPRF claims two members and Iabloko one. In Osh, none of the parties has representatives in the oblast administration or *kenesh*.

Political organizations in Osh and Samara have fared better in national parliamentary elections. The Democratic Party of Free Kyrgyzstan (Demokraticheskaia Partiia "Erkin Kyrgyzstan," or ErK) and the Party of Communists of Kyrgyzstan (Partiia Kommunistov Kyrgyzstana, or PKK) each had a representative in Osh's 26-member delegation to the two houses of the Zhogorku Kenesh. The president of an ethnic organization that is developing a political party is also a national deputy. Compared with their counterparts in Osh, parties in Samara have had even greater success with representation in the national parliament. Four of the six winners of single-mandate seats in Samara were nominated by an independent party – three by the KPRF and one by the Agrarian Party. The party in power nominated the remaining two.[37]

Although oblast party divisions nominate candidates for national office and help them campaign, the most successful contenders are local (or even national) notables who likely benefit more from their own prominence than their party affiliation. For example, the Osh branch of the Party of Communists of Kyrgyzstan supported Absamat Masaliev, who founded the national organization, ran for president of the country, and previously served as first secretary of the Kyrgyz SSR. Political organizations in the two provinces have made some progress toward representation in government; however, their greatest influence on government is through activism.

The work of political groups in the two regions – their revelations about government oversights, their nomination of opposition candidates, their protests against government policy, and their minimal success getting supporters into government offices – indicates that these organizations are not government organs masquerading as NGOs, as

---

[37] The greater party representation in Samara, as compared with Osh, is not surprising considering that the requirement that half of the seats in the Russian State Duma be filled by party list strengthened parties, which has spilled over into the single-mandate races. In Kyrgyzstan, legislators in both houses were elected from single-mandate districts.

Western observers have suspected. This is further confirmed by the founding stories and the financial status of these groups. None of the independent political groups was initiated by the authorities, and none is funded by the government.

With the greater freedom to form and maintain organizations in Samara and Osh, political groups in these provinces engage in meaningful activities. In Dahl's terms, the organizations help citizens "formulate their preferences" by informing people about public issues. Their specific missions and their support for particular candidates "signify preferences" that exist in the community. Without numerous representatives in local governments, these organizations have had greater difficulty ensuring that "preferences are weighed equally by officials." Yet, these freedoms are relatively new, and the skills of political groups will likely improve in regions like these where they can be put to use. Moreover, political organizations have provided the additional benefit of assistance to the public – a development that will help boost citizens' confidence in recent political changes.

Eligibility for Public Office

Entering an electoral race in Ul'ianovsk or Naryn requires a certain level of bravery because one may be subject to harassment by government officials. This is practically unheard of in Samara and Osh.[38] In none of the regions do electoral commissions or other "gatekeepers" prevent individuals from registering as candidates. However, in Ul'ianovsk and Naryn, local officials informally punish individuals who declare their intentions to run in key races and those who are highly viable candidates. Oblast officials will visit these contestants

---

[38] Analyses of electoral processes are based on the most recent elections at the time of fieldwork. For Samara, these are the December 1996 gubernatorial elections and the December 1997 oblast parliamentary elections. The most recent elections in Ul'ianovsk were the December 1996 gubernatorial elections and December 1995 oblast parliamentary elections. Kyrgyzstanis do not elect their governors, so the analyses are based on the February 1995 oblast parliamentary elections alone. Information in this section is drawn from interviews with 38 candidates, including both winners and losers, as well as regional campaign workers and election observers and regional and national election officials. Media representatives and other political activists provided confirming information. Further details appear in the section "Eligibility for Public Office and Right of Political Leaders to Compete for Support" in Appendix D.

after their announcement or registration of candidacy to discourage them from running, often by threatening their livelihood. This pressure can result in potential candidates opting not to run and registered candidates abandoning races – forms of self-censorship. During the campaign period and after the election, those who have entered and remained in the races may be fired from their jobs or experience pressure on their businesses. These candidates' campaign managers and volunteers face similar penalties. By destroying campaign teams, these livelihood punishments reduce candidates' ability to compete for support – the focus of the next section. Harassment of candidates and their supporters at any time discourages these individuals from participating in future elections, another form of self-censorship.

Punishments before, during, and after elections are most common in key contests, such as gubernatorial races in Ul'ianovsk and parliamentary contests against local luminaries in both Ul'ianovsk and Naryn. Because of the restricted autonomy of regional parliaments in Kyrgyzstan, campaign workers in races for oblast parliaments are less likely to suffer punishments than those assisting in national elections. Local officials have little incentive to interfere in oblast races because regional deputies have limited influence. In Ul'ianovsk and Naryn, contenders with little economic autonomy and particularly viable candidates, such as well-loved factory bosses, are especially likely to suffer punishments. These candidates face harassment regardless of their party affiliation; many are not even connected with a party.

Approximately half of the losing candidates interviewed in Ul'ianovsk and Naryn experienced government pressure at some time during the election. Of the winning candidates interviewed in the four provinces, only one in Naryn suffered reprisals, and no other harassment of winning candidates was reported. That harassment was more common among losers is not surprising considering how government officials helped their favored candidates win, as explained in the next section. At the same time, the fact that winning candidates and election observers in Naryn and Ul'ianovsk also described government pressure against certain contenders suggests that such reports were not simply concocted by sore losers.

In Table 4.4, I document the frequency of punishments based on samples of candidates. The percentages of punished candidates are not extraordinarily high because only certain types of candidates are targets

TABLE 4.4. *Comparison: Eligibility for Public Office and Right of Political Leaders to Compete for Support (given as the percentage followed by the ratio)*

	Russia		Kyrgyzstan	
Measures	Samara	Ul'ianovsk	Osh	Naryn
Candidates punished	0% (0/10)	18% (2/11)	0% (0/8)	44% (4/9)

Note: The ratios are the number of candidates that have been punished relative to the total sample of candidates. The total sample is a sample of winning and losing candidates for regional parliament and the post of governor in each Russian province and for regional parliament alone in each Kyrgyzstani oblast because governors are not elected in Kyrgyzstan: 10 for Samara, 11 for Ul'ianovsk, 8 for Osh, and 9 for Naryn, or 6 percent of the candidates in Samara, 9 percent in Ul'ianovsk, 5 percent in Osh, and 15 percent in Naryn. See Appendix D, "Eligibility for Public Office," for information about sampling and other details.

of government pressure, as described earlier. The number of candidates interviewed in each region is relatively small because it represents only one of many different groups of people I interviewed. Larger samples of candidates would have necessitated fewer interviews of members of other groups, such as journalists or party leaders. Moreover, in the Kyrgyzstani regions, where official candidate lists provide scant information and telephones and street signs are rare, unsuccessful candidates were quite difficult to find. Nonetheless, the sharp differences between the experiences of candidates interviewed in the regions of each country indicate that it is more difficult to run for office in Ul'ianovsk and Naryn than in Samara and Osh. Accounts from media representatives and other activists about harassment of additional candidates and campaign workers further support this conclusion.

Harassment of Candidates at the Outset. Prior to election campaigns, oblast officials in Ul'ianovsk and Naryn harassed those who entered or made public their plans to enter races against prominent incumbents and those who were local luminaries outside of the government. No candidates in Samara and Osh reported government pressure not to run. In Ul'ianovsk, a mid-level oblast administration official visited a well-respected factory director one day after the director registered as a gubernatorial candidate. The official tried to dissuade him from running, but the candidate remained in the race. This individual suffered negative repercussions at his workplace after losing the contest, as I describe in the next section, on electoral competition. In Naryn, a winning parliamentary candidate, who ran against the deputy head of an important county, recounted that oblast officials tried three times to convince him not to run, yet he stayed in the race. Another winning candidate in Naryn also confirmed cases where the oblast administration had pressured individuals not to seek parliamentary seats. By contrast, in Samara a deputy head of a county ran against the county leader for an oblast office, and the former suffered no harassment during the campaign and won the race.

As in the case of political groups, electoral candidates do not encounter harassment at the point of registration. The electoral commissions in the four regions did not illegally deny anyone the right to become a candidate, according to election watchers and media representatives.[39] Moreover, winners and losers in the four regions confirmed that the process of becoming a candidate followed the law and was not onerous. An unsuccessful gubernatorial candidate in Samara claimed that incumbents had an easier time gathering signatures – an initial step in the registration process – because they could recruit state managers to help: "Bosses of factories created teams and said, 'Sign for [the incumbent governor Konstantin] Titov!' whereas I only had volunteers [collect signatures]."[40] Nonetheless, even without the benefits of incumbency and managerial positions, contenders in Russia were able to collect the necessary signatures with the assistance of NGOs and friends. For example, office seekers affiliated with the KPRF could rely on this party's strong local networks to complete petitions. Winning and losing candidates in Kyrgyzstan found the process even easier than their Russian counterparts because contenders in Kyrgyzstan did not have to collect signatures. As a result, "any fool could run," according to an editor in Osh.[41]

---

[39] Potential candidates were only refused registration in two instances: first, when they collected too few signatures, and second, when the electoral commissions identified false signatures, which could not count toward the total. Media representatives in Ul'ianovsk also noted that people could not run if they submitted their documents past the deadline – another example of a legal refusal.

[40] Author's interview (140) with an unsuccessful candidate, Samara oblast, February 26, 1998 and March 4, 1998.

[41] Author's interview (61) with an editor of an independent media outlet, Osh oblast, May 6, 1998.

Self-Censorship by Candidates at the Outset. Individuals interested in running for public office can exercise self-censorship by never entering a race in the first place. Although measuring this phenomenon is like listening for dogs that do not bark, there are known cases of individuals deciding not to run because of government pressure. In one case, the oblast administration in Ul'ianovsk refused to give a potential candidate's organization its budgeted share of federal funds, and the governor resigned from the steering committee of the organization to protest the individual's possible candidacy. The head of the organization decided not to run for governor, and the organization now receives its share of federal money. Moreover, the potential candidate has become a political ally of the governor.

Individuals who stayed in the gubernatorial race in Ul'ianovsk included the incumbent and three candidates who were economically autonomous from local authorities, as described in the next chapter. Also remaining in the race were a fifth candidate, who after the election left his job to work for an oppositional mayor, and a sixth candidate, who was a "sitting duck," as Russians say, meaning he was put in the race by the incumbent. Fake candidates are common throughout the former Soviet Union, as they make the elections seem legitimate even if all the opposition candidates drop out. In the race, Duma deputy Aleksandr Kruglikov came in second with 33.71 percent of the vote, following incumbent Iurii Goriachev's win of 42.48 percent.[42] Kruglikov, who also heads the regional branch of the KPRF, is economically autonomous because of his position as a Duma deputy.

The Candidate Pool. The greater difficulty of running for office in Ul'ianovsk and Naryn is not reflected in the number of candidates or most of the characteristics of the candidates because registration for candidacy is not restricted and only particular candidates are harassed. The candidates do differ across the four regions in terms of employment sectors, suggesting that the threat of workplace harassment discourages some candidates from running and forces registered contestants out of the race. The next chapter presents the employment statistics,

---

[42] Election results are available from *Vybory glav ispolnitel'noi vlasti sub"ektov Rossiiskoi Federatsii, 1995–1997* (Moscow: Tsentral'naia Izbiratelnaia Komissiia Rossiiskoi Federatsii, 1997), 375.

TABLE 4.5. *Candidates per District (given as a percentage)*

Number of Candidates per District	Russia		Kyrgyzstan	
	Samara	Ul'ianovsk	Osh	Naryn
1	0	0	11	28
2	4	8	17	52
3	24	32	17	7
4	8	16	11	10
5	12	12	14	3
6	8	8	11	0
7	8	20	9	0
8	12	4	6	0
9	4	0	0	0
10	8	0	0	0
11	4	0	3	0
12	4	0	0	0
13	4	0	0	0

Sources: Information concerning the number of candidates comes from electoral coverage in the following newspapers: Samara's *Volzhskaia kommuna*, Ul'ianovsk's *Narodnaia gazeta*, and Osh's *EkhOsha*. For Ul'ianovsk, I also used a list of candidates from the oblast electoral commission. Data for the Naryn candidates come from electoral records available at the Naryn oblast parliament.

demonstrating the importance of economic autonomy, but here let us examine the number of candidates in each region and their other biographical characteristics.

The number of candidates who ran is comparable within each country, with an average of six contestants in each parliamentary district in Samara, five in Ul'ianovsk, and four and two in Osh and Naryn, respectively.[43] Table 4.5 provides the actual numbers. Slightly more than 10 percent of the precincts in Osh were uncontested, whereas nearly one-third of precincts in Naryn had only one candidate. Most likely, population density accounts for the different averages between Osh and Naryn: Osh and Naryn have 31 and 6 people per square kilometer,

---

[43] For the 25 parliamentary seats in each province, 158 and 114 candidates competed in Samara and Ul'ianovsk, respectively. There were five candidates per 100,000 residents in Samara and eight in Ul'ianovsk. In Osh, 147 candidates ran for 35 parliamentary seats, and in Naryn 61 candidates competed in 29 electoral districts. There were ten candidates per 100,000 residents in Osh and 23 in Naryn.

respectively. However, punishments related to eligibility for office may also account for a large number of uncontested races in Naryn. In the gubernatorial races, which occur in Russia but not Kyrgyzstan, there were three candidates in Samara and six in Ul'ianovsk.

Within each country, the candidate pools are quite similar. Table 4.6 compares the parliamentary candidates in Samara and Ul'ianovsk. The average candidate in both Samara and Ul'ianovsk is a male in his 30s, 40s, or 50s. He has a postsecondary degree in a technical science, such as engineering or agriculture, and he leads a state, private, or mixed-ownership firm. He was nominated for office by a group of coworkers or neighbors, not a political organization, and he is not a member of any party. Gubernatorial candidates in the two provinces are also middle-aged males, mostly with postsecondary technical degrees and positions of leadership in business or government.

In the Russian provinces, both nonelite contenders and the general public were aware of the overwhelming number of leaders in the candidate pools. A candidate in Samara raised this concern in his published statement and provided an insightful portrait of the average Russian's life.

> I...think that representatives of the average people should be elected to the Samara [oblast parliament] – not directors, businessmen, mayors, and their deputies who should serve the people but not represent them and [who should] not decide what is better for them and what they need. This is like "making the goat guard the cabbage." How can a mayor, businessman, or a director understand the problems of the ordinary worker? After all, they do not stand for an hour at the bus stop; they do not "allow themselves" to ride on the jammed buses; they do not cram with a few families into one apartment; they do not rent housing for 900,000 rubles; they do not run around the block in search of a working pay phone; and miserly pensions and salaries are not withheld from them. They do not fear falling ill, knowing that they have enough money for an operation and medicine; they do not fear criminals and hooligans: a healthy, strong guy guards them and their families. They are going to resolve such problems? The only worker among the candidates, I ask you to support me – one of you.[44]

---

[44] "Kandidaty v deputaty Samarskoi gubernskoi dumi: Tatishchevskii okrug N 13," *Volzhskaia kommuna*, December 2, 1997, 3.

TABLE 4.6. *Characteristics of Parliamentary Candidates in the Russian Regions (given as the percentage of candidates)*

	Samara	Ul'ianovsk
Gender[a]		
Male	93	84
Female	7	16
Year of birth[b]		
1900–1931	0	4
1932–1940	10	20
1941–1951	34	31
1952–1966	47	44
1967–1975	8	2
Source of nomination[c]		
Voter group	84	71
Organization	16	18
Self-nomination	0	10

	Samara	Ul'ianovsk
Field of education[d]		
Technical sciences	50	49
Social sciences	9	11
Medicine	9	11
Law	9	4
Humanities	3	0
Military sciences	3	2
Pedagogy	0	9
Multiple fields	17	12
None (school only)	4	4
Highest level of education[e]		
Graduate	9	9
Postsecondary	81	77
Vocational secondary	6	11
General secondary	4	3

	Samara	Ul'ianovsk[f]
Current employment position[f]		
Head	60	50
Deputy head	11	12
Division head	9	10
Deputy division head	0	1
Employee/Student	19	26
Unemployed/Retired	1	2

[a] The gender statistic is based on all the candidates from each oblast: 158 in Samara and 114 in Ul'ianovsk.

[b] The birth-year figures are based on 116 and 112 candidates from Samara and Ul'ianovsk, respectively.

[c] Data about nominations were available for all but one of the candidates from Samara and seven of the candidates from Ul'ianovsk.

[d] Field of education data are based on 117 candidates from Samara and 57 from Ul'ianovsk. Technical sciences include engineering, agricultural sciences, physics, and mathematics. Social sciences include economics, business, and finance. Humanities include languages, history, and journalism. Incorporating the fields of study of those who had multiple degrees did not change the relationship between the categories: Technical degrees still outnumbered all the other fields combined.

[e] Highest level of education data were available for 117 candidates in Samara and 64 in Ul'ianovsk. Graduate means the person obtained a *kandidat* or *doktor* degree or is currently studying for such a degree. Postsecondary includes those who studied at or obtained a degree from an *institut* or a military or pedagogical *uchilishche*. Vocational secondary refers to those who completed or attended *tekhnikum* or an *uchilishche* that was not military or pedagogical. General secondary means that the individual attended or completed only secondary school.

[f] From the statistics on current employment position, three candidates from Samara are missing and two candidates from Ul'ianovsk are missing.

Sources: For biographical data about candidates, I relied on newspapers, electoral records, and my own interviews with winners and losers. Oblast newspapers in Russia publish a detailed biography of each candidate.

There is no prevailing pattern for other characteristics, including Communist Party membership, government service, and ethnicity.[45] In both Samara and Ul'ianovsk, some candidates had joined the Communist Party at a young age, others joined later in life, and a third group had never joined. Likewise, when the Communist Party was banned, some candidates tore up their party cards, whereas others treasure them and never renounced their membership. Among the candidates, there were also experienced politicians and newcomers to the political arena, and the ethnic backgrounds of the contenders reflected the demographics of the provinces.

As in the Russian provinces, the average candidate in both Osh and Naryn was a male in his 30s, 40s, or 50s. He had at least a post-secondary education and was a leader at his workplace. A group of coworkers or neighbors nominated him for office, and he was not a member of any party.[46] Moreover, there was no prevailing pattern concerning Communist Party membership, government service, ethnicity, or clan.[47] Despite portrayals by scholars, journalists, and policymakers of clan identity directing events in Kyrgyzstan, there is no evidence that clan affiliation in either region is particularly helpful or harmful to becoming a candidate.[48] No particular clan or clans were dominant in the candidate pool. Overall, clan seems to have a neutral

---

[45] For this information, I relied on my interviews with a sample of candidates because this information is not published or available from the electoral commissions. I also drew on my interviews with campaign workers, election observers, media representatives, and other political activists.

[46] Published information about candidates in Kyrgyzstan is scant, so I cannot provide a chart of comprehensive data as I do for candidates in Samara and Ul'ianovsk.

[47] Ethnicity may not even be an influential category. Richard Rose found that education and economic position had a greater impact on attitudes toward democracy than religious and ethnic identities. See Richard Rose, "How Muslims View Democracy: Evidence from Central Asia," *Journal of Democracy* 13 (October, 2002), 102–111. Unlike the Russian office seekers, candidates in Kyrgyzstan were often deputies at other levels. In Naryn, more than half of the candidates I interviewed also served as deputies at another level, typically in a village *kenesh*. This practice seemed to exist in Osh as well, but it was less common. The preponderance of village deputies likely resulted from discussions during the 1994 village elections that village deputies would elect county and oblast deputies. As a result, notables throughout the country ran for these low-level positions.

[48] For example, see Kathleen Collins, "Clans, Pacts, and Politics in Central Asia," *Journal of Democracy* 13 (July, 2002); Collins, "The Logic of Clan Politics; Huskey, "Kyrgyzstan: The Fate of Political Liberalization," 267.

effect on activism.[49] Likewise, although respect for elders remains part of Central Asian culture, younger citizens ran against elders for posts.

Although the counts of candidates and the composition of the contestant pool suggest that it is equally easy for anyone to become a candidate within each country, in Ul'ianovsk and Naryn contestants face pressure to abandon the race. The candidates with the greatest chance of winning typically suffer the most harassment, and few individuals in Ul'ianovsk and Naryn can withstand punishments. Thus, as was the case with the Ul'ianovsk gubernatorial contenders described earlier, viable opposition candidates drop out of the race or likely never enter. Although opposition candidates do exist, the exit of the most viable ones reduces the degree of competition. In sum, eligibility for office is weaker in Ul'ianovsk and Naryn relative to Samara and Osh, respectively.

Right of Political Leaders to Compete for Support

Once an office seeker registers as a candidate, is he free to campaign among the voters, or do the tactics of his opponents or the behavior of government officials restrict his ability to compete? In all four regions, candidates try to undermine their opponents by spreading false information, for example, and government officials hinder fair competition by overtly supporting particular contestants. But, only in Ul'ianovsk and Naryn do government authorities take the additional step of punishing individuals who run against their favored contenders or who assist opposition candidates.[50]

---

[49] Collins argues that clan networks play a significant role in national elite politics. However, Jones Luong finds that these networks are more regional than clan-based. See Collins, "The Logic of Clan Politics"; Jones Luong, *Institutional Change and Political Continuity*.

[50] As in the previous section, analyses of electoral processes are based on the December 1996 gubernatorial elections and the December 1997 oblast parliamentary elections in Samara, the December 1996 gubernatorial elections and December 1995 oblast parliamentary elections in Ul'ianovsk, and the February 1995 oblast parliamentary elections in Osh and Naryn. I drew conclusions about the right of political leaders to compete for support primarily from interviews with 38 winning and losing candidates, as well as campaign workers and election observers in each region and national and subnational election officials. Media representatives and other political activists

Harassment of Candidates during and after the Campaign. The most famous case of government punishments in Ul'ianovsk involved the factory director who remained in the gubernatorial race despite pressure at the outset of his candidacy. He also faced negative repercussions in the year following the election. Twice the provincial authorities turned off his factory's gas, in one case for two weeks, causing the company to lose a significant sum of money. The provincial administration alleged that the enterprise lost power because it had not paid its bill; however, most firms owe the oblast administration for utilities, and the government has not turned the gas off at all these companies. Moreover, the oblast administration owes this federal factory money for services. President Yeltsin resolved the immediate conflict over utilities by calling the oblast administration and demanding that gas again be supplied. Nonetheless, the governor has continued to try to oust his former opponent from the factory, according to members of the media. The head of a political-rights organization recounted how another individual lost his job because he ran for the parliament in Ul'ianovsk. In Naryn, a winning candidate confirmed that numerous people had been fired from their jobs because they had run for the oblast *kenesh*.

Government pressure spilled over onto campaign workers as well. In Ul'ianovsk, a political activist described how he was fired from his state job because of his work in support of his party's candidates for oblast office. At least ten individuals in Naryn, including a deputy mayor and heads of *auls* (villages), were fired for backing opponents of candidates favored by the oblast administration. Three of these individuals were campaign workers for Ishenbai Kadyrbekov, a candidate for the Zhogorku Kenesh. Another of Kadyrbekov's campaign workers, who managed to retain his job, was asked by a top oblast administration official to stop supporting the candidate six weeks into the campaign period. A month later, oblast officials audited the institution the campaign worker directed, and the inspection lasted four times longer than is typical.

provided corroborating accounts. The section "Eligibility for Public Office and Right of Political Leaders to Compete for Support" in Appendix D provides additional details.

In Naryn, fear of job loss was so great that the head of the oblast division of an opposition party, also a government employee, refused to meet with the party's presidential candidate when the individual visited the region. Inactivity, however, can also cost people their jobs in Naryn. Some village heads lost their posts because they did not support the government candidate or, according to one journalist, even because the government's candidate lost. In Naryn, job loss was more likely in the national presidential and parliamentary elections because, as one media correspondent explained, "[the oblast parliament] does not mean much in our mentality."[51] In Kyrgyzstan, provincial parliaments have little power, so the stakes are considerably higher in national races.

Self-Censorship by Candidates after the Campaign. The candidate who has withstood pressure to drop out of a race and then suffers negative repercussions after the elections practices self-censorship by not running in future races for fear of further harassment. None of the candidates in the 1996 Ul'ianovsk gubernatorial race – the competition with the most severe government punishments – ran for governor in the next election in 2000. The field of candidates and one's family situation, among other factors, can influence an individual's decision to enter a race. Nonetheless, it is surprising that none of the earlier contenders returned for a second competition. Some of the candidates in 1996 most likely decided they had already suffered enough negative repercussions for their political involvement.

Unethical Campaigning. Government harassment has occurred only in Ul'ianovsk and Naryn, but this is not to suggest that authorities in Samara and Osh do not influence campaigning. In all four provinces, government officials tend to help favored candidates, thus hampering the campaigns of opposition candidates. Moreover, candidates themselves are no paragons of honesty. By giving gifts to voters, ignoring spending limits, and paying for media coverage, contenders also flout electoral laws. Government meddling during the campaign period and candidates' violations of campaign rules have a weaker impact on electoral outcomes than government harassment of contestants.

---

[51] Author's interview (5) with the head of a state media outlet, Naryn oblast, June 25, 1997.

Nonetheless, these campaign stories help complete the picture of post-Soviet elections.

GOVERNMENT MEDDLING IN CAMPAIGNS. Officials guilty of interfering with campaigns typically are not members of the electoral commissions. Instead, provincial and lower-level authorities running for office or partial to a particular candidate meddle in races. They influence contests by limiting certain candidates' access to voters, providing unequal media coverage, and using their positions to help themselves or others win office.

As part of their campaigns, most contestants in the four regions met with voters at schools, workplaces, apartment complexes, and public meeting places, such as teahouses and mosques in Osh. Gubernatorial candidates in Ul'ianovsk often found their access to voters restricted, but when the candidates contacted the Ul'ianovsk Oblast Electoral Commission, the commission resolved the problems immediately. As one losing candidate explained, "Conditions created for us were more difficult than for the other candidate,"[52] meaning the incumbent governor and victor Goriachev. For example, one candidate was denied access to the 20,000 workers of Ul'ianovsk Automobile Factory, whereas Goriachev could meet with the employees. Another candidate in Ul'ianovsk arrived at a public hall to find that a concert was taking place at the time designated for his meeting. In the end, he met with voters during the concert, against local authorities' wishes. Another gubernatorial candidate had lights turned off during his meetings in public halls, and he arrived at one location to be told that the building could not be opened.

Media coverage also favored government candidates in Samara and Ul'ianovsk, but it was a less contentious issue in Osh and Naryn, where the media provide little electoral information. Representatives of the state media in both Russian oblasts claimed that they were instructed to support the incumbent governor.

In my own review of election coverage by the state newspaper *Volzhskaia kommuna* in Samara, I found signs of bias toward state candidates. The newspaper printed biographies for all candidates, but it ran articles about only some of them. Specifically, the paper published

---

[52] Author's interview (201) with an unsuccessful candidate who is also an entrepreneur, Ul'ianovsk oblast, December 1, 1997.

articles about each of the following state officials running for office: the head of the Samara oblast division of the state pension fund, a mayor, a gas industry official, the head of Samara airport, the deputy head of the oblast social defense department, the head of an agricultural enterprise that was once a collective farm, a state factory head, a county administration head, and the first deputy director of the state concern Volgapromgaz. Most of these articles were directly related to the elections, and many were labeled "Elections-97" or had the name and number of the candidate's electoral district. Some also had a box with a check mark, evoking the idea of a ballot. The newspaper ran not only a biography but also two articles about the head of the oblast publishing house, one of the paper's owners. One story was entitled "Why I support [this candidate]...," and it had testimonials from members of the medical academy of sciences.[53] The head of the oblast parliament, who was running for reelection, received frequent front-page coverage in *Volzhskaia kommuna*. In the four weeks before the election, the paper ran at least one story about him on the front page of 10 of 12 issues. These articles did not simply report on his activities as chair: On eight occasions, the stories directly discussed his candidacy.[54]

---

[53] I. Ivanov, "Viacheslav Cherniavin: 'nastoiashchaia izvestnost' zarabatyvaetsia dobrymi delami, a ne skandalami: interv'iu po povodu," *Volzhskaia kommuna*, December 2, 1997, 2; "Vybory-97: Vladimir Lumpov: 'vy predlagaete – ia deistvuiu'," *Volzhskaia kommuna*, November 14, 1997, 2; L. Moliakova, "Vybory-97: v narode govoriat: 'Kogda trudno, vpered vykhodiat muzhchiny, a esli ochen' trudno – ikh zameniaiut zhenshchiny'," *Volzhskaia kommuna*, December 2, 1997, 2; V. Rubtsov, "Pokhvistnevskii izbiratel'nyi okrug N 24: Gennadii Kirdiashev: 'Interesy sel'chan v Dume smogut zashchitit' tol'ko deputaty-agrarii...'," *Volzhskaia kommuna*, December 2, 1997, 5; "Otradnenskii izbiratel'nyi okrug N 23: N. P. Gavrilin: kazhdyi dolzhen zanimat'sia svoim delom: monologs pristrastiem'," *Volzhskaia kommuna*, December 2, 1997, 5; V. Kirsanova, "Andrei Kislov: 'Moia programma ne gotovilas' k vyboram. Ia po nei zhivu'," *Volzhskaia kommuna*, November 26, 1997, 1–2; O. Arianina, "Za slovom-delo: sel'chane blagodariat Kosyreva, a tot nameren pomogat' im eshche bol'she," *Volzhskaia kommuna*, November 18, 1997, 1; V. Zhelezhniakov, "Vybory-97: Vasilii Ianin, mer Syzrani, kandidat v deputaty gubernskoi dumy po Syzranskomu izbiratel'nomu okrugu N 17. 'Moskva ishchet prezidenta cherez sud. A on zdravstvuet v Samare'," *Volzhskaia kommuna*, November 18, 1997, 2; V. Neverova, "Oleg D'iachenko: esli oblast' zarabatyvaet bol'she, ona i dolzhna zhit' luchshe," *Volzhskaia kommuna*, November 14, 1997, 4; S. Ishina, "Oleg D'iachenko: 'Ia gotov rabotat' po 16 chasov v sutki," *Volzhskaia kommuna*, November 12, 1997, 1.

[54] A. Petrov, "Kto v plenu u reform?" *Volzhskaia kommuna*, November 14, 1997, 1; A. Patreov, "Kandidat: chto skazhesh', predsedatel'?" *Volzhskaia kommuna*,

Government officials supported favored contenders directly by providing testimonials in campaign advertisements, meeting with voters, and arranging for better locations for campaign speeches. As one losing candidate in Naryn explained, "not clan but official clan played a role" in elections in Naryn.[55] In other words, ties to the government were more valuable than ties to a particular kin group.

CANDIDATES' BEHAVIOR. Government officials were not the only people who acted unethically during the campaigns. Candidates violated electoral laws even more severely and frequently by giving gifts, overspending, and paying for media coverage. In the four regions, a third party, not the candidate himself, typically distributed gifts to voters. An electoral commission official in Samara estimated that parliamentary candidates in 10 of 25 electoral districts had gifts given on their behalf. Often these goods were distributed through a charitable fund, such as one organized by the energy enterprise Volgapromgaz in support of its candidates.

In the Russian oblasts, gifts included vodka, tea, chocolate, boots, and free medicine. A gubernatorial candidate who did not distribute gifts in Samara was confronted by a voter during the campaign and asked, "Why didn't you bring boots?" because a candidate in an earlier race had distributed boots in the district. Gift-giving was less ubiquitous in Ul'ianovsk simply because there are few private businesspeople who have established large funds to back candidates.

Besides handing out tea, vodka, and sugar, candidates and their supporters in Osh and Naryn entertained voters. Relatives of candidates would "build a table" to entertain potential supporters in Naryn. One losing candidate in the provinces described how relatives threw a *toi* (social gathering) for him in the district where he was running.

November 12, 1997, 1; A. Slavin, "Prazdnik mitingu rozn'," *Volzhskaia kommuna*, November 11, 1997; A. Petrov, "Kontakt: chto khorosho dlia 'semerki'...," *Volzhskaia kommuna*, November 18, 1997, 1; A. Savin, "Vybory-97: vse li metody khoroshi?" *Volzhskaia kommuna*, November 28, 1997, 1; L. Savina, "Kandidat: u sela k Dume – svoi schet," *Volzhskaia kommuna*, November 21, 1997, 1; V. V. Nekipelov, "Vybory-97: Leon Koval'skii-eto vser'ez," *Volzhskaia kommuna*, December 3, 1997, 1–2; "Leon Koval'skii: 'Vybirat' nado delo, a ne obeshchaniia'," *Volzhskaia kommuna*, December 5, 1997, 1, 5; "Svad'ba pod predsedatel'stvom," *Volzhskaia kommuna*, December 3, 1997, 1; "Voprosy, otvety...i prazdnik," *Volzhskaia kommuna*, December 2, 1997, 1; G. Riblin, "Kontakt: u dobra – svoi zakony," *Volzhskaia kommuna*, November 25, 1997, 1.

55 Author's interview (21) with an unsuccessful candidate, Naryn oblast, June 26, 1997.

A candidate in Osh denied distributing gifts or entertaining voters
but then stumbled and referred to his campaign handouts as "invi-
tations."[56]

In the Russian oblasts, some candidates spent beyond the legal campaign limits. An electoral commission official in Samara estimated
that spending by parliamentary candidates in approximately 16 of the
25 electoral districts exceeded legal limits. The official's estimates are
based on the type of campaign a candidate ran and in some cases direct
evidence, such as an order for a television advertisement. An electoral
official in Ul'ianovsk suspects that gubernatorial candidates violated
spending limits because, although they had many advertisements, little money went through their official electoral accounts. A candidate
I interviewed in Ul'ianovsk acknowledged accepting unofficial donations because businesspeople feared pressure from the tax inspectors if
they gave money legally.

Campaign spending is a less salient issue in the Kyrgyzstani oblasts
because candidates received no money from the electoral commissions and spent little money overall. Most used money only for
transportation, and estimated expenditures ranged from no money to
10,000 soms. On average, candidates spent approximately 1,000 to
2,000 soms (or about two to four months' worth of income).

In all four regions, payment of reporters and editors was common.
Journalists received funds for favorable interviews with candidates,
reports from events candidates sponsored or attended, and glowing
analyses of candidates and their platforms. In addition to positive coverage, negative reports about opponents can be lucrative for media
outlets. A journalist with an independent newspaper in Samara estimated that 95 percent of candidates pay reporters or editors for hidden
advertisements, meaning positive coverage. Because many candidates
lack sufficient campaign funds, this figure is likely an exaggeration.
Nonetheless, half of the print journalists or editors in Samara with
whom I conferred about this practice claimed to have received offers
of rewards for positive coverage. In Naryn, a journalist recounted that
a national parliamentary candidate – evidently one of great means –
offered a Dictaphone, money, and a car in return for positive coverage.

---

[56] Author's interview (80) with a deputy in the oblast parliament, Osh oblast, May 19,
1998.

Payment for positive coverage also occurs in Ul'ianovsk, although in many cases rewards are not even necessary. One journalist in Ul'ianovsk claimed that his cohort was more likely to write positively about government candidates because they did not want to have problems with the oblast government and they feared losing their work.

Oblast candidates in Naryn are more likely to "entertain" media representatives than to bestow money or gifts upon them, according to one journalist there. He described how candidates would invite reporters to their homes or drive them to a picnic. The candidates would provide vodka and *zakuski* (snacks) in exchange for a pledge of favorable reporting. This current practice is analogous to the Soviet custom of having a party official and candidate meet with a reporter and instruct him to write positively about the candidate.

Campaign violations are committed by lower-level government officials and candidates in all four regions, reminding us that democracy is not fully developed in any of these provinces. These types of violations may have some impact on electoral outcomes. Yet, government punishments have a more troubling effect. Only in Ul'ianovsk and Naryn do oblast officials punish candidates who compete against favored contenders and campaign workers who assist opposition candidates. A likely result of these punishments is that viable candidates choose not to exercise their right to compete for fear of negative repercussions. Whereas campaign violations do not necessarily influence voters' decisions, government punishments limit the slate of candidates and thus reduce voters' choices.

NONDISTINGUISHING GUARANTEES

Providing alternative information, maintaining a political group, entering an electoral race, and competing in elections are more difficult in Ul'ianovsk and Naryn than in Samara and Osh, respectively. Other democratic freedoms, however, are equally easy to realize. Citizens in all four regions may express their ideas to their officials and peers openly. In each province, the right to vote is observed in registering voters and completing ballots. Elections have been free and fair in the sense that violations in ballot counting are minimal, and in each province institutions exist that ensure government policies depend on voters' preferences. Yet, in Ul'ianovsk and Naryn, the significance of these guarantees is minimal because the four other rights are difficult to exercise.

Freedom of Expression

A disgruntled citizen in any of the four provinces can criticize the regional leadership without fear of negative repercussions. In none of the oblasts do government officials fire, fine, jail, or otherwise harass individuals for speaking out. Instead, citizens freely complain about everyday problems as well as about the government's political direction. They express their ideas to their leaders directly through visits, letters, and telephone calls and indirectly through the media and protests.[57]

Direct Communication. In the four oblasts, citizens interact directly with provincial policymakers, including parliamentary deputies and administration officials. Typically, people contact government officials for assistance with personal problems, as noted in Table 4.7. In the four regions, the most common requests are for medical assistance and free or improved utilities. Otherwise, complaints and requests differ slightly within each country. People ask for capital for their enterprises in Samara but not in Ul'ianovsk. Whereas residents of Naryn asked for help finding employment, no officials in Osh reported receiving such requests. The greater obstacles to entrepreneurship in Ul'ianovsk and Naryn likely account for the differences within countries.

Requests also differ across countries, reflecting the fact that Russia has a more developed infrastructure but Kyrgyzstan has undertaken greater economic reforms. In Russia, people request improved housing services, such as trash removal, and financial privileges, such as tax breaks. In Kyrgyzstan, people complain that village councils enact land reform too slowly, and they request credit, repair of public

---

57 The findings in this section are based on 55 interviews I conducted with political and civic activists, including human-rights activists; 40 interviews I conducted with representatives of the local media; and 38 interviews I conducted with regional government officials, including administration officials and parliamentary deputies. My conversations with average citizens, my review of letters to regional newspapers, and my analysis of protest activities reported in media outlets also informed these conclusions. Additional methodological issues are addressed in Appendix D under "Freedom of Expression and Right to Vote."

TABLE 4.7. *Citizens' Requests and Complaints*

Request/Complaint	Russia		Kyrgyzstan	
	Samara	Ul'ianovsk	Osh	Naryn
Improve housing services	x	x		
Want a state privilege	x	x		
Need employment	x	x	x	x
Salary or pension not (yet) received	x	x	x	x
Need housing	x	x	x	x
Need home repairs	x	x	x	x
Provide free or improved utilities	x	x	x	x
Need medical assistance	x	x	x	x
Need legal advice	x	x	x	x
Mistreated by lower officials	x	x	x	x
Need credit			x	x
Land reform too slow			x	x
Need land			x	x
Construct something in my neighborhood			x	x
Public baths not working			x	x

Sources: I obtained this information from 38 interviews I conducted with regional government officials. I corroborated the information through interviews with media representatives and civic activists and conversations with informed citizens.

baths, and capital construction, such as bridges. On average, Russians already enjoy basic services such as public roads and indoor plumbing, whereas some citizens of Kyrgyzstan still lack these amenities. At the same time, residents of Kyrgyzstan were already concerned with the progress of land distribution, whereas land reform had barely begun in Russia.

Often voters make requests of a deputy that are specific to his job. In Ul'ianovsk, a legislator working in road construction receives requests for improving roads and bridges, whereas a doctor who serves in the parliament receives more pleas for medical assistance than other deputies. Citizens would, of course, approach these individuals for favors even if the individuals were not parliamentary deputies. However, by serving as deputies, they increase their visibility and voters expect them to have greater influence.

Once or twice a month, each legislator in Samara and Ul'ianovsk holds office hours in his or her district, and legislative assistants also meet with voters on the deputies' behalf. Office hours are less popular in the Kyrgyzstani provinces, in part because of transportation difficulties. Many deputies live in the provincial capital, not in their district, so it is difficult for people from distant counties to travel to the capital and to arrive at a designated time. Instead, deputies in Kyrgyzstan typically hold large public meetings four times a year in local clubs, schools, workplaces, or streets of their districts.

The number of residents who come to office hours and public meetings varies greatly within each oblast. A legislator in Samara reported an average of 25 to 30 visitors each time he held office hours. Another claimed 60 people came the first time he held office hours. Numbers for deputies in Ul'ianovsk fell within the same range. In both Osh and Naryn, attendance at public meetings ranged from 60 residents to upward of 100.[58]

Besides office hours and public meetings, social events and workplaces also provide opportunities for interaction between citizens and members of elected representative bodies. Deputies in Kyrgyzstan have contact with voters at frequent social events because, in their culture, respected members of the community are regularly included in families' celebrations. For example, a deputy in Osh explained that he has worked in his district for 30 years so people know him and often invite him to weddings and other social events. Nearly all deputies in the Russian and Kyrgyzstani provinces hold other jobs, so citizens also contact them at their workplaces, usually hospitals, schools, or businesses.

In both countries, governors and deputy governors meet with citizens, even though only the Russian governors were elected and thus

---

[58] These numbers are derived from the deputies' own estimates, the estimates of members of the mass media, and my own observation of contact between citizens and government officials. Data collected by the Gubernskaia duma suggest that the Samara legislators' estimates may be inflated, although the data are from a year earlier, and there has been an increase in contact with deputies in the past few years. According to the Duma data, 1,725 citizens visited deputies during their office hours in 1997, indicating that on average each legislator met with 69 constituents per year – considerably fewer than estimated. The deputies did encourage me to look at the official numbers, as they did not have the statistics with them during the interviews. "Vestnik Samarskoi gubernskoi dumy," 1 (January, 1998), 26.

directly accountable to voters. The four governors mainly interact with citizens during outings to workplaces, schools, and other institutions. The former governor of Ul'ianovsk, Goriachev, was famous – some say infamous – for his contact with voters. Goriachev preferred to solve problems locally, according to one of his staff members. To do this, the governor collected information directly from the voters during his Days of Open Letters. Four times each week, Goriachev traveled to a village or an industrial enterprise, met with voters, gave a speech, and answered questions, all of which was broadcast on state television. Goriachev's approach received mixed reviews: According to one media representative, "Between average people and the governor there is a direct connection.... [This has been] a phenomenon of our oblast for a long time. [Goriachev] knows what is going on below,"[59] whereas another complained that "[Days of Open Letters are a] self-advertisement on the government's bill.... He should not go deep into the countryside to personally resolve problems.... There is always a certain scene ... a club ... the governor with his sleeves rolled up ... it gives a strong impression to the voters."[60]

Deputy governors in each oblast primarily learn of voters' desires and complaints through the governor's interactions with citizens, but some have direct contact with voters. Administration officials who work in areas of interest to average people hold office hours. For example, in Samara the official in charge of economics and finance has regular office hours, whereas the official overseeing the industry and trade department does not.

Regional administrators and deputies also accept letters and telephone calls from voters. The number of letters and calls, as well as the number of visitors, varies dramatically among officials. Deputies

[59] Author's interview (182) with an editor of a state newspaper, Ul'ianovsk oblast, November 19, 1997.

[60] Author's interview (178) with an editor of an independent media outlet, Ul'ianovsk oblast, November 14, 1997. In contrast with Goriachev, the governor of Samara, Titov, has had more limited contact with voters because he was an active member of the upper house of the national parliament, the Federation Council. He headed the Council's tax and budget committee, so he spent one to two weeks each month in Moscow. In the late 1990s, he was meeting with voters in Samara only during his monthly or bimonthly visit to a village or when he made an appearance at a celebration, such as the opening of a new school, or the site of a tragedy.

who live in the provincial capital but represent a distant district are more likely to receive letters and calls.[61] Full-time deputies, administrators who work on issues of great interest to citizens, and members of political groups that mandate public contact interact the most with individual voters. The Communist Party is one organization that has made meeting with constituents part of its mission.

Events also affect the amount of contact public officials have with average people. During election campaigns, voters in the four provinces tend to contact their representatives more, and politicians hit the streets to meet and greet. An official in Ul'ianovsk reported getting more phone calls from residents when the temperature drops and when a flu epidemic develops because people need assistance heating their apartments and obtaining medical care.

Indirect Communication. Citizens express their opinions indirectly by writing letters to newspapers and periodically demonstrating in the street, refusing to work, and going on hunger strikes. In both Samara and Ul'ianovsk, as well as in Osh, independent newspapers will print highly critical letters, but state newspapers tend to shy away from them. Because no independent provincial media exist in Naryn, critiques of the governor or oblast parliament cannot reach a mass audience; however, these complaints may reach the officials themselves through direct forms of communication.

Public protests have occurred in each of the regions, as Table 4.8 indicates. Payment of wage arrears has been the most common demand, and demonstrators typically call on both oblast and federal officials for relief. Many of these protests have been in response to nationwide calls by unions to demonstrate against wage arrears. More political demands have also been heard. In 1998, residents of Ul'ianovsk protested government harassment of the local media.

Individuals have not suffered government punishments for participating in public protests in these regions. In general, government officials accepted criticism from individuals and did not try to stifle complaints. This suggests that freedom of expression is no weaker in one province than in another.

---

[61] The section on "Freedom of Expression" in Appendix D provides additional details about letters and phone calls.

TABLE 4.8. *Public Protests in the Four Regions*

Form of Protest	Date	Protestors	Demands	Description
Samara				
March	April 1995	Workers	Payment of wage arrears	Defense workers participated in a countrywide protest organized by the Federation of Independent Trade Unions of Russia. In a one-day protest, marchers carried coffins to represent the death of the defense industry.
Rally	August 1996	Workers	Payment of wage arrears	Approximately 2,000 employees of the airplane construction company Aviakor held a one-day rally to protest not having been paid since February.
Picket	March 1997	Retirees	Reduce housing rents	Pensioners protested the doubling of housing rents in 1997 by picketing the oblast legislature building.
Traffic blockade	February 1998	Workers	Payment of wage arrears	Approximately 1,500 workers from the Maslennikov factory, a defense plant in the provincial capital, blocked traffic and fought with police over several days. They demanded 5 million dollars (U.S.) in back wages from the oblast and federal governments.
Ul'ianovsk				
Rally	January 1998	Citizens	Freedom of press	Approximately 800 citizens protested government harassment of the media in a one-day rally in the provincial capital. Speakers at the demonstration called for the intervention of federal authorities.
Hunger strike	November/ December 1998	Teachers	Payment of wage arrears	As part of a countrywide protest, approximately 450 teachers in the oblast staged a hunger strike, demanding back wages. A 43-year-old teacher died and several were hospitalized. An estimated 1,500 people attended the teacher's funeral.

(continued)

TABLE 4.8 *(continued)*

Form of Protest	Date	Protestors	Demands	Description
Osh				
Strike	October 1995	Miners	End to corruption	Miners in Osh oblast held a strike in protest of management corruption and President Akaev's decision to hold early presidential elections. They adopted the latter complaint after citizens in Bishkek began to protest the decision.
Picket	April 1998	Elderly	Money to compensate investment losses	Approximately 300 elderly people demonstrated at the oblast administration building, demanding compensation for their losses in an investment scheme.
Naryn				
Picket	April 1999	Retirees	Payment of pensions	Approximately 40 people picketed the oblast administration building, demanding their pensions, which they had not received for three months.
Picket	August 1999	Citizens	Payment of social allowances	People picketed the oblast administration building twice in one month, demanding their pensions and social allowances, which they had not received for several months.
Rally	August 1999	Women	Payment of child allowances	Approximately 20 women protested in the provincial capital because they had not received benefits for their children since May.

Note: See "Freedom of Expression and Right to Vote" in Appendix D for information about the content analysis.

Sources: "Protestors Block Traffic in Samara," *IEWS Russian Regional Report*, vol. 3, no. 6, February 12, 1998; Penny Morvant, "Protest Preparations Continue," *RFE/RL Newsline*, March 26, 1997; Penny Morvant, "Workers across Russia Protest Unpaid Wages," *OMRI Daily Digest*, April 13, 1995; Anna Paretskaya, "Protests over Wage Arrears Continue," *OMRI Daily Digest*, August 28, 1996; Sergey Gorin, "Protest Rally for Press Freedom Staged in Ulyanovsk," *IEWS Russian Regional Report*, vol. 3, no. 4, January 29, 1998; L. B., "'Persecution' of Media Decried in Ulyanovsk," *RFE/RL Newsline – Russia*, January 29, 1998; J.A.C., "Teachers Strikes Continue," *RFE/RL Newsline – Russia*, November 25, 1998; J.A.C., "Striking Teacher Dies as Protest Actions Spread," *RFE/RL Newsline – Russia*, December 2, 1998; J.A.C., "Workers Launch New Protests," *RFE/RL Newsline – Russia*, December 4, 1998; Bruce Pannier, "Protests in Kyrgyzstan," *OMRI Daily Digest, Transcaucasia and Central Asia*, vol. 1, p. 191, October 2, 1995; "Aldangan va khurlangan otakhonlar onakhonlar," *Mezon*, April 24–May 1, 1998, p. 3; "Demonstration in Naryn," *Kyrgyz News*, e-mail service, April 5–12, 1999; "Demonstration in Naryn," *Kyrgyz News*, e-mail service, August 25, 1999; "Demonstration in Naryn," *Kyrgyz News*, e-mail service, August 27, 1999.

Right to Vote

Citizens' voices can be heard through the media and on the street, but can they also make their opinions known at the ballot box? Expressing concern through voting has been possible: Voters have not been excluded from registration lists, and illegal pressure to vote for a particular candidate and denial of the right to vote are rare. The few discrepancies in voting in the four oblasts occurred at the point of casting ballots – not in the voter registration process. In the Russian provinces, poll commissions allowed some voters to vote without the correct identification and perhaps cast false ballots, and in Osh and Naryn some citizens voted multiple times or received guidance about their selection from poll commission members. The oblast governments did not direct this illegal behavior and in most instances punished it. It was the poll commission members who were guilty of bending the rules.[62]

The most infamous alleged violation occurred in Samara, where leaders of the NGO For Honest Elections have claimed that voters at one poll cast ballots without the appropriate identification. At this poll, located in a hospital, people were allowed to vote using their health documents instead of their passports or other identification. The group alleges that the poll commission allowed this so that patients in the hospital would vote for the head doctor, who was running. The NGO also suspects that poll commission members may have cast false ballots for homebound voters. Observers calculated that the members were not gone from the poll long enough to visit all the homebound voters from whom they claimed to have collected ballots. During my stay in the region, oblast election officials and this group continued to debate these allegations. Overall, in Samara there have been four court investigations pertaining to the parliamentary elections and none related to the gubernatorial race.[63]

---

[62] Conclusions in this section are based on interviews I conducted with 38 candidates, including both winners and losers; 9 regional and national electoral officials and election observers, including members of electoral commissions' official observers, and journalists who provided systematic electoral coverage; and 55 political and nonpolitical NGO leaders and members, some of whom served as unofficial electoral observers for their organizations. I also relied on written media and NGO reports about the elections. The section on "Freedom of Expression and Right to Vote" in Appendix D considers other methodological issues.

[63] One unsuccessful parliamentary candidate challenged the results in his district, but he lost the court case because he had no evidence of violations. In another case, the KPRF sued a reelected incumbent because the party claimed he used his position to win. In

In Ul'ianovsk, a poll commission member allowed voters in the gubernatorial elections to vote without showing their passports as identification. However, other poll commission members forced him off the commission immediately. The Ul'ianovsk electoral commission also received a complaint that six ballots were completed by poll commission members instead of housebound voters.

In Osh and Naryn, the most common voting violation was family voting. Multiple, or family, voting is a legacy of the Soviet era, when the party pressured citizens to vote.[64] In Soviet times, often one individual in a family would vote for the other adult members to save them time, or an election monitor would submit ballots on others' behalf in order to improve turnout figures. With only a single party from which to choose, family or multiple voting did not influence outcomes; now, however, the slate of varied candidates has made voting meaningful. Nonetheless, a media representative in Osh who served on a poll commission saw instances where one person voted on behalf of his entire family. A member of the media in Naryn recounted how voters who saw violations at the polls would call him, and he and other media representatives would travel to the poll where violations were reported. They witnessed actual instances of multiple voting as well as signs of it, such as identical handwriting for several different voters. Another media representative reported that his neighbor voted on behalf of himself, his wife, and his son.

In the Kyrgyzstani oblasts, multiple voting seems to occur most often in rural areas, and there is a standard set of excuses for it. As one media representative in Osh explained, poll commissions tend to allow family voting if the person voting has each individual's documents and a good excuse, such as, "My wife is sick." Poll commissions are also more likely to allow multiple voting when turnout seems to be low, when a person would vote for the candidate that poll commission members prefer, or where the tradition of having the right to decide for one's wife still exists.

the two other instances, the oblast electoral commission was sued. A candidate sued during the campaign because he wanted the name of his district, not just Samara city, written under his name on the ballot. The candidate and commission compromised and his street address was included. The commission was also sued because it made a television announcement during the campaign that a candidate who was rumored to have dropped out remained in the race.

[64] White et al., *How Russia Votes,* 10, 187.

Despite the examples of multiple voting, the practice is not pervasive, and oblast officials have been effective in combating it. In the first round of the oblast and national parliamentary elections in Naryn, family voting did occur and some of the national parliamentary candidates complained. As a result, oblast electoral officials lost their posts, and poll commissions received better training information. Consequently, family voting was not as common in the second round.

Likewise, officials in Samara and Ul'ianovsk seem to have largely eliminated family and other forms of multiple voting, except for one instance in Ul'ianovsk. At one poll, commission members allowed citizens to vote on behalf of others as well as themselves. An observer for a candidate running for county office wrote a complaint to the oblast electoral commission, which forwarded it to the prosecutor, who investigated the claim. The prosecutor took the chair and members of the poll commission to court. The court found them guilty, and the oblast electoral commission threw out the results from this poll.

Overall, having a selection of candidates seems to have encouraged voters to value their vote and not allow others to vote for them. As one journalist explained, family voting rarely occurs because views concerning who is the best candidate often differ within a family.

A final violation was interference with voters' decisions, a problem reported but not widespread in Osh and Naryn. As one activist explained, older people are accustomed to the perfunctory elections of the Soviet era. Now they tend to ask, "Whom should I vote for?" A member of the poll commission says, "Vote for whomever you want." The voter says, "I do not care." The member responds, "Well, why don't you vote for [this candidate]," pointing to the ballot.

Oblast governments neither committed nor condoned these minor and infrequent violations in the voting process in the four oblasts. Poll commission members were the culprits. They broke rules in order to help voters or perhaps to pursue their own political views. Nonetheless, violations were rare and do not indicate that the right to vote is considerably weaker in one of the Russian or Kyrgyzstani provinces versus the other.

Free and Fair Elections

Once a voter has cast her ballot, she can be confident that it will be fairly counted in any of the regions. In each oblast, violations in vote counting were minor and rare, and people accepted the results. Moreover, the percentages by which successful candidates won and the characteristics of winners versus losers do not indicate that ballot tampering was a problem in one region more than another.[65]

Violations in Ballot Counting. Of the electoral officials, winning and losing candidates, observers, and media representatives I interviewed, only a few individuals reported or even suspected miscounting or falsification. In Samara, no one filed a complaint about ballot tampering in the parliamentary or gubernatorial elections. Two of the losing candidates I interviewed suspected falsification in their districts; however, they had no evidence.[66] In Ul'ianovsk, only a few media correspondents reported infrequent, insignificant violations, such as minor mistakes made on tally sheets. In Osh, one media representative saw some minor violations regarding ballot counting, and in Naryn only a few members of the media and a few losing candidates suspected ballot tampering. One candidate in Naryn believed ballots were changed or added because the vote count was not announced at the polls. The ballots then took a long time to reach the oblast capital, where the vote count was announced.

To discourage ballot tampering, the laws in each country permit candidates to have observers at the polls, and in all four provinces this right was widely exercised and enforced. Most candidates I interviewed in Samara and Ul'ianovsk had their own observers at 30 to 100 percent of the polls in their district. Nearly all the candidates in Osh and Naryn

---

[65] As in the previous section, findings about free and fair elections are based on interviews with 38 candidates, including both winners and losers; 9 regional and national electoral officials and election observers (members of electoral commissions, official observers, and journalists who provided systematic electoral coverage); 55 political and nonpolitical NGO leaders and members, some of whom served as unofficial electoral observers for their organizations; and written media and NGO reports about the elections. The section on "Free and Fair Elections" in Appendix D provides additional data.

[66] One candidate surmised that ballots were faked at the poll in his district where voters could use their hospital documents for identification, as described earlier. Another candidate believed that 20 percent of the ballots in his district were discarded because the number of voters his observers counted did not correspond with the final results. It is important to note, however, that electoral laws do allow for the discarding of ballots under certain conditions, so the discrepancy in numbers may have been for legal reasons.

had observers at all the polls, in part because many districts had fewer than six polls. In none of the oblasts were these observers denied access to polls. A few observers in the Russian oblasts were refused access initially, but a call to higher electoral officials rectified the situation. In Naryn, members of poll commissions instructed a few observers to sit in a certain place, thus restricting their movement. Similarly, one losing candidate in Naryn complained that poll commission members prohibited his observers from watching the counting of the ballots. Nevertheless, in each of the oblasts nearly all the observers worked unimpeded.

Provincial authorities neither ordered nor condoned the minor violations that did occur with regard to the counting of ballots and observation of the voting process. Instead, these violations occurred when poll commission members did not know electoral laws well or when they favored a certain candidate and illegally tried to help him or her. Members of poll commissions are more likely to commit violations because they are less knowledgeable about election laws than members of upper-level commissions, such as the oblast electoral commission. Also, poll commissions are not as politically balanced as higher-level commissions. In each province, members of nongovernmental groups have served on the oblast electoral commission; however, these organizations do not have enough people to have a representative on every commission in the region.

Acceptance of the Results. In light of the minor violations at the polls, do residents of each province accept the election results, or do they believe that violations were so great as to make the outcomes meaningless? In each province, those closest to the elections, including winning and losing candidates, election observers, election officials, and representatives of the independent and state mass media, accepted the outcomes of the races, with the exception of the gubernatorial race in Ul'ianovsk. In all four regions, people cited the presence of observers as a deterrent to violations. Observers were numerous, "like wolves in the forest," according to one candidate in Ul'ianovsk.[67] In the Kyrgyzstani provinces, those connected with the elections also stressed that the lack

---

[67] Author's interview (208) with a deputy in the oblast parliament, Ul'ianovsk oblast, December 1, 1997.

of parliamentary authority discouraged violations. Simply, the stakes in the election were not great enough to merit violations. For example, one losing candidate chose not to sue over perceived violations because "the oblast [parliament] is not worth the struggle."[68]

In Samara, residents feel that the gubernatorial and parliamentary elections were free and fair. Approximately 90 percent of the people I interviewed in the province believed that there were minor violations in the gubernatorial and parliamentary elections but that these did not change the outcome of the races. Most of the violations people knew of occurred during the campaign, not at the polls, and often the violators were candidates, not government authorities. Losers were no more likely than winners or observers to question the validity of the electoral outcomes.

In Ul'ianovsk, people accept the results of the parliamentary elections, but some suspect that Goriachev did not win the gubernatorial election fairly. Approximately half of the people I interviewed believed that Goriachev would not have won had there not been election violations. Doubters were losing candidates and members of the independent mass media, people who tend not to support Goriachev and his politics. One member of the independent media attributed the governor's victory to his "propaganda machine," explaining that this would have enabled him to win even without the violations.[69] Although urban elites doubted Goriachev's victory, all accounts, including independent journalists' own, suggest that voters in rural areas did, in fact, support him.

In the Kyrgyzstani oblasts, candidates, election officials, and media representatives indicated that small violations in the parliamentary elections did not undermine the election results. Even the losers in Osh and Naryn more or less accepted the results. Only one loser I interviewed doubted the outcome in his race, because people had promised to vote for him. Because he lost, he surmised that there must have been violations. Having chosen not to have his own observers at the polls, he had no evidence of the legality or the illegality of the voting and ballot counting.

---

[68] Author's interview (74) with an unsuccessful parliamentary candidate, Osh oblast, May 18, 1998.

[69] Author's interview (178) with an editor of an independent media outlet, Ul'ianovsk oblast, November 14, 1997.

Election Results. Election results also suggest that ballots were counted accurately. An overwhelming win could suggest that there was ballot tampering in favor of the winning candidate, but this was not the case. None of the parliamentary or gubernatorial candidates in the Russian provinces swept the election. On average, winning parliamentary candidates received 48 percent of the vote in Samara and 28 percent of the vote in Ul'ianovsk.[70] In the gubernatorial race in Samara, the incumbent governor won 63 percent of the vote, beating two other candidates. In Ul'ianovsk, the incumbent governor received 42 percent of the vote in a field of six candidates.[71]

If the pool of winners differed significantly from the pool of losers, ballot counting could have been biased against certain groups of people. However, a comparison of winners' and losers' characteristics suggests that personal characteristics, not counting violations, provide electoral advantages. Specifically, candidates who figured large in the community or had access to state resources, such as government media and support, were more likely to win.[72]

WINNERS IN RUSSIA. In the Russian oblasts, the age, profession, and employment position of the winners reflected their prominence in the community and their access to state resources. In Samara, the oldest and youngest candidates had an advantage, whereas in Ul'ianovsk older candidates were more successful. Older candidates have an advantage because they are usually local celebrities: They made their careers in the Soviet bureaucracy and now their connections and renown can help them win elections. In Samara, where entrepreneurial opportunities are

---

[70] See Table D.4 in Appendix D in the section on "Free and Fair Elections" for the specific races.

[71] This information was not available for individual candidates in parliamentary elections in Osh and Naryn. See *Samarskaia oblast': 1996 ofitsial'nyi spravochnik*, (Samara: Fedorov, 1997), 118; *Vybory glav ispolnitel'noi vlasti sub"ektov Rossiiskoi Federatsii*, 372.

[72] Neither being of a particular gender nor holding a particular position in an organization provided an advantage in the Russian provinces. Eighteen percent of the women who ran and 16 percent of the men who ran in Samara won. Twenty-two percent of the women and 22 percent of the men who ran in Ul'ianovsk won. Ethnic identity is not listed in official biographical information, and only a few candidates mention their ethnicity in their own campaign materials. From my interviews with candidates and information about oblast parliaments, I found that legislative bodies in Samara and Ul'ianovsk reflected the ethnic composition of the population. Samara is largely homogeneous, and at least one of the 25 members of Ul'ianovsk's parliament is Tatar. Furthermore, no one in any of the oblasts claimed that his or her rights as a candidate were violated because of his or her ethnicity.

greater relative to Ul'ianovsk, young businesspeople have also made names for themselves.

Medical degrees also increased candidates' probability of success in the Russian provinces. Doctors and veterinarians are respected, widely known members of the community, and in some cases they can offer medicine and hospital privileges to voters. In Ul'ianovsk, candidates with a pedagogical education also did well, most likely because teachers are well-known locally, having helped raise many of the region's children. In Samara, no one with only a pedagogical degree ran.

According to Table 4.9, a degree in the technical sciences offered a considerable advantage in Samara. However, it is the candidates' current positions – not their technical degrees themselves – that are advantageous. In the Soviet era, individuals with technical degrees often became leaders in government, and now these individuals are mayors and heads of large state concerns or companies that have only recently been privatized. It is the state resources, not the technical degrees, that give them an advantage in elections. In Ul'ianovsk, candidates also benefit from state resources, but those candidates tend to head state farms. Some directors of state farms have technical degrees, but others have veterinarian degrees, thus helping to explain the large proportion of winners with a medical education in Ul'ianovsk. In Samara and Ul'ianovsk, candidates with graduate or postsecondary degrees had an advantage over those with only a vocational or general secondary education. This reflects global voting patterns: Voters tend to elect elites, not the common person. Higher education is also likely to provide access to personal contacts, material resources, and leadership positions – all useful in winning elections.

WINNERS IN KYRGYZSTAN. In the Kyrgyzstani regions, differences between winners and losers seemed to be slight.[73] In Osh, candidates I interviewed who had a technical education were more likely to win than lose, whereas in Naryn a medical education offered an advantage. Also, businesspeople in Osh were more likely to win, perhaps because

---

[73] Little information is published about candidates in Kyrgyzstan, so I cannot provide a chart of comprehensive data as I do for winners and losers in Samara and Ul'ianovsk. Because full biographies are not published for the candidates in the Kyrgyzstani provinces, conclusions about all characteristics except gender are based on samples of candidates. I also drew on my interviews with campaign workers, election observers, media representatives, and other political activists.

they had greater financial resources. Heads of organizations had an advantage over deputy heads and employees in Naryn, suggesting that citizens tend to vote for elites.[74]

Other characteristics appeared to provide no advantage in the Kyrgyzstani provinces.[75] Men and women had a similar likelihood of winning parliamentary races in each oblast. No women won parliamentary seats in Osh, but only four percent of the candidates were women. In Naryn, 40 percent of the female candidates won seats, and 48 percent of male contenders were victorious.

Differences in age, source of nomination, ethnicity, and clan between winners and losers were also not significant. Ethnicity is a relevant issue in Osh, where nearly 30 percent of the population is Uzbek, but not in Naryn, where 98 percent of the population is Kyrgyz.[76] Nonetheless, in Osh, Uzbeks are represented in the *kenesh*. Some losing candidates I interviewed in Osh blamed their defeats, in part, on the ethnic makeup of their districts. One loser, a Kyrgyz, claimed that an Uzbek candidate won because there were more Uzbeks in his district. However, neither this perception nor this voter practice is ubiquitous: In another district in Osh, an Uzbek candidate was victorious over a Kyrgyz contender even though Kyrgyz outnumber Uzbeks in the district.

Likewise, despite outsiders' predictions, clan seems to have played little role in these regional elections. In both Osh and Naryn, a few losing candidates blamed their losses on clan allegiances, but many contenders overcame clan identities in order to win. A winner in Naryn managed to prevail over clan allegiances and his opponent's high stature. His opponent was a high-ranking local official and a member of a different clan, which composes 40 percent of the district. The victor's clan made up only 10 percent of the district. The winner explained, "No one believed I would win....I was also doubtful...because of clan and the position [of my opponent]. Clan influenced [the results] in the first round. Clan was less important in the last [round]....[Voters] do not care who [a person is]. It is more important who works and

---

[74] In Osh, my sample of candidates included only heads of organizations.

[75] All the candidates I interviewed in the two oblasts were well-educated, so I could not evaluate whether little education was a disadvantage.

[76] These data were obtained directly from the National Statistics Committee for the beginning of 1997.

TABLE 4.9. *Characteristics of Winners and Losers in Russian Regional Parliamentary Elections (percentages)*

	Samara		Ul'ianovsk	
	Winner	Loser	Winner	Loser
Gender[a]				
Male	92	93	84	84
Female	8	7	16	16
Year of birth[b]				
1900–1931	0	0	4	3
1932–1940	14	10	28	17
1941–1951	32	35	24	33
1952–1966	45	48	44	44
1967–1975	9	7	0	2
Source of nomination[c]				
Field of education[d]				
Technical sciences	75	44	50	49
Social sciences	10	8	0	14
Medicine	10	4	21	7
Law	0	10	0	5
Humanities	5	3	0	0
Military sciences	0	4	0	2
Pedagogy	0	0	21	5
Multiple fields	0	21	7	14
None (school only)	0	5	0	5
Highest level of education[e]				
Current employment position[f]				
Head	64	59	64	46
Deputy head	16	11	4	14
Division head	4	9	8	10
Deputy division head	0	0	0	1
Employee/Student	16	20	20	28
Unemployed/Retired	0	1	4	1
Field of employment[g]				
Business	24	33	20	44
Government	44	22	8	7
NGO	12	15	4	16

Voter group	92	83	75	70
Organization	8	17	21	17
Self-nomination	0	0	4	12
Graduate	10	8	19	6
Postsecondary	90	79	75	77
Vocational secondary	0	7	6	13
General secondary	0	5	0	4
Education/Research	4	8	16	10
Police/Military	0	5	4	5
Farming	4	2	20	5
Medicine	4	3	8	7
Media	0	4	8	2
Unemployed/Retired	0	1	4	1
Multiple	8	8	8	3

[a] The gender statistic is based on all the candidates from each oblast: 158 Samara and 114 in Ul'ianovsk.

[b] The birth-year figures are based on 116 and 112 candidates from Samara and Ul'ianovsk, respectively.

[c] Data about nominations were available for all but one of the candidates from Samara and seven of the candidates from Ul'ianovsk.

[d] Field of education data are based on 117 candidates from Samara and 57 from Ul'ianovsk. Technical sciences include engineering, agricultural sciences, physics, and mathematics. Social sciences include economics, business, and finance. Humanities include languages, history, and journalism. Incorporating the fields of study of those who had multiple degrees did not change the relationship between the categories: Technical degrees still outnumbered all the other fields combined.

[e] Highest level of education data were available for 117 candidates in Samara and 64 in Ul'ianovsk. Graduate means the person obtained a *kandidat* or *doktor* degree or is currently studying for such a degree. Postsecondary includes those who studied at or obtained a degree from an *institut* or a military or pedagogical *uchilishche*. Vocational secondary refers to those who completed or attended *tekhnikum* or an *uchilishche* that was not military or pedagogical. General secondary means that the individual attended or completed only secondary school.

[f] From the statistics on current employment position, three candidates from Samara are missing and two candidates from Ul'ianovsk are missing.

[g] The field of employment statistic is based on all the candidates from each oblast.

Sources: For biographical data about candidates, I relied on newspapers, electoral records, and my own interviews with winners and losers. Oblast newspapers in Russia publish a detailed biography of each candidate.

who helps."[77] Likewise, a winning candidate in Osh calculated that he won only because members of other clans supported him. Increasingly, voters overlook clan membership in order to choose the most effective leader.

The profiles of winning and losing candidates, as well as the extent and types of violations, attitudes toward the elections, and winners' percentages, suggest that ballot tampering is not widespread in any of the regions. In Samara, Ul'ianovsk, Osh, and Naryn, a ballot cast is typically a ballot counted.

Institutions for Making Government Policies Depend on Preferences

Because publishing alternative information, maintaining a political group, and competing for elected seats are more difficult in Ul'ianovsk and Naryn, it is less likely that the demands of citizens in these regions will reach the halls of government. Yet, those preferences that do reach regional officials are as likely to shape government policy as demands in Samara and Osh. The design, operation, and effectiveness of formal government institutions are similar in the Russian provinces and in the Kyrgyzstani regions.[78]

On paper and in practice, administrations have been the most influential entities in regional politics. Governors in the Russian oblasts have derived their power from their status as elected officials and from their significant legal authority. In Kyrgyzstan, governors are influential because they are presidential appointees and the law grants them substantial powers. In the four regions, the administration prepares the budget, presents proposals to the parliament, and implements new programs. The governors carry out their responsibilities with the help of a team of deputy governors and department heads, each of whom focuses on a particular area of oblast affairs, such as economic development.

---

[77] Author's interview (29) with a deputy in the oblast parliament, Naryn oblast, July 8, 1997.

[78] Findings in this section came from my review of national and oblast legislation, 38 interviews I conducted with regional parliamentary deputies and administration officials, conversations with informed citizens, and direct observation of the parliaments in the Russian provinces.

It is rare that judges can independently fulfill the demands of the public. In the four oblasts, residents perceive that the regional executives wield considerable influence over the judiciary. By contrast, parliaments do respond to voters' preferences. Admittedly, as entities, the parliaments are significantly weaker than the governors, particularly in the Kyrgyzstani provinces. Deputies in Osh and Naryn consider their legislative function as only a supplement to the work of the national parliament and president. The national parliament creates the legislative base for the country, and the oblast parliaments pass decisions primarily on social policy, according to one deputy in Osh. The oblast parliaments also receive "commands and assignments" from the president. As an official in the administration of Naryn oblast explained, "Nothing depends on [regional] deputies. . . . Deputies ask for help, we help . . . deputies have no money, no power. . . . We provide [the regional parliament] with tasks."[79] However, individual deputies do have an independent impact in the four oblasts.

All deputies can resolve small, everyday problems for their constituents. One deputy was able to get free medicine for an invalid, and another described how he obtained a "charity" phone for a person who could not afford a commercial phone and who did not want to wait in the long line for a donated one. Deputies with positions of authority in the community or parliament can also implement larger projects, such as those promised on the campaign trail. A senior deputy in Samara with a long history of parliamentary service earlier promised to help agricultural production by improving the water supply system, and during his previous terms he was able to convince his colleagues to pass a water supply program for the oblast. A deputy working in transportation in Osh managed to create additional routes for express buses. Another deputy who promised to create new jobs in Osh opened a photography laboratory, auto service shop, and a press, using capital from his private advertising and information agency.

To carry out their legislative duties, deputies in Samara and Ul'ianovsk work in committees that focus on broad issues such as industry and trade. A committee may meet as often as once a week or as rarely as once a month. Each committee hears testimony from

---

[79] Author's interview (30) with an administration official, Naryn oblast, July 4, 1997.

experts and prepares reports and proposals for review and approval at monthly legislative sessions. The chair, the director of the apparatus, and a few full-time deputies manage the daily business of the parliaments. Full-time deputies are typically chairs or deputy chairs of parliamentary committees, and they, along with the chair of the parliament, are the only deputies to receive salaries.

The elected representative bodies in the Kyrgyzstani regions operate in a comparable fashion. Committees in Osh and Naryn perform similar functions, and most meet for a day before each session and perhaps a few additional times each year. The *kenesh* hold approximately four sessions per year, and each session lasts about one day. Typically, the chair of the *kenesh* calls the session. In contrast to the Russian legislatures, in the Kyrgyzstani *kenesh* only the chairs work full-time and receive a salary. Moreover, deputies in the Russian provinces elect their parliamentary chairs, whereas in Kyrgyzstan the president recommends a chair from among the elected deputies in each region. The *kenesh* can reject or accept the candidate, and, in instances of rejection, the president simply proposes another candidate.

The Russian Parliaments in Action. In Samara and Ul'ianovsk, I had the opportunity to observe a session of parliament.[80] The two legislatures operate similarly with the exception of the degree of accessibility the institutions grant the media. Media outlets in Ul'ianovsk can obtain bills and can observe their fates in the session; however, the discussion and arguments that preceded the proposals are less transparent. In Ul'ianovsk, media representatives are prohibited from observing extrasessional meetings, in contrast to their counterparts in Samara. The parliamentary restrictions on newspapers and broadcasting firms in Ul'ianovsk reflect the general difficulty of providing an alternative source of information in the oblast.

In Samara, I observed the third meeting of the newly elected Gubernskaia duma, which took place on February 3, 1998. It was the first session in which the deputies discussed substantive instead of administrative matters. The meeting hall is traditional in design, with a dais in

---

[80] I was not able to watch sessions of parliament in the Kyrgyzstani oblasts because they are not held according to a schedule. While I was in the oblasts, the chairs did not happen to call a session.

front and desks and armchairs for deputies. Next to the dais, the chair sits with a deputy chair on each side, and slightly above the dais on each side are places for the governor and presidential representative. The governor was not present at this session, but he usually attends if he is in town. Behind the deputies were deputy governors and other members of the administration scheduled to speak or merely interested in the topics of discussion. Guests and members of the media sit in a balcony above. Big screens at the front of the room show the speaker, and during breaks nature videos with classical music are broadcast. Large computerized boards, which reveal the secret votes are attached to the walls.

While supporters of the Communist Party and the LDPR protested outside, the Samara deputies began the session by standing for a hymn and then approving the agenda. Members of a committee left to elect their chair, while the head of the committee on families, motherhood, and childhood spoke about a bill on guardianship. During the session, the deputies passed this bill, as well as others concerning funds from mineral production, a vaccination program for 1998–2000, a forestry development program for 1998–2005, and an inventory of cultural monuments not subject to privatization. For three proposals that received committee recommendations, the legislators decided to interrupt the speaker and vote immediately. Deputies voted that a proposal to remove segments of the oblast charter that contradicted federal legislation required more work, and they sent another bill on charter amendments to a compromise committee composed of deputies and administration officials. During the session, deputies also discussed the fund for mandatory medical insurance, and, in organizational matters, the deputies considered the status of their assistants and their six-month plan of work. At the end of the session, one deputy rose to encourage his colleagues to ask questions of the deputy governors who attended, and another suggested structural changes in the parliament so that members could work more effectively.

During the session of the Samara parliament, television cameras were filming and were fairly intrusive. Members of the media received copies of the bills and proposals from the parliamentary press service, and during the break some media representatives interviewed deputies on the floor. Correspondents, as well as guests, had easy access to the deputies because to reach the balcony we had to walk across the floor where the deputies sat, and some visitors took advantage of this opportunity. According to a parliamentary staff member, all meetings, even committee meetings, are usually open to the mass media. This staff member could not remember a time when a meeting was closed, but hypothetically the media would be excluded if deputies did not want their personal disagreements aired. "They are like a family," in the sense that sometimes they squabble.[81]

The work of the Ul'ianovsk parliament, the Zakonodatel'noe Sobranie, is less transparent. Prior to each session, deputies attend a hearing, where they "raise technical, working questions," according to a staff member.[82] These hearings were instituted about six months after the parliament began operating, and they are closed to the press. The deputies found it easier to solve problems of a detailed nature before facing the media at the sessions.

The session I attended took place on November 27, 1997. The legislators met in a narrow rectangular room and sat around a long table at one end of the room, and the chair and deputy chair sat at another table at the head of the legislators' table. Support staff and representatives from the administration sat two-by-two in desks alongside the long table, and members of the media sat in rows at the other end of the room. The cameras were intrusive, and the media representatives were often noisy. Prior to the meetings, members of the media could pick up a folder with an agenda and copies of the bills. In their speeches, some deputies seemed to be speaking to the media instead of to their colleagues.

At this session of the Ul'ianovsk parliament, the deputies considered nominations for court staff members. Not having an electronic voting system, they indicated their approval by raising their hands. The deputies also passed proposals on road construction, the epidemiological welfare of the population, the publication of laws, and the hiring and certification of civil servants. In the long and busy session, the members of parliament also made decisions about mandatory

---

[81] Author's interview (150) with a staff member in the oblast parliament, Samara oblast, February 3, 1998.
[82] Author's interview (216) with a staff member in the oblast parliament, Ul'ianovsk oblast, November 27, 1997.

medical insurance, prevention of child neglect and juvenile crime, and the accreditation of media representatives for the purposes of observing parliament. Another approved proposal granted a tax credit to a company that had not paid taxes and had thus been fined. The deputies also discussed the 1997 oblast budget, amendments to the oblast charter, laws on referenda, and regulations on the status of deputies' assistants.

A large portion of the Ul'ianovsk session focused on the governor's socioeconomic program. Besides setting goals for economic stabilization, lower unemployment, and increased industrial and agricultural production, the program called for attracting more investors. An administration official cited Chase Manhattan's ranking of the investment potential of Russian provinces. The bank rated Ul'ianovsk oblast highly on human and natural resources but noted that the province needed to improve its image.

A program for small businesses also generated considerable discussion among the Ul'ianovsk legislators. Deputies debated the proposal, weighing whether to adopt it immediately or require a committee to make further changes. One deputy argued that because the committee had already reviewed the proposal, the bill was ready. This deputy urged the parliament to respect the committee's work.

A review of laws passed by the Samara and Ul'ianovsk parliaments indicates that the topics I heard discussed are typical. The Samara legislators have adopted laws on economic matters, including the oblast budget, taxes, investment, and natural resource use, and they have made decisions about housing, medical privileges, and insurance. They have also passed laws about the operation of government, including electoral regulations and administration divisions. A review of the bulletin of the Ul'ianovsk parliament reveals laws on economic matters, such as taxes, and decisions on provincial appointments. Ul'ianovsk legislators have also adopted laws to bring oblast legislation into compliance with federal law.[83]

---

[83] *Sobranie zakonodatel'stva Samarskoi oblasti*, Vols. 1, 2 (Samara: Samarskaia gubernskaia duma, 1997); Zakonodatel'noe sobranie Ul'ianovskoi oblasti, *Informatsionnyi biulleten'*. Ul'ianovsk: Zakonodatel'noe sobranie Ul'ianovskoi oblasti. (March 1996–October 1997). March 1996 was the first issue.

Within each country, the authority of the different branches of regional government, the operation of administrations and parliaments, and the successes and failures of deputies are similar. To the extent that citizens' preferences reach these governmental bodies, the demands are likely to be treated comparably in Samara and Ul'ianovsk and in Osh and Naryn.

In sum, the key difference between the provinces in each country is the ability to effectively challenge incumbents through participation in the civic sphere. Because restrictions on activism undermine the operation of the new democratic institutions, it is accurate to say that democracy is weaker in Ul'ianovsk and Naryn. The challenges to activism are in the form of government punishments and self-censorship – not the operation of formal institutions. Government harassment comes in the form of attacks on the livelihood of activists. Media in Ul'ianovsk face groundless state inspections, loss of utilities and office space, government lawsuits, pressure on advertisers, and other forms of harassment. Leaders and members of political organizations in Ul'ianovsk have suffered firings, threats of job loss, or state inspections as a result of their activism. Candidates in key races and viable opposition candidates in Ul'ianovsk and Naryn experienced pressure from local officials to drop out of the race, and those that remained in the competition endured job loss and challenges to their businesses after the election. Campaign workers for these candidates faced an identical fate. Fearing reprisals, activists in Ul'ianovsk and Naryn practice self-censorship. Most independent media outlets in Ul'ianovsk do not report oblast corruption and do not challenge regional authorities. Journalists in Naryn are so wary of harassment that they have not even created independent media companies. Leaders of political organizations in Ul'ianovsk have responded to government punishments by disbanding their groups or limiting their activities. Members and contributors have deserted the groups or maintain only secret, superficial connections through anonymous donations. In Naryn, the single political group to form in the oblast disbanded for fear of government punishment. Potential activists have avoided the risk of government harassment by not forming groups. Likewise, harassment of candidates discourages people from entering races, and some existing candidates drop out of competitions and opt not to run in the future.

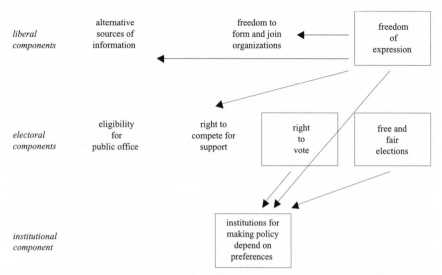

FIGURE 4.1. Interaction among the eight guarantees in Ul'ianovsk and Naryn. Note: The absence of a box around a guarantee indicates that it is weak or absent.

INTERACTION AMONG THE GUARANTEES

At first glance, the finding that only four of the guarantees are violated in Ul'ianovsk and Naryn might encourage optimism. Yet, applying the model of interaction among components to Ul'ianovsk and Naryn reveals how democracy as a whole is weaker than the strength of four of eight guarantees would suggest. Government interference and self-censorship in the spheres of media, NGOs, and candidacy in Ul'ianovsk and Naryn effectively undermine the four realized rights. Only 6 of the 24 possible connections among components are strong in these two provinces, as depicted in Figure 4.1.

In Ul'ianovsk and Naryn, individuals take advantage of freedom of expression, challenging the government through letters to officials and infrequent, small-scale protests. However, the self-censorship of political NGOs and the independent press in Ul'ianovsk and absence of these societal structures in Naryn mean that people's views cannot be disseminated widely. The impact of harassment and self-censorship on free speech in Ul'ianovsk is not quite as dire as in Naryn because in Ul'ianovsk a few independent presses have been able to challenge local authorities. These media outlets are likely to continue to criticize local provincial officials as long as the firms can maintain their economic autonomy.

Without independent media in Naryn, casting of ballots – or the right to vote – is less meaningful because voters' abilities to judge candidates are limited. In both oblasts, weak or defunct political groups cannot effectively support candidates for office, reducing the number of contenders or at least the number of viable contenders. Voting becomes even less significant when the government has coerced its opponents into dropping out of electoral races and perhaps never running for office again or when officials have pressured campaign workers into abandoning their candidates and perhaps never working on a campaign again. In both Ul'ianovsk and Naryn, harassment of opposition candidates during and after the electoral period effectively limits the candidate pool to those individuals who support or at least do not threaten the provincial government.

The importance of counting the ballots – or free and fair elections – is questionable when the candidate pool has already been limited. Moreover, without independent media and nongovernmental organizations, the number and quality of observers decline. In Naryn, observers were limited to state journalists and the friends and family of specific candidates. Although the latter had incentives to challenge the results, the lack of associations backing them up hindered their effectiveness. In Ul'ianovsk, observers from political parties and the independent press could complain only to the extent that their organizations could withstand government punishments. Also, electoral commissions are likely to be less objective if opposition groups do not hold seats on them.

Finally, government institutions' ability to develop policies to respond to citizens' preferences is severely hamstrung by weak or absent independent media, nongovernmental organizations, and opposition candidates. Independent media and NGOs are sources of information about societal conditions and citizens' wishes. Without these channels, officials in Naryn must rely on accounts from individual citizens and the glowing reports of the state media. Information flow to officials in Ul'ianovsk is limited to the extent that media and political groups self-censor. The weakness of these civic institutions in Ul'ianovsk and their absence in Naryn means that there is little or no public assessment of the responsiveness of government policies.

Such information can shape public opinion and encourage mass action, thus perhaps encouraging or forcing greater responsiveness. Because of harassment of opposition candidates during and after the electoral periods, citizens in Ul'ianovsk and Naryn who disagree with current policies cannot be represented in government institutions.

The interaction among the components results in only democratic façades in Ul'ianovsk and Naryn. In general, citizens participate but do not challenge. By examining the interactions among the components in the two provinces, it is also clear that democracy is weaker in Naryn than in Ul'ianovsk. Comparing provinces in two highly different settings yields little empirical advantage, but it does underscore the importance of interactions among components of democracy. Naryn's lack of independent media and nongovernmental political organizations is even more damning in light of how the absence of these components undermines so many other aspects of democracy. In Ul'ianovsk, the collective impact of independent media and political groups on 13 other components is weaker than in Samara and Osh, but at least the relationships exist. (One could draw these lines very faintly on Figure 4.1.) In Samara and Osh, all the connections among the guarantees exist and are relatively strong. This has created in these two provinces not perfect democracies but at least ones that offer both participation and contestation.

5

Illustrations of Economic Autonomy

The concept of economic autonomy can account for the greater difficulty of engaging in oppositional activity in Ul'ianovsk and Naryn relative to Samara and Osh. Yet, the utility of this concept is not limited to post-Soviet provincial politics of the 1990s. The idea of economic autonomy remains relevant in Russia and Kyrgyzstan today, helping us understand how economic and institutional changes may affect democratic development. Economic autonomy also illuminates why democracy has flourished in some regions of the world more than others.

ECONOMIC AUTONOMY IN THE FOUR PROVINCES

Any explanation for differences in oppositional activity must account for why government punishments and self-censorship are common in Ul'ianovsk and Naryn but not in Samara and Osh, as enumerated in Table 5.1. Moreover, it must be able to answer two questions embedded within this larger puzzle: Why do journalists and members of political organizations practice self-censorship in Naryn even though there have not been punishments on the media and political groups? Also, why are some individuals in Ul'ianovsk and Naryn activists, despite harassment and tendencies toward self-censorship in these regions?

Five types of information demonstrate that economic autonomy is the answer. First, data about individuals' professions indicate that current activists hold only those jobs that afford protection from local

TABLE 5.1. *Comparison: Punishment and Self-Censorship (given as the percentage followed by the ratio)*

Measure	Russia		Kyrgyzstan	
	Samara	Ul'ianovsk	Osh	Naryn
Independent media punished	0% (0/3)	80% (4/5)	0% (0/3)	No independent media (0/0)
Independent media that self-censor	0% (0/3)	40% (2/5)	0% (0/3)	No independent media (0/0)
Independent political groups punished	8% (1/12)	89% (8/9)	0% (0/6)	0% (0/1)
Independent political groups that self-censor	0% (0/12)	22% (2/9)	0% (0/6)	100% (1/1)
Candidates punished	0% (0/10)	18% (2/11)	0% (0/8)	44% (4/9)

Notes: The media ratios are the number of independent media that have been punished or that practice self-censorship relative to the total number of media. The total number represents all the independent media outlets that cover provincial news in a nontabloid fashion: three for Samara, five for Ul'ianovsk, three for Osh, and zero for Naryn. Although the absolute numbers are small, meaningful conclusions can be drawn from the data because they represent the entire populations, not samples. See Chapter 4 and Appendix D, "Alternative Sources of Information," for further details.

The ratios for political groups are the number of independent political groups that have been punished or that practice self-censorship relative to the total number of political groups. The total number represents all the current and former political parties and human-rights organizations that were active at one time: 12 for Samara, 9 for Ul'ianovsk (one of which is defunct), 6 for Osh, and 1 defunct party for Naryn. Although the absolute numbers are small, meaningful conclusions can be drawn from the data because they represent the entire populations, not samples. See Chapter 3 and Appendix D, "Freedom to Form and Join Organizations," for further details. Percentages are rounded to whole numbers.

The candidate ratios are the number of candidates that have been punished relative to the total sample of candidates. The total sample is a sample of winning and losing candidates for regional parliament and the post of governor in each Russian province and for regional parliament alone in each Kyrgyzstani oblast, because governors are not elected in Kyrgyzstan: 10 for Samara, 11 for Ul'ianovsk, 8 for Osh, and 9 for Naryn, or 6% of the candidates in Samara, 9% in Ul'ianovsk, 5% in Osh, and 15% in Naryn. See Chapter 3 and Appendix D, "Eligibility for Public Office," for information about sampling and other details.

authorities in Ul'ianovsk and Naryn, provinces with little economic autonomy. Activists who have abandoned their civic pursuits earn their income under the "thumb" of local officials. By contrast, activists work in spheres within and outside the reach of local leaders in Samara and

Osh, regions that provide substantial economic autonomy. Second, the accounts of activists in the four provinces show that individuals' decisions about political engagement are based on their personal economic autonomy. Third, financial information about independent media outlets demonstrates how economic autonomy enables them to challenge local authorities. Fourth, the fact that financial backers of activism provide secret support in Ul'ianovsk and open support in Samara and Osh also lends credence to the argument about environmental economic autonomy. Finally, descriptions of the economies of the provinces demonstrate that economic autonomy is, in fact, more limited in Ul'ianovsk and Naryn relative to Samara and Osh, thus suggesting an explanation for the different frequencies of government harassment.

Professions of Current and Former Activists

In Samara and Osh, activists work in a variety of professions, whereas activists in Ul'ianovsk and Naryn hold only those jobs that are outside the reach of local authorities. Furthermore, in Ul'ianovsk and Naryn, individuals who work under the influence of government officials have abandoned their political activities.[1] This suggests that economic autonomy influences political activism. Activists in Samara and Osh can afford to work in jobs under the control of local officials because they know they can find work independent of authorities if they lose their current jobs. In Ul'ianovsk and Naryn, regions that provide little economic autonomy, only those individuals with personal economic autonomy can risk political activism.

Approximately 30 percent of the leaders of independent political organizations in Samara and Osh hold jobs controlled by the local authorities, as noted in Table 5.2. These individuals include analysts in government departments and workers at state-owned firms. These activists did not express a fear of losing their livelihoods because employment opportunities free from local government influence are available. In Samara, one of these leaders, a schoolteacher, claims to

---

[1] Unless otherwise noted, information in this and the following three subsections is based on interviews I conducted with current and former leaders of political organizations, winning and losing candidates, media editors, and businesspeople in the four regions.

TABLE 5.2. *Professions of Leaders of Political NGOs (given as the percentage followed by ratio)*

Measure	Russia		Kyrgyzstan	
	Samara	Ul'ianovsk	Osh	Naryn
Job under control of local authorities	30% (3/10)	0% (0/8)	33% (2/6)	0% (0/1)
Job independent of local authorities	70% (7/10)	100% (8/8)	67% (4/6)	100% (1/1)

Notes: The ratios are the number of independent political leaders that do or do not work under the control of local authorities relative to the total number of political leaders. The total number represents the current and former political parties and human-rights organizations that were active at one time: 10 for Samara, 8 for Ul'ianovsk, 6 for Osh, and 1 inactive party for Naryn. For two of the 12 political groups in Samara, I do not have information about the professions of their leaders. With the inclusion of these two, the percentages for Samara would be 33 and 67, 42 and 58, or 25 and 75, depending on their professions. The leader of one of the political groups in Ul'ianovsk dissolved the organization in the face of livelihood punishments, so professional data about that leader do not appear here. Percentages are rounded to whole numbers.

Source: These data come from my interviews with leaders of political NGOs. At the end of each interview, I collected biographical information, including place of employment.

have lost his job because of his oppositional activity; however, there is no evidence that the directive came from the administration. Regardless, he found other work and continues to protest regional policies.

By contrast, consider the jobs of those who head political organizations in Ul'ianovsk and Naryn. In Ul'ianovsk, none of the leaders of independent political organizations work for provincial, county, city, or village government. One activist works for a successful private firm, where employees own the shares. A leader who heads two political groups earns income from a profitable independent sports association. A third party head receives his salary from a federal government institution. A fourth works for a federal enterprise located in the oblast.

Party activists in Ul'ianovsk who work as entrepreneurs have considerably more economic autonomy than the average businessperson in the province. One leader established an equipment-leasing business that operates in other regions of Russia. The head of another party has a business in the food sector. Although he would not reveal details of his venture, counterparts in other provinces of Russia described this enterprise as being financially successful and perhaps associated with the Russian mafia. In Naryn, a doctor of an oblast hospital "heads" the

TABLE 5.3. *Professions of Candidates for Provincial Office in the Russian Regions (given as the percentage followed by the ratio)*

Measure	Samara	Ul'ianovsk
Work in oblast, raion, city, or village government	26% (40/154)	8% (9/116)

Notes: A *raion* is a subdivision of an oblast. The ratios are the number of candidates in these positions relative to the total number of candidates. I excluded four full-time incumbents in Samara and one full-time incumbent in Ul'ianovsk from the counts. Other incumbents have jobs outside their elected office. Percentages are rounded to whole numbers.

Sources: The information was calculated from biographical data I collected from newspapers, electoral records, and my own interviews with winners and losers.

one independent political organization, the dissolved party. Although he continues to call himself the leader of this party, so many members have left out of fear of workplace harassment that the party is defunct.

The professions of those forced out of the civic sphere in Ul'ianovsk reflect the impact of weak economic autonomy as well. The party leader in Ul'ianovsk who abandoned his organization worked at a school, which is under the purview of local authorities. The entire "democratic" bloc in Ul'ianovsk suffered, according to one former activist, when a key leader had to give up politics. He was a struggling entrepreneur whose business could not survive pressure from the administration.

Electoral candidates' professions also demonstrate the connection between employment and activism. Significantly more candidates in Samara were local government employees than was the case in Ul'ianovsk, as Table 5.3 describes. In Samara, candidates included police officers, government lawyers, employees of the oblast departments of trade and social services, and workers in various county and city offices. These candidates were not government lackeys but in many cases serious opposition candidates. This suggests that they did not fear finding work outside the reach of local officials if they lost their state jobs. The frequency of government workers running for office in Samara as compared with Ul'ianovsk indicates that government workers can risk political engagement in Samara but not in Ul'ianovsk. As one newspaper editor in Ul'ianovsk noted, "All *biudzhetniki* [government employees] are afraid of losing their jobs"[2] if they engage in oppositional activities.

In the gubernatorial elections in Ul'ianovsk, three of the five "challengers" were economically independent of local authorities. One gubernatorial candidate owns a large, successful business. Another earns income from a job in Moscow. The third heads a federal factory. The fourth challenger left, or possibly lost, his job after the elections. Perhaps he miscalculated the employment risks of running for governor. The fifth candidate was not a challenger but the fake candidate.

In the 1999 gubernatorial elections, held after I completed my field research, economic autonomy enabled Vladimir Shamanov to successfully challenge Governor Goriachev. Vladimir Shamanov was a commander in the Russian army, so he did not rely on local officials for his income. Moreover, reports indicate that firms from outside the provinces funded his campaign.

The professions of the candidates in the Kyrgyzstani provinces also demonstrate the importance of economic autonomy. The candidate pool in Osh was diverse, whereas in Naryn doctors and government officials were common among the contenders. Most doctors were opposition candidates, whereas government officials ran with the blessing of higher authorities. Candidates in Naryn were more likely than contenders in Osh to hold medical degrees because a medical degree is one of the few ways to withstand government punishments in Naryn.

The candidates in Ul'ianovsk and Naryn who experienced government pressure yet still decided to run were outside of the direct reach of regional authorities. For example, the gubernatorial candidate in Ul'ianovsk who headed a federal factory easily ended workplace harassment by complaining to officials in Moscow. A parliamentary candidate in Naryn who had a medical diploma could ignore authorities' demands that he abandon politics because he could threaten to work elsewhere if necessary.

Accounts of Current and Former Activists

Current and former activists in the four provinces discuss livelihood risks when they recount their choices about political engagement.

[2] Author's interview (179) with the editor of an independent media outlet, Ul'ianovsk oblast, November 17, 1997.

Individuals in Ul'ianovsk and Naryn attributed their decisions to initiate and either continue or abandon civic pursuits to their degree of personal economic autonomy. In Samara and Osh, people stated that civic activities did not put their livelihood at risk because of the economic autonomy their provinces provided.

The Ul'ianovsk school director quoted at the beginning of Chapter 1 described how he miscalculated the risks of creating a political party. Unable to find other work, he explained that he would only become politically active again if government reprisals came to an end.

Another political party leader in Ul'ianovsk took a different approach. When he was fired from his state job for his activism, he decided to look for another job so that he could continue his oppositional activities. He managed to find a job at a private firm run by an individual who is willing to afford him some protection. His boss "will sometimes close his eyes [to the activist's pursuits]."[3]

Yet another party leader in Ul'ianovsk contrasted his own decision to remain an activist with those of former members of the organization. Because the leader earns income from beyond the borders of the province, he can withstand the risks of activism. He explained that others, however, are in a different position. "A head of an enterprise left the party because of this indirect pressure, and he has not experienced any more incidents. [We've] lost many members from this indirect pressure," the leader recounted. The head of the party described how some members found another means of opposition. "All members do not work actively. Some just give money. They asked for anonymity."[4]

Activists in Ul'ianovsk and Naryn indicated that they do not base their judgments about their individual economic autonomy solely on the extent to which their current jobs afford them protection. They also consider the degree to which their skills and the regional economic environment offer alternative employment outside the reach of local authorities. For example, a doctor in an administrative post in Naryn, who served as a campaign manager, credited his medical diploma for his resistance to government attempts to dissuade him from oppositional activity: "If I lose work as head doctor, I can work as a regular doctor.

---

[3] Author's interview (186) with a political party leader, Ul'ianovsk oblast, November 22, 1997.
[4] Author's interview (189) with a party leader, Ul'ianovsk oblast, November 29, 1997.

I have a medical diploma," he stated.[5] Another doctor who ran for office in Naryn explained how officials on the oblast level tried three times to convince him not to run but that he refused because his status as a doctor protected him. "How could I face [my supporters if I dropped out].... I have a medical diploma."[6]

In Osh and Samara, activists described how environmental economic autonomy reduced their fears of political engagement. Consider the comment of an activist in Osh who claimed that even "government officials and workers are less and less afraid to support a candidate independent of their bosses' wishes because these lower individuals are creating their own business on the side. In other words, if they lose their state jobs, they have an alternative income."[7] Whereas an activist in Naryn said that "[Potential activists] are fearful because they all work in the government...they are all subordinates."[8] Like their counterparts in Osh, activists in Samara draw a connection between economic opportunities in the region and political activism. A journalist with an independent firm compared the Russian provinces, explaining that "in Samara, as compared to Ul'ianovsk, business is not afraid of taking part in politics. Firms are larger and stronger. There may be administrative pressure, through tax inspections for example, but business in this oblast can withstand this pressure."[9]

Protection for Opposition Media

Political leaders and candidates calculate the risks that activism poses to their individual livelihood. In the case of the media, not just one activist but an entire firm can come under attack. Like any company, media outlets can better withstand government harassment if they are financially strong and if they have outside contacts. For newspapers, the ability to print on nongovernmental presses is also helpful.

[5] Author's interview (29) with a deputy in the oblast parliament, Naryn oblast, July 8, 1997.
[6] Author's interview (21) with an unsuccessful candidate, Naryn oblast, June 26, 1997.
[7] Author's interview (61) with an editor of an independent media outlet, Osh oblast, May 6, 1998.
[8] Author's interview (6) with a journalist for an independent media outlet, Naryn oblast, July 2, 1997.
[9] Author's interview (108) with an editor of an independent media outlet, Samara oblast, January 26, 1998.

In these ways, the three opposition media outlets in Ul'ianovsk are able to criticize local authorities without succumbing to government harassment, whereas others are not. As described in the previous chapter, a newspaper that risked losing its lease successfully threatened to use its contacts in the international mass media to cause a scandal. To pay legal fees to fight government lawsuits, the newspaper has relied on its earnings from advertising, subscriptions, and sales at kiosks. The firm has managed to keep its expenses low by paying its staff very little. However, the economic position of this newspaper is even more precarious because local authorities have scared away some of its advertisers. Nonetheless, the editorial collective has refused offers to be purchased by city and oblast government organs, as well as numerous large businesses. Instead, the staff has begun to publish special thematic sections, such as one on cars, in order to increase advertising revenue.

Another newspaper in Ul'ianovsk has been able to endure government financial harassment because it is part of an interregional corporation. The corporation also owns a television station and a children's magazine called *Arbus*, and the firm has divisions in Moscow, Samara, Nizhegorod, Murmansk, Saratov, and St. Petersburg, among other regions. The newspaper in Ul'ianovsk has some protection in terms of distribution as well. According to a competitor, this newspaper owns the controlling share in a firm that distributes periodicals to stores and kiosks. The third opposition newspaper is also part of a larger successful media corporation, and this has enabled it to withstand government punishments. When the government has responded to critical articles by refusing to print the publication at its printing house, the staff has printed the newspaper in Nizhegorod oblast instead. Financial strength and outside contacts help opposition media in regions with little economic autonomy, such as Ul'ianovsk, endure government punishments.

In Samara and Osh, the relatively stronger business environments have created economic autonomy for media outlets in these provinces. In Samara, a young banker supports numerous newspapers and owns 12 printing presses.[10] His ownership of presses has broken the regional government monopoly on printing. The higher density of small businesses and people in Osh relative to Naryn has helped independent

---

[10] Laura Belin and Peter Rutland, "Regional Press Fights Political Control," *Transition* 1 (September 7, 1995).

media outlets in this region to survive economically. Electoral candidates purchase advertisements in the media, and people buy congratulatory announcements broadcast for friends and family. Moreover, a media director in Osh described how connections to economically autonomous individuals in the community help protect his firm. "It is better to befriend the government, all the more so if you are a private company. The government has the ability to prevent one from working. . . . You need to respect power. . . . The laws are such that in any private company [the tax inspectors] can find a mistake." A person's risk depends on "who stands behind him, who is his *krysha* [roof]," he explained. A "roof " is an economically autonomous individual who can provide support, typically financial, if an organization has trouble with the authorities. Before reporting on corruption, he "would speak with [his] own roof and ask 'Can you guarantee me help?' With a corruption story you put your work and family at risk."[11]

Behavior of Financial Supporters

Economic autonomy has an impact on the decisions of those directly engaged in politics. It also influences the behavior of those who provide financial backing to electoral candidates, independent media, and political groups. Businesspeople in Ul'ianovsk secretly support political activists, whereas business leaders in Samara and Osh provide assistance openly. In Naryn, financial backing of activism is less common.

In Ul'ianovsk, companies make secret and thus illegal donations to electoral campaigns because they fear government reprisals. As a gubernatorial candidate in Ul'ianovsk explained, "Businessmen are afraid to give money officially. They fear inspections, such as tax inspections."[12] A business owner clarified: "Those who go against the governor, the administration, are punished."[13] Business leaders in Samara, on the other hand, tend to make legal donations and even publicly back candidates. Overall, more candidates in Samara seem to receive

---

[11] Author's interview (53) with the deputy director of an independent media outlet, Osh oblast, April 27, 1998.

[12] Author's interview (201) with an unsuccessful candidate who is also an entrepreneur, Ul'ianovsk oblast, December 1, 1997.

[13] Author's interview (223) with a party leader who is also an entrepreneur, Ul'ianovsk oblast, November 29, 1998.

commercial backing, reflecting the richer business environment in the province.

Entrepreneurs in Ul'ianovsk also are less likely to openly sponsor a media outlet or to advertise in the independent media. An editor explained that "business people will refuse to advertise... for political reasons. This has happened more than once.... They will say, 'If we put in an advertisement, there will be unhealthy attention toward our company from the oblast administration.' "[14] The editor recounted that business leaders were so fearful of government harassment that the head of a large enterprise visited him and asked the editor not to tell anyone he was ever there. The government held no shares in the enterprise, yet "even without the government as a shareholder, the governor still affects whether a tax inspection takes place and whether credit can be obtained."[15] In Samara, by contrast, businesses play a public role in the media. Oil and gas companies openly own shares of a newspaper distribution firm and a large media company, and editors at media outlets with different political orientations have never experienced refusals to advertise for political reasons.

Whereas business support for activism is relatively common in Osh, it is rare in Naryn. In Osh, firms sponsor the activities of some political groups, and businesspeople and electoral candidates buy advertisements in the media. Businesspeople and editors in Osh recounted that economic, not political, concerns are the only deterrents to placing advertisements in the media. Advertising in independent media is not an issue in Naryn, where no private newspapers or broadcasting companies exist.

Even if businesses do not press for greater democracy themselves, they contribute indirectly to responsive government by encouraging political activism. Donations to opposition candidates, advertising in independent media, and sponsorship of political groups support three guarantees of democracy – the ability of political leaders to compete for political support, the provision of alternative sources of information, and the formation of organizations. This is not to suggest

[14] Author's interview (179) with the editor of an independent media outlet, Ul'ianovsk oblast, November 17, 1997.
[15] Author's interview (179) with the editor of an independent media outlet, Ul'ianovsk oblast, November 17, 1997.

that businesses are always supportive of political activism. After purchasing shares in two newspapers, businesspeople in Samara's city of Tol'iatti had one editor beaten and another killed because their staffs refused to work under the new owners.[16] Nonetheless, on balance, businesses typically serve as a positive counterweight to the government through their backing of activism. Limited economic autonomy in Ul'ianovsk forces firms in this region to support activists secretly, whereas greater economic autonomy in Samara and Osh allows companies to openly back activists.

Provincial Characteristics

Activists' behavior and words suggest that little environmental economic autonomy exists in Ul'ianovsk and Naryn relative to Samara and Osh, respectively. But, are activists' perceptions of the degree of economic autonomy in their province accurate, and what are the sources of economic autonomy? Earning income without the interference of local authorities is, in fact, hampered in Ul'ianovsk as compared with Samara; Ul'ianovsk companies lack healthy profits and strong foreign ties, and the governor's monopoly on business stifles entrepreneurship in the oblast. Similarly, residents of Naryn are more dependent on local authorities than are people in Osh because of the lack of marketable goods produced in the region and the limited access to established trade routes.

Capitalism's role in creating economic autonomy is evident in Samara and Osh, regions that offer greater economic independence. These provinces are not paragons of capitalism, yet capitalist features of these regions produce economic autonomy nonetheless. Financial success, international investment, and pro-market policies in Samara and tradeable goods and market access in Osh are key components of capitalism. Financially successful companies and foreign investors create employment options independent of local authorities in Samara. Local officials encourage the development of these alternatives through

---

[16] Francesca Mereu, "Defending Press Freedom No Easy Chore in Regions." *The Russia Journal*, June 24, 2000. Available at http://www.russiajournal.com/weekly/article.shtml?ad=3115.

their pro-market policies. Coveted products and market access in Osh enable people to construct their own jobs outside the state sector.

Samara and Ul'ianovsk. Both Samara and Ul'ianovsk are primarily industrial, dominated by the automobile and aircraft industries as well as food processing, electrical power production, and chemical and petrochemical manufacturing. The disintegration of the Soviet economic system created severe problems in both oblasts. Large industrial complexes face declining state orders, disruptions of inputs, shrinking markets, and the expense of converting defense plants to other uses. However, financial success, international contacts, and the pro-market orientation of the regional government afford companies in Samara greater economic independence than their counterparts in Ul'ianovsk.

Enterprises in Samara have the benefit of monopolizing Russian and, in one case, even world markets. By improving their chances for financial success, the monopoly status of firms in Samara gives them bargaining power with local authorities. Samara is home to the manufacturers of 18 percent of the goods that monopolize the Russian market.[17] The local automobile manufacturer AvtoVAZ produces more than 70 percent of all Russian cars, nearly six times more than the next largest manufacturer.[18] AvtoVAZ provides half the regional tax revenue, so it has influence over the provincial administration.[19] In contrast, UAZ, Ul'ianovsk's automobile plant and one of its leading companies, built 14 times fewer cars than AvtoVAZ in 1997 and only one-quarter of the trucks manufactured in the country.[20]

Besides Samara's AvtoVAZ, the region's metallurgical plant is the only producer of some semifinished goods in Russia and the only manufacturer of some products in the world. Samara oblast also supplies

---

[17] Aleksei Novikov, an analyst at Institut Ekonomiki Goroda, provided this information.
[18] European Bank for Reconstruction and Development, *Russian Federation 1999 Country Profile* (London: European Bank for Reconstruction and Development, 1999), 32; Business Information Service for the Newly Independent States, *Samara Regional Report*. Samara: Business Information Service for the Newly Independent States, 1999. Available at http://bisnis.doc.gov/bisnis/country/991101samararegrep.htm.
[19] "Sweetly Flows the Volga," *The Economist*, June 5, 1999, 62.
[20] The Ul'ianovsk Automobile Factory is a leader, although not a monopolistic one, in minibus manufacturing, having produced nearly three times more than the next largest company. See European Bank for Reconstruction and Development, *Russian Federation 1999 Country Profile*, 33.

Russia with 30 percent of its synthetic rubber, used mainly for tires, and the province provides the Volga River region with 40 percent of its locally generated electrical power. Furthermore, the Rossiia chocolate factory and Samara Cable Company are the largest of their kind in the country. Samara's aerospace companies have made the province a leader in the production of aircraft, aircraft engines, spacecraft, and satellites, and the oblast is home to one of the main bearing plants in the country. The region has also become a financial hub, housing one of eight foreign-currency exchanges and one of eight securities-trading floors in the country.[21]

In contrast to Samara, Ul'ianovsk is a leader only in heavy air freight – a single somewhat narrow industry. Volga-Dnepr Airlines in Ul'ianovsk operates the world's largest air freighters, some of which are produced by the local aircraft manufacturer Aviastar. Most other enterprises, such as UAZ and the Volzhanka confectionary company, produce goods similar to those manufactured in Samara. Thus, they face monopolistic or at least Goliath-sized competition.

Ties to foreign markets and access to foreign capital further increase the economic independence of Samara businesses relative to those in Ul'ianovsk. Samara exports 25 times more goods to countries outside the Commonwealth of Independent States (CIS) and nearly six times more within the CIS than Ul'ianovsk,[22] as Table 5.4 indicates. Even taking into account the fact that Samara has twice as many people, these are significant differences. Samara's AvtoVAZ earns large sums of hard currency by selling cars in Asia and third world countries, and the aerospace, petrochemical, machine-building, and beverage industries provide additional export income. Ul'ianovsk's Volga-Dnepr, which offers service to North America, Asia, Europe, and the Middle East, and the factories that export automobiles and machines do not match the might of the Samara companies.[23]

---

[21] Philip Hanson, "Samara: A Preliminary Profile of a Russian Region and Its Adaptation to the Market," *Europe–Asia Studies* 49 (May, 1997), 416, 420. Business Information Service for the Newly Independent States, *Samara Regional Report*; *The Economist*, "Sweetly Flows the Volga."

[22] Calculated from *Regiony Rossii, 1999: statisticheskii sbornik*, vol. 2 (Moscow: Goskomstat Rossii, 1999), 846.

[23] Business Information Service for the Newly Independent States, *Samara Regional Report*; Samara Research Group, "Two Military-Industrial Giants," in *The Russian Enterprise in Transition: Case Studies*, ed. Simon Clarke (Cheltenham: Edward

TABLE 5.4. *Economic Characteristics of the Russian Regions*

Measure	Samara	Ul'ianovsk
Exports to countries outside the CIS, 1997 (millions of U.S. dollars)	1,794.9	71.4
Exports to CIS countries, 1997 (millions of U.S. dollars)	235	41.2
Foreign direct investment, 1997 (thousands of U.S. dollars)	68,210	2,364
Foreign direct investment, 1996 (thousands of U.S. dollars)	29,594	104
Firms and organizations with foreign capital, 1998 (entities)	84	13
Workers at entities receiving foreign funds, 1998 (people)	31,000	1,500

Note: This table provides data from the years I conducted research in the regions, with the exception of foreign direct investment, for which I also provided 1996 data.
Source: *Regiony Rossii, 1999: statisticheskii sbornik*, Vol. 2 (Moscow: Goskomstat Rossii, 1999), 814–815, 846, 848–849.

Samara's economy received nearly 29 times more foreign direct investment than Ul'ianovsk's in 1997 and nearly 285 times more in 1996. Most of this foreign capital went into industry. Almost seven times as many companies with foreign capital operate in Samara, and 20 times as many workers are employed at enterprises and organizations that receive foreign assistance.[24] The foreign presence in Samara includes Coca Cola and Pepsi-Cola bottling plants, the Danone Volga production facility, a partnership between AvtoVAZ and General Motors/Packard Electric Division, and an agreement between Samara Cable Company and Corning Incorporated to produce optical cable for residents of the former Soviet Union. In addition, Nestle Food LLC owns 49 percent of the Rossiia chocolate factory, GTS provides digital telephone services, and Lufthansa offers direct flights to Frankfurt. With fewer than half the number of foreign joint ventures, Ul'ianovsk's

Elgar, 1996), 275; Hanson, "Samara," 411; Samara State University, *Samara Region: Investments*. Samara: Samara State University. Available at http://www.samara.ru/business/indexen.asp; Volga-Dnepr Airlines, *Volga-Dnepr Airlines: Company Background*. Ul'ianovsk: Volga-Dnepr Airlines. Available at http://voldn.ru/compbarc.htm.
[24] Calculated from *Regiony Rossii, 1999: statisticheskii sbornik*, 814–815, 848–849.

most significant international partnership involves Volga-Dnepr. The company collaborates with Heavy Lift Cargo Airlines of London and the Chinese government.[25]

Strong profits and foreign connections afford large companies some protection from local authorities, but in relatively decentralized Russia the firms still may be subject to the policies of antimarket or corrupt local governments. Moreover, successful smaller companies with foreign contact have little bargaining power because they provide little revenue and employ few people. For these reasons, a pro-business government policy is also a component of economic autonomy in Samara. The Samara regional administration supports market reform and entrepreneurial ventures. The government helps old and new companies, but it does not interfere in their operations. In contrast, the Ul'ianovsk regional government has been antimarket, and Governor Goriachev created a political–economic monopoly.

Entrepreneurs in Samara say that provincial authorities have never tried to impede their business pursuits. This does not mean that businesspeople in Samara are completely content with authorities' decisions but merely that in this province there is "no strict control of business"[26] and "no one will break you if your business is honest."[27] Instead, the regional government has encouraged business development through its Department of Support of Entrepreneurship and Small Business. The department has centers in almost all towns in the region. These centers provide information about credit and leasing through state and private banks, and they suggest additional resources for business development.[28] The founder of an independent media company explained that "if you have a desire, you can create it [in Samara oblast]."[29] In spite of the government support, an administration official "referred

[25] Business Information Service for the Newly Independent States, *Samara Regional Report*; *The Economist*, "Sweetly Flows the Volga"; European Bank for Reconstruction and Development, *Russian Federation 1999 Country Profile*; Volga-Dnepr Airlines, *Company Background*.

[26] Author's interview (111) with the head of an independent media outlet who is also an entrepreneur, Samara oblast, January 28, 1998.

[27] Author's interview (109) with the deputy editor of a state media outlet, Samara oblast, January 26, 1998.

[28] Samara State University, *Samara Region: Small Business*. Samara: Samara State University. Available at http://www.samara.ru/investments/smallen.asp.

[29] Author's interview (111) with the head of an independent media outlet, Samara oblast, January 28, 1998.

to any enterprise that does not have much involvement with the political authorities as 'a success for our policies, because it is fending for itself.'"[30] This statement emphasizes the market philosophy of the administration.

The supportive business climate in Samara has been attributed to Governor Titov, a former economist and a newcomer to politics who supports marketization. Under Titov's leadership, Samara introduced market reforms at the earliest opportunity. The governor also demonstrated his comfort with the new economic and political rules in Russia, traveling frequently to Moscow to lobby on behalf of Samara and visiting foreign nations in order to win support for the province and for his proposal for countrywide economic reform. "The receptive nature of the local government" toward foreign investment is emphasized on Samara's official Web site. The site notes that "[t]he authorities consider assistance to the increase of investment activities in the Region and attracting investment as the main task of the present stage of economic reforms."[31] Titov's policies have repeatedly drawn support from the international community. A partnership between local banks and Technical Assistance to the Commonwealth of Independent States (TACIS) provided financing for more than 350 small businesses. In 1998, Samara earned one of only three spots in the Russian–American program Regional Investment Initiative, which encourages U.S. companies and government programs to develop projects in regions of Russia.[32]

In Ul'ianovsk, an entrepreneur described the business environment there in this way: "There is a monopoly held by the governor's entourage. One hundred percent. If you want to create a business – a

30 Hanson, "Samara," 423.
31 Business Information Service for the Newly Independent States, *Samara Regional Report*; Samara Region Administration, *Samara Region Administration: Economy and Business*. Samara: Samara Region Administration. Available at http://www.adm.samara.ru/econom/invprjen.asp.
32 Samara State University, *Samara Region: Small Business*; European Bank for Reconstruction and Development, *Regional Venture Funds*. London: European Bank for Reconstruction and Development. Available at http://www.ebrd.com/english/opera/Country/rus05.htm; European Bank for Reconstruction and Development, *Russia Small Business Fund*. London: European Bank for Reconstruction and Development. Available at http://www.ebrd.com/english/opera/Country/RSBF08.htm; Business Information Service for the Newly Independent States, *Samara Regional Report*.

business in a new sphere that is not part of [their] monopoly – officials will simply say, 'No.' Officials give a blank stare when you propose something and say, 'I will think about it.' Oblast officials are crazy – like zombies."[33]

Businesspeople in Ul'ianovsk recounted how only those individuals in the favor of the governor could create new businesses, and for existing businesses to survive, owners need to have good relations with the governor. "[Entrepreneurs] are under his influence," according to a representative of the media who covers regional economic issues.[34] The governor created a finance group, giving his own friends and family and those of other top administration officials key business posts, such as the chairmanship of a leading local bank.[35] The governor also granted these people privileges. For example, his son sells cash registers, so the governor decreed that all vendors in the outdoor market in the provincial capital must begin to use cash registers purchased from his son.[36]

---

[33] Author's interview (193) with a civic leader who is also an entrepreneur, Ul'ianovsk oblast, December 3, 1997.

[34] Author's interview (179) with the editor of an independent media outlet, Ul'ianovsk oblast, November 17, 1997.

[35] The development of monopolies in Russia was to some extent intended, as a goal of voucher privatization was to concentrate ownership in order to improve corporate governance. Monopolies were also a result of the structure of Soviet society. Because the Soviet government controlled most resources and party functionaries "stole the state" in the late Soviet era, the party elites, along with black-market entrepreneurs, were the only ones with the capital to take advantage of market opportunities in the post-Soviet period. At the regional level, in particular, these party elites remained in power, and many used their political privileges, including access to information and the right to grant licenses, to benefit from marketization. (In their study of regional political elites in Russia, David Lane and Cameron Ross found that slightly more than half had previously held a Communist Party position.) See Hilary Appel, "Voucher Privatisation in Russia: Structural Consequences and Mass Response in the Second Period of Reform," *Europe–Asia Studies* 49 (December, 1997), 1434–1435; David S. Lane and Cameron Ross, *The Transition from Communism to Capitalism: Ruling Elites from Gorbachev to Yeltsin*, 1st ed. (New York: St. Martin's Press, 1999), 150–152; Steven Lee Solnick, *Stealing the State: Control and Collapse in Soviet Institutions* (Cambridge, MA: Harvard University Press, 1998).

[36] A survey of 70 shops in the city of Ul'ianovsk in the spring and summer of 1996 corroborates these accounts of the difficulty of running a business in the region. The survey was not conducted in Samara but was conducted in Smolensk, a similarly pro-market region, and Moscow, known for the mayor's political–economic monopoly, thus providing some comparative data. Of the respondents in Ul'ianovsk, 48.7 percent said the government hinders business, 46.2 percent said it had a neutral effect, and 5.1 percent said it was helpful. The comparable percentages for Smolensk

The governor's actions have been attributed less to greed than to his history as a former communist leader who prefers the Soviet economic system. As governor, he perhaps tried to monopolize business in order to secure his position in the new economic and political order. Goriachev tried to maintain the Soviet economic system for as long as possible, continuing with ration cards for food staples until mid-1996 and not holding auctions to privatize municipal property until June 1997.[37] His policies have extended to the international sphere, manifested in refusals to woo foreign capital, accept foreign charity, or speak with foreign journalists. As a result, international small business and investment programs have not set up offices in Ul'ianovsk as they have in Samara.[38]

Many businesspeople have left Ul'ianovsk oblast or they work primarily outside the region while continuing to reside in Ul'ianovsk, as one entrepreneur phrased it, to escape this "nightmarish dream."[39] Although no concrete figures exist, remaining entrepreneurs and journalists estimate the percentage of large businesses that have left to be as high as 50 percent. One administration official, a relatively pro-market outsider, acknowledged that some businesspeople have left the oblast because the market came late. Statistics on general migration do suggest that Ul'ianovsk is a less favorable place to live than Samara. In 1997, Samara and Ul'ianovsk gained approximately 17,874 and 1,342 people, respectively.[40]

---

were 34.2, 61.8, and 3.9, respectively, and the percentages for Moscow were 17.1, 72.9, and 10, respectively. Businesses in Ul'ianovsk were inspected by government agencies almost 22 times a year versus approximately 16 times in Smolensk and Moscow, and the Ul'ianovsk shops were fined on 38 percent of the visits in contrast with 19 percent in Smolensk. The percentage was similar to Moscow's 37 percent. Shops were also more difficult to open in Ul'ianovsk, requiring nine permits and five months for registration. See Timothy Frye and Ekaterina Zhuravskaya, "Rackets, Regulation, and the Rule of Law," *Journal of Law Economics and Organization* 16 (October, 2000), 11–12, 33.

37 Darrell Slider, "Russia's Market-Distorting Federalism," *Post-Soviet Geography and Economics* 38 (1997), 450–451.

38 European Bank for Reconstruction and Development, *Regional Venture Funds*; European Bank for Reconstruction and Development, *Russia Small Business Fund*.

39 Author's interview (193) with a civic leader who is also an entrepreneur, Ul'ianovsk oblast, December 3, 1997.

40 Calculated from *Regiony Rossii, 1999: statisticheskii sbornik*, 32, 68.

The differing economic policies of Samara and Ul'ianovsk are reflected in statistics on privatization and small businesses. Approximately four times as many enterprises and apartments have been privatized in Samara since the beginning of the national campaign than in Ul'ianovsk.[41] By 1996, nearly 96 percent of trading enterprises, dining establishments, and services were privatized in Samara compared with 47 percent in Ul'ianovsk.[42] The government continued to own approximately 15 percent of industrial enterprises in Ul'ianovsk and only 2 percent in Samara in 1997. Among industrial workers in the region, nearly twice as many worked for the government in Ul'ianovsk. By that year, there were nearly four times as many small businesses, as well as small business employees, in Samara compared with Ul'ianovsk.[43]

In sum, residents of Samara, relative to people in Ul'ianovsk, are more economically independent of regional authorities because local industries enjoy monopoly status, foreign capital, and international partnerships. Furthermore, the policies of the Samara oblast administration have not interfered with the private sector but instead have enabled it to grow larger.

Osh and Naryn. The degree of economic independence also distinguishes the Kyrgyzstani provinces; however, the sources of autonomy are not the same as in the Russian regions. Residents of Osh are more economically independent of local authorities than their neighbors in Naryn because the topography of Osh oblast allows for production of more desirable goods and better access to markets outside the region. These outside contacts afford people in Osh protection from local authorities.

Osh oblast is part of the Ferghana Valley, an area surrounded by high mountains and populated by more than 10 million people of southern Kyrgyzstan, eastern Uzbekistan, and northern Tajikistan. The province has plains and hills in the north, the Pamir Mountains in the south, and the Ferghana Mountains of the Tien Shan range in the east. In

---

[41] Calculated from Ibid., 328, 354.
[42] *Predprinimatel'skii klimat regionov Rossii: geografiia Rossii dlia investorov i predprinimatelei* (Moscow: Nachala-Press, 1997), 276.
[43] *Regiony Rossii, 1999: statisticheskii sbornik*, 318, 366.

contrast, Naryn, situated within the Tien Shan Mountains, is isolated and remote. Seventy percent of Naryn oblast is mountainous, and the remainder consists of high mountain valleys. More than 95 percent of the oblast sits higher than 1,000 meters above sea level.[44]

Because Kyrgyzstan is not very industrialized, geography has dictated the economies of Osh and Naryn. Melting snow from the Pamir and Ferghana mountains irrigates farms in the lower lands, making Osh one of the best regions for agriculture in the country. Cattle, sheep, and goat herding dominate the agricultural industry, followed by the cultivation of cotton, tobacco, subtropical fruits, and nuts. In Naryn, only animal husbandry is possible because of the topography and climate of the region.

The value of goods produced in Osh and the greater access to markets mean that residents in this province enjoy greater economic independence. Farms in Osh sell much of their produce directly to independent traders, and independent processing of agricultural products has increased.[45] Produce from Osh sells particularly well in nearby countries with less hospitable climates and topographies. For example, in southern Russia, small-scale traders from Osh exchange fruits for construction materials to sell in Kyrgyzstan.

A relatively efficient transportation network radiating from Osh facilitates long-distance sales. Entrepreneurs can drive trucks 262 kilometers from Osh city to Irkeshtam in China or 754 kilometers to Khorog in southern Tajikistan. They can even take a bus to Iran. Traders can also fly from two airfields and an airport, one of only two international airports in the country. Besides flights to northern Kyrgyzstan, the Osh airport offers daily flights to Almaty (Kazakhstan) and Omsk (Russia) and weekly flights to Moscow and Novosibirsk (Russia). There are also regular flights to Istanbul and

---

[44] United Nations Human Development Programme in Kyrgyzstan, *National Human Development Report for the Kyrgyz Republic 1999*. Bishkek: United Nations Human Development Programme in Kyrgyzstan, 1999. Available at http://www.undp. bishkek.su/english/publications/nhdr1999/chapter 5.html; Kyrgyzstan Development Gateway Project, *Regions*. Bishkek: State Committee of the Kyrgyz Republic on Foreign Investments and Economic Development. Available at http://kyrgyzinvest. org/en/country/regions.htm.

[45] State Commission on Foreign Investment and Economic Assistance, *The Kyrgyz Republic: Osh Regional Economic Strategy* (Bishkek: State Commission on Foreign Investment and Economic Assistance, 1996), 25.

frequent charter flights to Beijing, Urumchi (China), Delhi, and numerous cities in Pakistan, Saudi Arabia, and the United Arab Emirates.[46]

Trading within the Ferghana Valley is even more common than long-distance business. Small-scale traders sell products from Osh outside the province, buy consumer goods, and then resell them. "Most of the economically active population is now in the bazaar," according to a regional official.[47] In the northern and western parts of Osh oblast, where most people live, the "border economy" generates nearly all the income. Most of the cities and larger towns of the province are located along the northern border, across from which are Uzbekistani and Tajikistani towns. Andizhan (Uzbekistan) is only a one-hour car or bus ride from Osh city. From the northwestern town of Batken, Kokand (Uzbekistan) is only three to five hours away and Khojent (Tajikistan) is only three to six hours away, depending on the road conditions and mode of transportation. The bazaar economy is most visible in the center of Osh city, where one of the largest open markets in Central Asia operates.

Alongside the traders in Osh oblast, other entrepreneurs have created and privatized enterprises to provide services, such as haircuts and dining. This economic activity is reflected in the fact that more than one-third of Osh's gross product is from services, as compared with less than one-fifth of Naryn's.[48] Table 5.5 provides the specific numbers. Nowadays, it is easy for chefs and lawyers to find work in Osh, according to a media representative and small business owner.

Opportunities for trading are more limited in Naryn. The province is sparsely populated, and it shares an international border only with China. The trip from the provincial capital, Naryn, to Kashgar, the

[46] Witt Raczka, "Xinjang and Its Central Asian Borderlands," *Central Asia Survey* 17 (1998), 373–407; United Nations Human Development Programme in Kyrgyzstan, *National Human Development Report*; Nancy Lubin and Barnett R. Rubin, *Calming the Ferghana Valley: Development and Dialogue in the Heart of Central Asia* (New York: Century Foundation Press, 1999), 70; State Commission on Foreign Investment and Economic Assistance, *The Kyrgyz Republic: Osh Regional Economic Strategy*; Kyrgyzstan Development Gateway Project, *Regions*; Business Information Service for the Newly Independent States, *General Investment Opportunities in Osh Oblast.* Washington DC: Business Information Service for the Newly Independent States, 1997. Available at http://bisnis.doc.gov/bisnis/country/kgosh4.htm.
[47] Lubin and Rubin, *Calming the Ferghana Valley*, 66.
[48] United Nations Human Development Programme in Kyrgyzstan, *National Human Development Report*.

TABLE 5.5. *Economic Characteristics of the Kyrgyzstani Regions*

Measure	Osh	Naryn
Gross product derived from services, 1997 (percentage)	36.2	17.2
Foreign direct investment, 1995–1999 (millions of U.S. dollars)	71	3.98

Note: This table provides data from the years I conducted research in the regions, 1997 and 1998.
Sources: "Chapter V: Regions," *National Human Development Report for the Kyrgyz Republic 1999*, The United Nations Human Development Programme in Kyrgyzstan, http://www.undp.bishkek.su/english/publications/nhdr1999/chapter_5.html; The Kyrgyzstan National Statistics Committee on the former Web site of The Kyrgyzstan Development Gateway Project, State Committee of the Kyrgyz Republic on Foreign Investments and Economic Development.

most accessible Chinese city, can take two to three days. Moreover, because the border was closed for 25 years during the late Soviet era, there is no tradition of trade between the peoples living on each side. The historical lack of trading between Naryn and Xinjiang is reflected by the fact that towns do not exist near the border point, Torugart, which is instead quite isolated. Air travel is also not an option for Naryn residents, as the airport has no regular flights – only infrequent chartered ones.

The strength of trade and other services in Osh, as compared with Naryn, dates back centuries, when Osh was home to sedentary peoples engaged in trade and agriculture and Naryn was a region of nomads. Historically, the city of Osh was a main stopping point on the Silk Road, which linked traders in the Ferghana Valley with the rest of the world. The fact that the valley was a single political unit under the Kokand khanate for 250 years prior to Russian rule further contributed to Osh's "thriving tradition of trade."[49]

Soviet policies also help account for the rich trading and service environment in Osh today. Moscow never industrialized the southern part of Kyrgyzstan as much as the northern part of the country. As a result, the service sector continued to be a mainstay of Osh's economy

[49] Lubin and Rubin, *Calming the Ferghana Valley*, 36, 39; State Commission on Foreign Investment and Economic Assistance, *The Kyrgyz Republic: Osh Regional Economic Strategy*.

during the Soviet era. In fact, under socialism, much of this activity went underground, feeding the organized crime of the Ferghana Valley.[50] Soviet road construction facilitated cross-border trading in particular. The economies of the Soviet republics were designed to be interdependent, so the roads from one republican city to another often passed through a second republic. This strengthened cross-border trade in the Soviet era, and this road network continues to facilitate it today. Soviet separation of ethnic groups and even families by borders also encourages trading. Residents of one country of the Ferghana Valley often have kin in another. For example, members of the large Uzbek population in Osh oblast still have family ties in Uzbekistan.

Differences in products and market access also distinguish large-scale enterprise trade in Osh and Naryn. Along the Osh rail lines, which are well-connected with those of other CIS countries, tobacco, cotton fiber, coal, produce, and processed foods travel to Uzbekistan and more distant nations. The Haidarkan Mercury Combine and the Kadamjai Antimony Combine supply the world market. The centrifugal borehole pump factory, one of only two in the Soviet Union, continues to have strong sales throughout the CIS.[51] Reflecting the relatively attractive goods and transportation in Osh, nearly 18 times more foreign direct

---

[50] Lubin and Rubin, *Calming the Ferghana Valley*, 43–44.

[51] Unlike these other products, illicit opium did not become a major trading good in the region during the mid-1990s. Cultivation in post-Soviet Central Asia was limited to small personal plots, and the smallest amount was grown in Kyrgyzstan. Furthermore, demand was relatively low in Kyrgyzstan, with only 0.1 percent of the population ages 15 and above using heroin as compared with 0.9 in Russia and 0.3 in the United States. At this time, Afghanistan was one of the largest producers of opium, and cultivation increasingly developed near the border of Tajikistan as security along Iranian and Pakistani borders grew tighter. Concern grew that trafficking would increase from Khorog (Tajikistan) to Osh in order to reach CIS, European, and world markets. However, the United Nations International Drug Control Programme began working in Osh, and trafficking along this route was minimal. Moreover, it seemed to involve Russian border guards and military personnel more than the local population. More recently, there have been reports that former members of the radical group the Islamic Movement of Uzbekistan have been engaged in drug trafficking. See United Nations, *Global Illicit Drug Trends: 2001* (New York: United Nations, 2001), 19–20, 22, 125; "Kyrgyzstan Confronted by Narcotics Nightmare as Drug Trade Booms," EurasiaNet, 2004; United Nations International Drug Control Programme, "UN Drug Programme to Launch Regional Law Enforcement Project Linking Kyrgyzstan, Tajikistan and Uzbekistan," Press Release (May 2, 1997); Lubin and Rubin, *Calming the Ferghana Valley*, 72, 92; State Commission on Foreign Investment and Economic Assistance, *The Kyrgyz Republic: Osh Regional Economic Strategy*.

investment went to Osh oblast than to Naryn oblast between 1995 and 1999.[52]

In spite of its status as a Free Economic Zone, Naryn has few products ready for consumption beyond its borders. The infrastructure has not been built to exploit its ore deposits, and electricity generated from the Naryn River does not reach China. Established in 1993, the Free Economic Zone offers tax and customs privileges to businesses with foreign investors and export potential.[53] Yet, most of the businesses neither collaborate with foreign firms nor export goods. One success story is the Chinese-backed firm Ak-Moor, which exports packaging and labels. Another is Orgtekhnika, which exports pens, pencils, macaroni, and parts for agricultural machinery to other CIS countries.[54] Despite the success of these companies, the zone has little effect on employment, providing jobs for only 1,062 people.[55] With barriers to developing trade and services and a lack of industrial jobs, residents of Naryn rely heavily on income from animal herding and on subsidies from Bishkek.

In sum, citizens of Osh have greater economic autonomy relative to residents of Naryn because Osh oblast offers more marketable goods and better market access. These opportunities for external economic contacts are due more to geography than to regional economic policy. In Kyrgyzstan's unified system of government, national leaders set policy and subnational officials are expected to implement it. Neither region's administration has defied national authorities on the issue of market reforms. For example, privatization has occurred equally in the regions.[56] This subnational obedience is not surprising considering that regional governors are appointed and those who impede market reforms can easily be removed.

These broad economic, cultural, and institutional factors shape the economic autonomy and thus the frequency of self-censorship

---

[52] I obtained these data from the Kyrgyzstan National Statistics Committee on the former Web site of The Kyrgyzstan Development Gateway Project, State Committee of the Kyrgyz Republic on Foreign Investments and Economic Development.

[53] The staff of the Free Economic Zone provided this information.

[54] Kyrgyzstan Development Gateway Project, *Investment Projects*. Bishkek: State Committee of the Kyrgyz Republic on Foreign Investments and Economic Development, July 14, 2000. Available at http://kyrgyzinvest.org/en/economy/invest_projects.htm.

[55] The staff of the Free Economic Zone provided this information.

[56] This conclusion is based on data provided by provincial-level privatization officials.

and harassment in the four regions. These distinct environments also illuminate smaller differences in political activism. It is not surprising that gift giving during election campaigns is more common and grand in Samara, where business thrives, than in Ul'ianovsk, where entrepreneurs struggle. Likewise, it is logical that a larger percentage of winning candidates in Samara are entrepreneurs than in Ul'ianovsk. Economic differences between Osh and Naryn account for the larger number of commercial sponsors for political activity in the former.

How do we know that the different degrees of economic autonomy in these regions are a cause and not a result of democracy? Perhaps democracy creates jobs outside the state sector. Undoubtedly, there is some feedback between democracy and economic autonomy, as the transparency and government responsiveness that accompany democracy enable entrepreneurs to operate more easily. Nonetheless, the causal chain clearly runs from economic autonomy to democracy. In both Russia and Kyrgyzstan, certain basic democratic reforms, such as elections and glasnost, were introduced throughout the countries in the late Soviet period, and in Russia these reforms led to different economic policies, as described earlier. In Kyrgyzstan, geographical and historical differences preceded the nationwide reforms of the late Soviet era and structured the post-Soviet economies. These varied economic environments in Russia and Kyrgyzstan, in turn, influenced the extent of democracy. Furthermore, the accounts of individual activists in the four provinces reveal a causal link from economic autonomy to democracy: Citizens explain that their political activities are less oppositional or that they have discontinued them because they fear losing their state jobs in an environment of limited economic autonomy.

The dire predictions made by two scholars of post-Soviet politics in the early 1990s have come true. Kathryn Stoner-Weiss foresaw that economic concentration within Russian regions might exclude new social groups in the future,[57] and Mary McAuley cautioned that "the presence or absence of a 'democratic' political environment counts for little, given the concentration of economic resources."[58] Specifically, the economic strength of some local governments relative to other groups in society prevents the functioning of democratic institutions.

[57] Stoner-Weiss, *Local Heroes*, 199.
[58] McAuley, "Politics, Economics, and Elite Realignment in Russia," 87.

Citizens are fearful of losing their jobs if they challenge authorities, and officials punish those who risk activism. The good news is that some regions, such as Samara and Osh, have broken out of these economic monopolies.

ECONOMIC AUTONOMY OVER TIME

The degree of economic autonomy in a territory is not static but can increase or decrease with economic, institutional, and cultural developments over time. Russia and Kyrgyzstan have experienced significant economic and institutional changes since I conducted this study in the late 1990s.[59] The growth of big business in Russia and the increasing challenges to international trade in Kyrgyzstan have considerable, but opposite, impacts on economic autonomy. Institutional changes, namely declining national support for democracy and altered center–periphery relations in both countries, have likely had a minimal influence on economic autonomy. Together, these developments bode well for democracy in Russia and poorly for democracy in Kyrgyzstan.

Economic Changes

The growth of big business in Russia has likely increased economic autonomy. In the mid-1990s, a small number of bankers and industrialists came to dominate the Russian economy. Although the financial crisis of 1998 weakened certain economic oligarchs, it provided opportunities for new ones to emerge. Today, many of the large economic groups are concentrated in the natural resource industry. Their businesses boost economic autonomy because they provide opportunities for people to earn income independent of state authorities. As Andrew Barnes notes, these firms are in a strong position relative to regional authorities because they are large in size and broad in geographical scope. These companies intentionally "expand their holdings across regional boundaries... to give them leverage over any single regional government, and the practice has grown more extensive over

---

[59] Significant cultural change, such as the development of a tradition of trade, is unlikely to have occurred in this short time span.

time."[60] Because of the relative strength of these economic groups, their employees are likely to have economic autonomy from state authorities. Large private companies have also purchased independent media outlets, funded political campaigns, and established charities to do good work in the name of electoral candidates. Their support enables electoral candidates and independent media to better withstand financial harassment from local authorities. One drawback of the political involvement of big business is that these companies do not act through political parties, thus serving as yet another damper on the Russian party system.[61] Nonetheless, their business and political activities boost economic autonomy. Although profit is likely the primary, or even exclusive, motive of Russian companies, their business and political activities contribute to pluralism in society. In this respect, Russian companies play a role similar to those in the West, as described by Lindblom.[62]

By contrast, opportunities for economic autonomy in Kyrgyzstan have decreased as the tightening of borders between countries has hampered international trade. Despite Central Asian officials' formal calls for improved trade relations, they have increasingly restricted border crossings for security and economic reasons. Following raids by the Islamic Movement of Uzbekistan in Kyrgyzstan in 1999 and in Kyrgyzstan, Tajikistan, and Uzbekistan in 2000, countries in the region imposed additional customs duties and visa requirements. The growing strength of the nonviolent international Islamic group Hizb ut-Tahrir has also encouraged border restrictions. Uzbekistan has mined its borders, largely without marking the minefields, thus resulting in the deaths of civilians. Kyrgyzstan's neighbors increased restrictions on the movement of its citizens in response to President Akaev's ouster in March 2005, and Uzbekistan closed checkpoints into Kyrgyzstan following the uprising within its own boundaries in May 2005. In addition to security threats, maintenance of its state-controlled economy has motivated the Uzbekistani government to limit the movement of traders. Shuttle traders undermine government attempts to control the economy, and they emphasize the weaknesses of the country's economic

---

[60] Barnes, "Russia's New Business Groups and State Power," 175, 179.
[61] Hale, "Why Not Parties?"; McFaul, *Russia's Unfinished Revolution*, 318.
[62] Lindblom, *Politics and Markets*.

policies. As a result of border restrictions, trade has become increasingly unprofitable and dangerous. As one analyst explained, "Many villagers used to live off profits from an annual trip to sell fruit in lucrative Russian markets.... Now, those lorries stand idle, as border taxes and controls make the trade uneconomical."[63] The inability to sell goods outside of their home provinces also reduces citizens' economic autonomy.

Institutional Changes

Unlike economic developments, the focus and impact of institutional changes have been similar in Russia and Kyrgyzstan. The countries witnessed a decline in the national leadership's support for democracy and attempts to alter relations with subnational officials. Although these developments are important in their own right, their impacts on economic autonomy and regional activism are minimal.

Since President Putin came to power in 2000, the national government of Russia has closed independent media outlets and arrested and threatened to arrest political challengers under the guise of cracking down on illegal business practices. The arrests represent a new type of government punishment. Nonetheless, economic autonomy may ward off arrests and jail time in two ways. First, an activist with significant autonomous funds could perhaps buy off government officials; however, this is unlikely in national prosecutions because top government officials have political stakes in these high-profile cases. Second, to the extent that an activist's economic autonomy derives from international ties, the arrest of the activist may generate an influential international outcry. Yet, cases, such as the conviction of businessman and political donor Mikhail Khodorkovsky, demonstrate that Russian officials have not been receptive to at least the murmur of international outrage.

Although the attacks on national opposition figures and media outlets hinder the practice of democracy at the national level, they are unlikely to completely destroy democracy in Russia. High-profile

---

[63] Political geographer Nick Megoran, quoted in Alisher Khamidov, "Kyrgyz–Tajik Border Riots Highlight Building Inter-Ethnic Tension in Central Asia," EurasiaNet, 2003. Available at http://www.eurasianet.org/departments/insight/articles/eav010803.shtml.

arrests do not undermine the economic autonomy of the small-scale activists in the provinces. If regional leaders were to increasingly use arrests as a form of harassment, it is unlikely that this approach would be as effective at the subnational level. Whereas national activists must seek refuge from harassment in a foreign country, local activists can easily escape by moving to another province. Limited cooperation among regional authorities in Russia and the national governments' lack of interest in local political spats in both countries suggest that authorities outside the province will not pursue activists. Because of the ease of exit, the threat of arrest is less credible and therefore perhaps less likely to be employed at the subnational level.

In Kyrgyzstan, Akaev's government also increasingly harassed independent media firms and arrested opposition figures on trumped-up charges of corruption, fraud, and abuse of power. As a result of his overthrow, promises of democracy again emanated from national government buildings as opposition leaders claimed power. Yet, national support for democracy does not guarantee that people throughout the country will be able to exercise their democratic rights. Without economic autonomy, activists in the provinces will remain wary of challenging local authorities.

Restructuring relations with subnational authorities has also been a focus in both countries. Putin has tried to strengthen the national government by reducing the power of the regional executives. Most significantly, Moscow now appoints regional leaders. The national government has also diminished regional executives' authority by introducing seven presidential envoys to oversee their work, removing them from the upper house of the Russian parliament, increasing its share and control of tax revenue, revising bilateral treaties to create greater regional symmetry, and working to bring regional laws in line with federal legislation. In contrast, Akaev tried to bolster his position by devolving power to local authorities. Through a constitutional referendum in 2002, the national government of Kyrgyzstan mandated that local representatives be elected. Bishkek also granted greater budgetary and policy authority to local representative bodies, as well as local governments. Yet, regional governors remain presidential appointees with considerable authority over the makeup of local governments. The devolution of authority helped Akaev gain local leaders' support for the referendum. This provided a legal means to end calls for

Akaev's resignation, although ultimately extralegal means removed him from office. The Akaev administration hoped the redistribution of power would ease tensions between the north and the south as well. The new government could extend, maintain, or reverse this devolution of power. Regardless, these moves toward centralization in Russia and decentralization in Kyrgyzstan are not likely to significantly influence economic autonomy. As this study demonstrates, economic autonomy facilitates democracy under both federal and unitary governments.[64]

Overall, opportunities for economic autonomy have likely expanded in Russia and contracted in Kyrgyzstan, in both cases because of economic, not institutional, developments. However, these trends are clearly reversible. For example, greater state control over the natural resource sector could reduce economic autonomy in Russia, and Central Asian policies promoting international trade could increase economic autonomy in Kyrgyzstan.

ECONOMIC AUTONOMY OUTSIDE THE FORMER SOVIET UNION

Outside the former USSR, the idea of economic autonomy from the state is most salient in countries where the government monopolizes the economy. The economic role of the state and thus the degree of economic dependence exist along a spectrum. Economic autonomy from the state is most important to democratization in postcommunist and communist countries. In the Middle East and Africa, the state has also played a significant role in the economy; therefore, economic autonomy from the state is critical to democratic development there as well. Economic autonomy from the state has been least important to democratization in Europe and the Americas. Instead,

---

[64] Gordon Hahn suggests that the campaign to bring regional laws in Russia in line with federal legislation has encouraged civic groups to use the national government as an ally against regional authorities. This is not a new practice, although it may have intensified as the harmonization campaign has demonstrated to local activists that the national government is interested in regional violations. Evidence in this study, such as the experience of the gubernatorial candidate in Ul'ianovsk who sought Yeltsin's support, indicates that, even prior to Putin's centralization attempts, ties to the national government could help activists oppose regional authorities. See Gordon M. Hahn, "The Impact of Putin's Federative Reforms on Democratization in Russia," *Post-Soviet Affairs* 19 (2003), 114–153.

economic autonomy from dominant classes, such as aristocracies and large landowners, has been critical.

Economic autonomy is most relevant in communist countries, such as China. Market reforms in China have increased citizens' economic autonomy from local officials, and this has reduced their fear of engaging in protest.[65] Despite marketization, economic independence has not grown as much in China as it has in the postcommunist world. In China, the national government has maintained considerable control over market forces. As a result, Chinese activists who work in the new economy are at greater risk of workplace harassment than their counterparts in the postcommunist world. Moreover, in China, economic prosperity, coupled with government supervision of market forces, has meant that national and local officials continue to control resources that citizens need.[66] By contrast, most local governments in the postcommunist world are short on resources, such as capital.[67] This further reduces citizens' economic dependence on the state for resources.

In many countries of the Middle East and Africa, citizens rely on the state for their livelihood. Governments in this part of the world are typically the chief employers, bankers, exploiters of natural resources, and owners of the means of production. State support for capitalist development has discouraged traditionally pro-democratic classes, such as capitalists and labor, from pressing for political reform. These groups already receive benefits from the state, so they do not have any incentive to encourage the government to be more responsive overall.[68] Yet, in the Middle East and Africa, large informal sectors have developed, and individuals from this sector have challenged the

---

[65] Kevin J. O'Brien, "Rightful Resistance," *World Politics* 49 (October, 1996), 31–55. By contrast, Andrew Walder describes the period prior to market reform. Workers would not protest because they relied on local party secretaries for their jobs and social services. See Andrew G. Walder, *Communist Neo-Traditionalism: Work and Authority in Chinese Industry* (Berkeley: University of California Press, 1986).

[66] Jean Oi describes how market reforms in China have provided peasants with more economic choices, yet many rural residents nonetheless remain dependent on village officials for resources and assistance. See Jean C. Oi, *State and Peasant in Contemporary China: The Political Economy of Village Government* (Berkeley: University of California Press, 1989), 187–214.

[67] Slider, "Russia's Market-Distorting Federalism," 445–460.

[68] Bellin, *Stalled Democracy*.

government. These campaigns have triggered the liberalization that has occurred.[69]

The sequence of events in the Middle East and Africa distinguishes this region of the world from postcommunist countries. In the Middle East and Africa, citizens are acquiring economic autonomy from the state prior to democratic transition or even political liberalization, whereas in postcommunist countries that have introduced democratic institutions, citizens still struggle to increase their economic independence from the state in order to engage in oppositional activity. This difference facilitates democratization in the Middle East and Africa relative to the former Soviet Union.

Economic dependence has been important in the Americas and Europe, too, but here economic reliance on dominant classes, not the state, has been the greater obstacle to democracy. In these regions, capitalist development broke this dependency, empowering pro-democratic classes to press for reform. The new capitalist class pressed for rights to protect its financial ventures, and workers demanded that the rights initially granted only to the capitalists be extended to them.[70]

Among this group of countries, it is useful to distinguish Latin American states. In Latin America, particularly during periods of import substitution industrialization (ISI), the state played a significant role in the economy, especially through the provision of subsidies. By contrast, in colonial America, the government had little influence in the agrarian economy, and farmers were largely independent.[71] Nonetheless, although Latin American states have been interventionist, they have also been relatively weak and repeatedly forced to build coalitions with powerful economic elites in order to implement state policies.[72]

---

[69] Henry Bienen and Jeffrey Herbst, "The Relationship between Political and Economic Reform in Africa," *Comparative Politics* 29 (October, 1996), 29; Farhad Kazemi and Augustus Richard Norton, "Hardliners and Softliners in the Middle East: Problems of Governance and the Prospects for Liberalization in Authoritarian Political Systems," in *Democracy and Its Limits: Lessons from Asia, Latin America, and the Middle East*, ed. Howard Handelman and Mark A. Tessler (Notre Dame, IN: University of Notre Dame Press, 1999), 73; Alan Richards and John Waterbury, *A Political Economy of the Middle East*, 2nd ed. (Boulder, CO: Westview Press, 1996), 274–275.

[70] Moore, *Social Origins of Dictatorship and Democracy*; Rueschemeyer et al., *Capitalist Development and Democracy*, 47–51, 277.

[71] Dahl, *Democracy and Its Critics*, 254; Dahl, *Democracy, Liberty, and Equality*, 136.

[72] Hector Schamis's account of politics during ISI periods highlights the power of economic actors relative to the state. For example, he writes, "A broad coalition formed

Thus, in Latin American countries, as well as in North America and Europe, economic reliance on dominant classes, not the state, has been the impediment to democratization.

The relationship between economic autonomy from dominant groups and oppositional activity was also evident in the American South of the 1960s. Blacks were typically dependent on local whites for their income. For example, laborers worked on white-owned plantations, and teachers were employed by white-dominated school boards. This economic dependency depressed black voter turnout even after the government had reduced legal obstacles to voting. Research from this era indicates that blacks feared job loss as a result of voting rather than fearing violence.[73]

The salience of economic autonomy across space and time might also be captured in findings concerning economic development and democracy. In a statistical analysis examining political transitions worldwide from 1850 to 1980, Carles Boix and Susan Stokes found that fragmented property systems – family farms instead of concentrated land ownership, for example – are positively associated with democracy.[74] The causal mechanism linking property and democracy might, in fact, be economic autonomy.

by domestic-oriented manufacturing, organized labor, and the urban middle sectors sustained ISI for most of the postwar period in Chile. [When the government backed away from ISI], all propertied groups – landowners, industrial groups, and the middle classes – came together against the UP (Popular Unity) government and in support of the military." Similarly, Guillermo O'Donnell describes how in many Latin American countries the state has been "impelled by and allied with the large bourgeoisie." He also demonstrates how the greater autonomy of the popular sector from the dominant classes in Argentina helped topple the bureaucratic–authoritarian regime in that country. M.A. Centeno documents the historical weakness of Latin American states, emphasizing that economic elites in the 1800s did not care which regime governed their territory, as they were so independent. See M. A. Centeno, "Blood and Debt: War and Taxation in Nineteenth-Century Latin America," *American Journal of Sociology* 102 (May, 1997), 1589, 1594; Guillermo O'Donnell, "State and Alliances in Argentina, 1956–1976," *The Journal of Development Studies* 15 (October, 1979), 3, 14; Hector E. Schamis, "Distributional Coalitions and the Politics of Economic Reform in Latin America," *World Politics* 51 (January, 1999), 245, 250.

[73] U.S. Commission on Civil Rights, Hearings, Jackson, Mississippi, February 16–20, 1965 (Washington, DC: U.S. Government Printing Office, 1965), I, 209, cited in Lester M. Salamon and Stephen Van Evera, "Fear, Apathy, and Discrimination: A Test of Three Explanations of Political Participation," *The American Political Science Review* 67 (December, 1973), 1294, 1296.

[74] Boix and Stokes, "Endogenous Democratization."

Examining politics in other parts of the world helps to demonstrate the generalizability of the relationship between economic autonomy and democracy. As Gerardo Munck suggests, "The introduction of a new variable should thus push researchers to show how it applies to all cases – either in terms of its absence, its presence, or its degree of presence . . . "[75]

This exercise also illuminates how democratization in the postcommunist region is distinct from reform attempts in other regions of the world. Since the early 1990s, scholars have contemplated how reform in the "East" might differ from the democratization of the "South," meaning Southern Europe and Latin America. Studies have suggested that the different global environments, weak civil societies, the need for state-building, and modes of transition, among other factors, would make democratization more difficult in postcommunist countries.[76] Although these factors are important, my investigation suggests that the greater role of the state in postcommunist economies is the foremost influence. During more than half a century of socialism, landed and other economic elites were absent in this part of the world. Instead, the state was the dominant economic actor. Valerie Bunce characterizes the socialist state as one that owned the means of production, directed labor, distributed capital, produced goods and services, and set prices.[77] Despite the disintegration of the Soviet state, the governments of the 15 new countries of the former Soviet Union continue to play substantial roles in their economies. Even in countries that have undertaken market

---

[75] Munck continues, "and to conduct an empirical investigation of how the diverse ways in which it applies affect the process under consideration." The cross-regional empirical investigation will have to be left to another study, but the cross-regional exploration in this book begins to illuminate this issue. See Munck, "The Regime Question," 134.

[76] As examples, see Valerie Bunce, "Regional Differences in Democratization: The East Versus the South," *Post-Soviet Affairs* 14 (July–September, 1998), 187–211; Valerie Bunce, "Should Transitologists Be Grounded?" *Slavic Review* 54 (Spring, 1995), 111–127; Grzegorz Ekiert, "Peculiarities of Post-communist Politics: The Case of Poland," *Studies in Comparative Communism* 25 (December, 1992), 349, 356; Howard, *The Weakness of Civil Society*; Linz and Stepan, *Problems of Democratic Transition and Consolidation*, 386–388; Michael McFaul, "The Fourth Wave of Democracy *and* Dictatorship: Noncooperative Transitions in the Postcommunist World," *World Politics* 54 (January, 2002), 212–244; Sarah Meiklejohn Terry, "Thinking About Postcommunist Transitions: How Different Are They?" *Slavic Review* 52 (Summer, 1993), 334, 336.

[77] Bunce, "Elementy."

reform, such as Russia and Kyrgyzstan, states continue to own more enterprises and control more resources than is typical under capitalism. In addition, many firms that have become private are now merely in the personal portfolios of government leaders and their friends and families.

In sum, the concept of economic autonomy demonstrates "the complex interaction among postcommunist institutions and the communist substrate on which they have been constructed," to use a phrase written by Charles King.[78] Namely, the communist legacy of a state economic monopoly has hindered the functioning of democratic institutions. It is this legacy that distinguishes the "East" from the "South" and helps account for both democratic successes and failures. Overall, postcommunist states play a greater role in the economies of their countries than states in the "South." Yet, within postcommunist countries there are pockets of economic autonomy that have strengthened democracy. The varying importance of economic autonomy throughout the world suggests that scholars of postcommunist democratization may want to shift their focus. Existing cross-regional studies have assessed political reform in postcommunist countries relative to the democratization experiences of the West and "South" – Southern Europe and Latin America in particular. The argument about economic autonomy indicates that we may learn more about the processes and prospects for democracy in the former Eastern bloc through comparisons with the liberalization attempts of communist, Middle Eastern, and African countries, where state control of the economy is relatively greater than in Europe and the Americas.

---

[78] Charles King, "Post-communism: Transition, Comparison, and the End of 'Eastern Europe,'" *World Politics* 53 (October, 2000), 155–156.

6

Hybrid Regimes

The third wave of democratization – beginning in 1974 with a military coup in Portugal and washing over much of Latin America, Asia, Africa, and the Eastern bloc during the next two decades – raised expectations among scholars, activists, and journalists that democracy would flourish in regions outside of Western Europe and North America.[1] Political leaders in third wave countries had circumvented socioeconomic conditions not conducive to democratic development by opting to dismantle old regimes and craft new political institutions. Yet, in the 21st century, our euphoria over these extractions from authoritarianism has dissipated as many of these new governments have shown themselves to be hybrid regimes; in other words, they combine elements of democracy and authoritarianism.[2] Nearly half of all countries worldwide can be characterized as having hybrid regimes.[3] Typically, these regimes hold elections without guaranteeing the civil

---

[1] Credit for the concept of the third wave goes to Samuel Huntington. See Huntington, *The Third Wave.*
[2] Thomas Carothers, "The End of the Transition Paradigm," *Journal of Democracy* 13 (January, 2002), 5–21; Larry Diamond, "Thinking About Hybrid Regimes," *Journal of Democracy* 13 (April, 2002), 23, 25.
[3] Of the remaining countries, 38 percent have democratic regimes and 25 percent have authoritarian regimes, or in Larry Diamond's terms liberal democratic regimes and politically closed authoritarian regimes. These numbers are based on my calculations of regime classification published by Diamond. See Diamond, "Thinking About Hybrid Regimes," 26.

liberties that make electoral outcomes accurate expressions of citizens' preferences.[4]

Why have hybrid regimes proliferated? The concept of economic autonomy and the model of interaction developed in this book offer some clues. Interventionist states had developed in many of the third wave countries by the time democratic institutions were introduced there. The emergence of interventionist states robbed citizens of their economic autonomy and thus enabled governments to more easily harass their opponents. The interaction among components of democracy compounded the problem by allowing government officials to undermine entire nascent democracies through the restriction of only a few civil liberties.

A PROLIFERATION OF HYBRID REGIMES

The increase in hybrid regimes is troubling on a number of counts. The democratic component of these regimes offers the false promise to citizens that government leaders will respond to their needs and wishes. Because elections serve as a democratic window dressing, hybrid regimes are often able to win praise for being "democratic" from the international community, which may not have the knowledge or incentives to unmask the charade. This situation leaves citizens of hybrid regimes frustrated over the hypocrisy of their leaders and the international community. If citizens believe the claims of their officials and international actors that their country is democratic, people's faith in democracy diminishes. The proliferation of hybrid regimes is all the more troubling because there is no guarantee that they will evolve into democracies. The hybrid nature of these regimes might, in fact, increase their stability.[5]

---

[4] Approximately 81 percent of hybrid regimes have exhibited this behavior based on my calculations of Larry Diamond's regime classifications. Diamond deems the remaining hybrid regimes difficult to categorize, but they likely display this behavior as well. See Diamond, "Thinking About Hybrid Regimes."

[5] Valerie Bunce, "Comparative Democratization: Big and Bounded Generalizations," *Comparative Political Studies* 33 (August/September, 2000), 724; McFaul, *Russia's Unfinished Revolution*, 310, 335.

In response to the growth of hybrid regimes, scholars have coined new terms, including "electoral democracies" and "illiberal democracies," contributing to a list of more than 550 subtypes of democracy – more types than countries being studied.[6] A smaller number of subtypes of authoritarianism, such as "electoral authoritarianism" and "liberalized autocracy," have also emerged.[7] However, analysts have devoted less attention to explaining the proliferation of hybrid regimes. Most scholars would agree that the dominance of liberal ideology following the disgrace of communism and the end of the Cold War encourages many government officials, even those who do not support democracy, to adopt a mantle of democracy. Government leaders have an incentive to establish democratic institutions to increase their legitimacy in the international community or,[8] in the case of local leaders, in the national political arenas of democratizing countries.[9] Yet, what explains the common approach of holding elections but limiting civil liberties?

---

[6] David Collier and Steven Levitsky, "Democracy 'with Adjectives': Conceptual Innovation in Comparative Research," in *Working Paper Series: The Helen Kellogg Institute for International Studies* (Notre Dame, IN: University of Notre Dame, 1996). Since Collier and Levitsky counted the terms, other terms have been added to the list. See, for example, Harley Balzer, "Managed Pluralism: Vladimir Putin's Emerging Regime," *Post-Soviet Affairs* 19 (2003), 189–227; Diamond, "Is the Third Wave Over?"; Diamond, "Thinking About Hybrid Regimes," 32; Zakaria, "The Rise of Illiberal Democracy."

[7] Michael Bratton, Robert B. Mattes, and Emmanuel Gyimah-Boadi, *Public Opinion, Democracy, and Market Reform in Africa* (New York: Cambridge University Press, 2005); Diamond, "Thinking About Hybrid Regimes." See also Steven Levitsky and Lucan A. Way, "The Rise of Competitive Authoritarianism," *Journal of Democracy* 13 (April, 2002), 51–65; Lucan A. Way, "Pluralism by Default in Moldova," *Journal of Democracy* 13 (October, 2002), 127–141.

[8] Diamond, "Is the Third Wave Over?"; Human Rights Watch, *Human Rights Watch World Report* (New York: Human Rights Watch, 1996); Levitsky and Way, "The Rise of Competitive Authoritarianism," 54, 61.

[9] Subnational authorities are clearly aware of international democratic norms. In Ul'ianovsk, the importance of the norms was apparent in legislators' discussion of the governor's economic plan. The plan noted that Chase Manhattan rated the oblast as being in the top 20 percent of Russian regions for human potential, resources, and social protection. The administration and many legislators agreed with the bank's assessment that the problem was the oblast's image. The talk at the legislative session was not of greater reform but of improving the province's image in order to appeal to the international community. Similarly, the independent newspaper in Ul'ianovsk that faced a government plan to revoke its lease scared officials away by threatening to inform its "friends in the international mass media" of the situation. The editor of the newspaper warned that these friends would create an international scandal.

INTERVENTIONIST STATES AND INTERACTIVE GUARANTEES

Allowing elections but restricting civil liberties is a cost-effective means for nondemocratic elites to maintain their rule while masking their authoritarian practices. The rise of interventionist states facilitates this process. Many of the countries of the third wave followed state-led development plans from the end of World War II through the 1970s.[10] As a result, by the time these countries began to democratize in the 1970s and 1980s, their states had come to play a large role in their economies. Without democratic institutions, particularly links between officials and civil society, these states had not grown to be particularly responsive or effective in the prior decades. Nonetheless, they had become economically powerful relative to their citizens.[11] This created a situation in which citizens did not have the economic autonomy to engage in the oppositional activity necessary to ensure that the democratic institutions later introduced functioned properly. With the dominance of liberal ideology following the Cold War, nondemocratic leaders had an incentive to allow the shells of these democratic institutions to continue to operate. Leaders of the new post-Soviet states, facing the same incentive and having a history of an extremely interventionist state, then followed in their footsteps.

This account suggests that leaders of hybrid regimes are acting from a position of strength. They limit democracy because weak economic autonomy in their societies grants them the ability to do so. By contrast, other explanations of hybrid regimes focus on poor state capacity, arguing that government elites are unable to restrict all components of democracy.[12] Yet, the model of interaction demonstrates that government officials need restrict only a few components of democracy in order to undermine the system. Therefore, this reasoning suggests that government officials curb only some components not necessarily because this is the most they can do but because this is all they must do.

---

[10] Bishwapriya Sanyal, *Cooperative Autonomy: The Dialectic of State–NGO Relationship in Developing Countries* (Geneva: International Institute for Labour Studies, 1994).

[11] Atul Kohli, *Democracy and Discontent: India's Growing Crisis of Governability* (Cambridge: Cambridge University Press, 1990), 29–31.

[12] See, for example, Levitsky and Way, "The Rise of Competitive Authoritarianism."

To undermine democracy, leaders need only to restrict alternative media, NGOs, and opposition campaigns. When these guarantees are weak, democratic institutions cannot function effectively, as the model of interaction indicates. Compared with freedom of expression, these three guarantees pose a greater threat to nondemocratic officials because these forms of activism are organized. Unlike an individual's complaint to an official or letter to an editor, media outlets, political groups, and opposition campaigns bring together large numbers of aggrieved people. In contrast to street protests and votes, these civic pursuits challenge officials on a regular basis for long periods of time. The collective nature and potential endurance of alternative media, NGOs, and opposition campaigns enable them to recruit large numbers of people to opposition causes.

Dispersing protestors, destroying formal institutions, banning voting, and tampering with ballots are more costly because they spoil the democratic façade. These nondemocratic behaviors are more difficult to hide from international and national democracy promoters than punishments of media, NGOs, and candidates. The international community, particularly human-rights organizations, has increasingly monitored, exposed, and investigated incidents of state violence.[13] This development could deter authorities from disbanding street protests. Outsiders can easily monitor the formal design and operation of government institutions by reviewing laws.[14] They need only be present for a short period in order to observe procedures at the polls.[15] Violence against demonstrators, attacks on formal institutions, voting bans, and ballot tampering are also not adequate means of squelching opposition in countries where other means of effective legal protest – the independent media, political NGOs, or opposition campaigns – exist. These other forms of activism help people formulate and express their opinions independent of formal institutions and electoral processes.

---

[13] Keck and Sikkink, *Activists Beyond Borders*.
[14] H. E. Chehabi and Juan J. Linz, "A Theory of Sultanism 1: A Type of Nondemocratic Rule," in *Sultanistic Regimes*, ed. H. E. Chehabi and Juan J. Linz (Baltimore: Johns Hopkins University Press, 1998), 18; Levitsky and Way, "The Rise of Competitive Authoritarianism," 62.
[15] Diamond, "Is the Third Wave Over?"; Levitsky and Way, "The Rise of Competitive Authoritarianism," 55; Zakaria, "The Rise of Illiberal Democracy."

Relative to the other components of democracy, alternative media, NGOs, and opposition campaigns are easy for authorities to undercut. With little effort, government officials can identify members of media outlets, political NGOs, and opposition campaigns. Unlike a voter or a picketer, these activists must be prominent in order to be successful: To sell papers, recruit supporters, and win votes, these activists need to be public figures. Because media, NGOs, and campaigns operate for extended periods, authorities also have multiple opportunities to locate and punish their members. These individuals are more vulnerable than crowds in the street or at the polls. Because media outlets rely on the government for resources, such as information and printing services, officials can easily apply pressure to these organizations as well as to journalists and editors individually. Officials may not even need to harass all opposition candidates because only some offices are worth the fight. For example, if representative bodies are weak, as is the case in many post-Soviet polities, only races for executive offices require attacks.

In addition to providing a façade of democracy, allowing elections, formal institutions, and free expression preserves resources. Complete repression would require a large security force to conduct surveillance and mete out punishment. Moreover, even limited democratic freedoms can serve as a pressure valve, allowing people to air their grievances. Without this pressure valve, complaints may compound, anger may intensify, and greater repression may be required to prevent an effective opposition from developing.

STRONG ON PARTICIPATION, WEAK ON CONTESTATION

Besides limiting only certain components of democracy, leaders of hybrid regimes also seem to allow participation but stealthily undermine contestation. Elections enable citizens to participate, but constraints on liberal components of democracy make races essentially noncompetitive. Moreover, often citizens can engage in some civic pursuits, such as forming a political group, but they must limit their opposition to government authorities by censoring the content of their participation. Allowing participation but restricting contestation reduces the risk of international exposure, as outsiders have greater difficulty monitoring the latter. Furthermore, this approach reflects a trend where government leaders have responded to democracy promoters' tactics by punishing local activists in a particular way.[16] Authorities do not harass activists at the beginning of their civic pursuits or at the points of official contact with the state, although these techniques would perhaps be the easiest for government leaders. Instead, media outlets, political groups, and candidates are allowed to form and register freely, so harassment is not reflected in the numbers of the activists. This approach creates a positive paper trail that can be paraded to outsiders. Threatening and punishing NGO members and leaders and candidates through their workplaces, for example, leaves a less visible antidemocratic paper trail than harassing associations during registration. Although firing individual activists and inspecting media outlets creates a paper trail, it is one of business problems, not political confrontations.

Perhaps the general idea of "strong on participation, weak on contestation" is a more useful heuristic term than the multitude of specific labels scholars have created to describe hybrid regimes. The descriptions of different hybrid regimes are a good step toward building a general theory. From the data provided by these descriptions, we can begin to explore whether these subtypes represent a single phenomenon. In "Democracy with Adjectives," David Collier and Steven Levitsky worked toward this goal by aggregating scholars' approaches into diminished subtypes, "precising" the definition, and shifting the overall concept. However, they did not consider the question of whether these scholars are describing an overarching phenomenon.[17] The fact that the hybrid regimes in this study require yet another label because they do not fit existing ones emphasizes the point that it is time to begin to aggregate the subtypes of hybrid regimes.[18]

---

[16] Argentinean leaders secretly kidnapped and executed people, having "learned" from the international response to the mass executions and imprisonments following the Chilean coup. See Keck and Sikkink, *Activists Beyond Borders*, 104.

[17] David Collier and Steven Levitsky, "Democracy with Adjectives: Conceptual Innovation in Comparative Research," *World Politics* 49, no. 3 (April, 1997), 430–451.

[18] Current labels do not describe the hybrid regimes of Ul'ianovsk and Naryn. For example, free speech is observed, yet opposition candidates are harassed, so these provinces are not "electoral" or "illiberal" democracies. The regions also do not exhibit signs of "competitive authoritarianism" because they lack strong parliamentary oppositions, a key indicator of this form of government. The governor of Ul'ianovsk won less than 50 percent of the vote, disqualifying the regime as "hegemonic electoral authoritarianism," where the executive wins 75 percent or more of the vote. Finally, "managed pluralism" does not seem to apply because in Ul'ianovsk and Naryn government

"Strong on participation, weak on contestation" may well describe the general phenomenon of hybrid regimes. The preceding analysis suggests that this may be a common pattern because of relationships among components of democracy and the international monitoring of democracy. Using Dahl's participation and contestation dimensions is also useful because the idea is grounded in a theory of democracy instead of simply a checklist of indicators.[19]

The degree to which "strong on participation, weak on contestation" describes an overarching phenomenon is an empirical question requiring careful research. Because of international incentives for officials to present a democratic face, scholars must be wary of relying on counts of independent media outlets, political groups, and other manifestations of democracy. What matters is the degree to which these groups can practice freely and ultimately perform functions of democracy, not how many exist on paper. We should also keep in mind that certain democratic behaviors, such as elections, are more visible than others. For this reason, on-the-ground evaluations of multiple components of governance are essential for accurately characterizing hybrid regimes. Finally, the fact that the extent of democracy or authoritarianism can vary within countries should caution us to avoid focusing on only national institutions and behaviors.

PROMOTION OF DEMOCRACY

How can the problem of hybrid regimes be addressed? The model of interaction and the concept of economic autonomy offer some guidance about how to facilitate the further democratization of these regimes. The model of interaction indicates that some components of democracy should appear before others in the democratization process. Resources

---

officials have focused on limiting oppositional activity, not the groups themselves. See Balzer, "Managed Pluralism," Collier and Levitsky, "Democracy 'with Adjectives'" – *Working Paper series*; Diamond, "Is the Third Wave Over?"; Diamond, "Thinking About Hybrid Regimes," 32; Levitsky and Way, "The Rise of Competitive Authoritarianism"; Way, "Pluralism by Default in Moldova"; Zakaria, "The Rise of Illiberal Democracy."

[19] Thomas Carothers's division of hybrid regimes into two categories, "feckless pluralism" and "dominant-power politics," also helps aggregate the subtypes. His analysis, although more developed than a checklist, is not tied to an underlying theory. See Carothers, "The End of the Transition Paradigm."

and opportunities will be wasted if domestic reformers and international organizations try to hold honest, multicandidate elections in societies that lack independent media, political groups, and free speech. Such elections can discredit democracy in a country, making further reforms more difficult. Even when societal momentum for democracy exists, domestic reformers and the international community would be wise to focus first on civic institutions. In its advice and funding, the international community can set expectations that civic development should come before electoral development, thus helping to reduce frustration among pro-democratic societal actors.

Both civic and electoral institutions are routinely copied from advanced democracies, but these institutions cannot function properly if the environment differs substantially from that of the capitalist societies in which they developed. In the first wave of democratization in the 1800s and early 1900s, democracy emerged naturally with capitalism, whereas more recently these democratic institutions have been introduced into societies where the state historically has controlled the economy. For this reason, economic autonomy should be a priority for democracy promoters as well.

Market reform might be one means to increase economic autonomy from the state. By shrinking the state sector, marketization reduces the number of employees who are economically dependent on government officials. This relationship might help account for the seemingly varied influence of market reform on democratic development throughout the world.[20] For example, marketization and democratization seem compatible in the former Eastem bloc: Postcommunist countries that have implemented the most extensive market reforms have the most competitive political systems.[21] Because the communist state enjoyed an economic monopoly, economic autonomy was an essential first step to political contestation in these countries. In Latin America, by

---

[20] Valerie Bunce identifies this relationship, but she offers a different explanation that focuses on governments' electoral mandates, political inclinations, and policy agendas. See V. Bunce, "Democratization and Economic Reform," *Annual Review of Political Science* 4 (2001), 44–45, 55–58.

[21] M. Steven Fish, "Democratization's Requisites: The Postcommunist Experience," *Post-Soviet Affairs* 14 (1998), 212–247; Joel S. Hellman, "Winners Take All: The Politics of Partial Reform in Postcommunist Transitions," *World Politics* 50 (January, 1998), 203–234.

comparison, market reforms seem to have been less beneficial to democratic development. Government leaders concentrated power in order to implement market reforms,[22] and these reforms reduced the ease with which some societal actors could challenge government policies. In Latin America, economic autonomy from the state was not a significant by-product of market reform because states did not have economic monopolies. In fact, the existence of powerful economic interests, such as business elites and unions, encouraged government leaders to use decree powers to implement market reforms. Economic liberalization, in turn, dispersed interests and weakened social institutions, reducing urban and rural workers' abilities to mobilize and contest government policies.[23]

Worldwide market reform's impact on democratic development seems mixed. Other studies of the interaction between market and democratic reforms have examined groups and their interests and organizational capacity.[24] By focusing instead on individuals and their risk calculations, this book reveals that market reform is critical to democratic development to the extent that it can break state economic monopolies. Without economic autonomy from the state, individuals will not engage in the civic activities that enable institutions to function democratically.

---

[22] Stephan Haggard and Robert R. Kaufman, *The Political Economy of Democratic Transitions* (Princeton, NJ: Princeton University Press, 1995); Luiz Carlos Bresser Pereira, José María Maravall, and Adam Przeworski, *Economic Reforms in New Democracies: A Social–Democratic Approach* (Cambridge: Cambridge University Press, 1993), 208; Hector E. Schamis, *Re-Forming the State: The Politics of Privatization in Latin America and Europe*, Interests, Identities, and Institutions in Comparative Politics (Ann Arbor: University of Michigan Press, 2002), 188.

[23] Marcus J. Kurtz, "The Dilemmas of Democracy in the Open Economy: Lessons from Latin America," *World Politics* 56 (January, 2004), 262–302; Marcus J. Kurtz, *Free Market Democracy and the Chilean and Mexican Countryside* (Cambridge: Cambridge University Press, 2004).

[24] Valerie Bunce, "Comparative Democratization: Lessons from Russia and the Postcommunist World," in *After the Collapse of Communism: Comparative Lessons of Transitions*, ed. Michael McFaul and Kathryn Stoner-Weiss (New York: Cambridge University Press, 2005); Hellman, "Winners Take All"; Kurtz, *Free Market Democracy*; Schamis, *Re-Forming the State*.

Appendix A

Description of Surveys

In Moscow in the early spring and summer of 1997, a colleague and I asked experts to rate regions according to Dahl's definition of democracy.[1] I conducted a similar survey in Bishkek in May 1997. This appendix describes the selection process for the respondents, the structure of the surveys, the validity and reliability of the results, and the results themselves.

RESPONDENTS

Twenty-six experts in Russia completed the survey,[2] and 23 respondents filled out the questionnaire in Kyrgyzstan. The respondents from Russia included representatives of universities and research centers in Moscow, members of the Russian presidential administration and the Federation Council, and foreign scholars residing in Moscow at the time of the survey. The Kyrgyzstani experts were members of universities and research centers in Bishkek and staff in the administrations of the president and prime minister.

---

[1] I am grateful to Nikolai Petrov of the Carnegie Moscow Center for collaborating with me on the survey in Russia. He helped design the questionnaire and administered it.

[2] For a more detailed consideration of the strengths and weaknesses and the results of the Russian survey, see Kelly M. McMann and Nikolai V. Petrov, "A Survey of Democracy in Russia's Regions," *Post-Soviet Geography and Economics* 41 (April–May, 2000), 155–182.

I used a snowball sample to select respondents in each country because there is no defined group of experts on regional politics and, as a group, experts are more difficult to reach than other populations, such as the public. The snowball sample was generated as follows: I worked with a local scholar of regional politics in each country to create an initial list of regional experts, and in the questionnaires I then asked respondents to suggest additional experts. My colleagues and I distributed the survey to those recommended according to a number of conditions. We selected people who are knowledgeable about regional politics, as evidenced by their work, and we tried to maintain a balance between people in academic, research, and government positions. For example, as the proportion of respondents who were government workers grew in my survey in Bishkek, I sought out academics instead. We also had to be able to reach the suggested individual. This proved particularly difficult in Bishkek, where telephone books are rare. Respondents would often suggest people they had heard of but did not know personally. I then faced the challenge of finding the individual; I failed in nine cases. We no longer sought out additional respondents once approximately 25 respondents had completed the survey in each country. None of the conditions we employed seems likely to have affected the ratings of democracy in the regions.

The small number of respondents in each country reflects the limited pool of regional experts. Not many people have in-depth knowledge of politics in all or most regions of their country. This is true in Russia, where there are many regions, and in Kyrgyzstan, where the expert community is small.

In each country, a few experts declined to complete the survey. In Russia, those who refused claimed they did not have knowledge of many regions or that they were not familiar with the particulars of their politics. Three people declined to complete the survey in Bishkek. One did not consider himself qualified to complete the survey, and two did not have time. It is unlikely that the few refusals in Moscow or Bishkek introduced bias into the survey. The reasons for refusal do not seem connected with evaluations of democracy in regions.

We limited the pool of respondents to residents of the capital cities of Russia and Kyrgyzstan. Moscow and Bishkek are centers of government and scholarship, thus enabling us to choose from a larger pool of potential respondents than would have been possible in any other city. This is particularly true in Kyrgyzstan, where Bishkek is the only city with numerous universities and research centers. Concentrating on experts in one city enabled me to reduce the costs of the surveys. In the section on reliability and validity, I consider the possibility that selecting experts from capital cities introduced bias into the responses.

SURVEY STRUCTURE

The survey consisted of a written questionnaire. In part one of the survey, experts in each country ranked the regions according to their own conceptualizations of democracy. No definition of democracy was provided. In Russia, experts rated provinces, specifically the 49 oblasts and 6 *krais* (large administrative divisions), as well as the two federal cities. Ethnoterritorial regions were not part of the Russian survey, as these administrative units do not exist in Kyrgyzstan.[3] The respondents in Russia selected the ten most democratic regions of their country and the ten least democratic regions of their country and then rated these 20 from one to ten, with ten being the most democratic. The experts in Kyrgyzstan rated all the regions of their country using this scale.

In part two of the survey, I asked the experts to rate the regions in the same manner but using Dahl's definition of democracy, which I provided.[4] It is this rating based on Dahl's definition that I used to investigate the unevenness of democracy and to select the four provinces. I requested that experts first rate the regions based on their own understandings of democracy so that I could evaluate whether they actually used Dahl's definition in part two of the survey.

RELIABILITY AND VALIDITY

I evaluated the reliability and validity of the data by examining the extent to which the respondents' judgments are free from random

---

[3] Even though Kyrgyzstan does not have *krais*, I included them in the group of Russian regions because in structure and function they are similar to oblasts.

[4] Nikolai Petrov, who administered the survey in Russia, requested that respondents not look at part two of the survey before completing part one. I administered the survey in Bishkek, and I did not give respondents part two of the survey until they had completed part one.

error and the extent to which their ratings likely reflect actual levels of democracy, as defined by Dahl.

Reliability

Because of the large number of regions in Russia and the small number in Kyrgyzstan, I included a specific measure of reliability only on the Russian survey. In the process of selecting the most and least democratic regions and rating them on the scale of one to ten, the respondents in Russia may have made careless mistakes. To evaluate the reliability of their responses, my colleague and I asked experts also to rate eight regions on a scale of one to ten, ten being the most democratic. (The eight regions were Volgograd, Saratov, Orel, Kursk, Rostov, Krasnodar, Irkutsk, and Krasnoyarsk.) I examined whether the respondents rated regions consistently by comparing results from this section with their other selections. For example, I examined whether a respondent repeatedly ranked Rostov lower than Volgograd but above Krasnodar. We selected regions that we expected to fall neither at the more nor less democratic end of the spectrum but in the middle. Consistent ratings of these more confusing cases would increase our confidence in the reliability of our measures. At the same time, we selected pairs of neighboring regions, from different parts of Russia, that exhibited political differences. For example, political orientations of the regional leaders vary within the set and in some cases within a pair. These differences helped us evaluate whether our experts used the rating scale in a similar fashion.

Our experts' responses were fairly reliable. Of the 23 respondents who completed the section of eight regions, three confused the direction of the scale. Otherwise, five experts' ratings in this section differed from their previous responses. Of these five, three respondents each gave two oblasts the same score in part one of the survey and scores differing by one point in the section of eight regions. A fourth expert reversed the order of two oblasts. The two regions differed only by one point. The fifth expert rated two regions identically at first and as differing by one point in the second section. The experts' evaluations were more or less consistent across sections, so we concluded that respondents' mistakes were not too detrimental to our results.

From the ratings of these eight regions, we also found that our respondents used the democracy scale similarly. Nearly all of the experts placed the regions in the middle of the scale, as we would expect. None of the respondents rated all of the regions on either end of the spectrum, and only a few experts gave this set of regions a wide range of ratings, such as from one to eight, on the scale of one to ten. Overall, there was consistency in how the respondents used the rating scheme.

Validity

Whether the respondents were knowledgeable enough to rate democracy in the regions and whether they abided by my request to use Dahl's definition in part two of the survey were salient issues for both the Russian and Kyrgyzstani surveys. To evaluate knowledge and compliance, I conducted two tests of familiarity with the regions and two tests of conceptualizations of democracy.

As a first measure of familiarity with the regions, I asked respondents to list the name of the leader of each region. Respondents in Russia listed the name of the leader of regions they selected, and respondents in Kyrgyzstan listed the names of all the leaders. With this information, I could better evaluate respondents' familiarity with the current politics of each region.

Respondents in Russia listed the correct leaders for 85 percent of their selections. Three percent were incorrect answers, and the remainder were left blank.[5] Approximately three-quarters of the incorrect answers were for Nizhegorod, where elections for a new governor were taking place during our administration of the survey. (Respondents wrote the name of the previous governor and "former.") Two questionnaires accounted for half of all the blanks.

Considering that we asked respondents in Russia to consider 57 regions, an 85 percent correct response rate indicates that these

---

[5] Two respondents did not list leaders for either the most democratic or least democratic section, and one respondent did not list leaders for both sections. Because they left entire sections blank, we assume they either did not see the request or did not have time to fulfill it.

respondents are knowledgeable about regional politics. The responses also suggest that most of the individuals kept current on changes in the regions. For example, respondents knew that a new individual had recently replaced the former governor of Kemerovo.

In Kyrgyzstan, respondents named the correct leader 61 percent of the time. Eight percent of their answers were incorrect, and 30 percent were blank. Three respondents were responsible for 41 percent of the blanks. Two of these individuals did not write any names, suggesting that they overlooked the section. Without these three respondents, 70 percent of answers were correct, 9 percent were incorrect, and 21 percent were incomplete.

In Kyrgyzstan, recall of leaders' names is lower and this test is likely less effective because provincial governors are not pivotal figures in Kyrgyzstani society. The president appoints governors in Kyrgyzstan, so these officials do not mount large election campaigns that catch the attention of residents in the capital. Furthermore, regional leaders do not tend to become national political figures. Rotation of governors is common, so it can also be difficult for political observers to keep track of who currently heads a provincial administration. Overall, this measure of familiarity suggests that the respondents in Russia and Kyrgyzstan are knowledgeable about regional politics.

As a second measure, I asked the respondents to indicate their level of knowledge of the regions. They selected as many of the following choices as applied:

a. personal experience with the region,
b. personal contact with representatives of the region,
c. familiarity with materials from the region, and/or
d. knowledge of the situation in the region through the central mass media.

Experts in Russia indicated their familiarity with those regions they selected, whereas respondents in Kyrgyzstan noted their familiarity for all seven regions in their country.[6]

---

[6] The familiarity measures were in part one of the survey. Because the ratings in part one and part two of the survey are highly correlated, the familiarity measures also indicate the validity of the rating in part two (based on Dahl's definition).

TABLE A.1. *Russian Survey: Knowledge of Regions*

Source of Knowledge	Percentage of Choices
Personal experience with the region (at least)	34
Personal contact with representatives (but no personal experience)	17
Familiarity with regional materials (but no personal experience or contact with representatives)	32
Knowledge through the central media (but no personal experience, contact with representatives, or familiarity with regional materials)	16

The results from this measure of familiarity, provided in Table A.1, confirm that our Russian respondents are experts. In contrast to non-experts, our respondents had personal experience with many regions and familiarity with numerous regional materials, such as newspapers: They did not simply rely on the central media in order to understand regional politics.

Respondents in Kyrgyzstan are even more familiar with regions of their country, as Table A.2 indicates.[7] The considerable direct and indirect personal contact with the regions is because of the small size of the country, migration patterns, and cadre policy. People who excel in their fields often move to the capital city in order to work at the best academic institutions or the highest levels of government; therefore, respondents were often from regions other than Bishkek and the surrounding province, Chui. Also, according to government cadre policy, officials rotate throughout the country, so an official working in Bishkek now is likely to have worked in other regions previously. Reliance on materials from the regions was low (13 percent), reflecting the paucity of regional publications, including newspapers and statistical studies.

In the Russian survey, I found that the respondents were more knowledgeable about the regions they chose as more democratic than about the regions they selected as less democratic, as Table A.3

---

[7] Five respondents in Kyrgyzstan did not complete the familiarity section. Because they did not rate their familiarity for any of the regions, the omissions were likely an oversight.

TABLE A.2. *Kyrgyzstani Survey: Knowledge of Regions*

Source of Knowledge	Percentage of Choices
Personal experience with the region (at least)	54
Personal contact with representatives (but no personal experience)	24
Familiarity with regional materials (but no personal experience or contact with representatives)	13
Knowledge through the central media (but no personal experience, contact with representatives, or familiarity with regional materials)	10

TABLE A.3. *Russian Survey: Knowledge of Most and Least Democratic Regions*

Source of Knowledge	Percentage of Choices	
	Most Democratic	Least Democratic
Personal experience with the region (at least)	77	44
Personal contact with representatives (but no personal experience)	43	18
Familiarity with regional materials (but no personal experience or contact with representatives)	61	52
Knowledge through the central media (but no personal experience, contact with representatives, or familiarity with regional materials)	26	31

describes. Seventy-seven percent of their more democratic selections and only 44 percent of their less democratic choices were based on personal experience. Likewise, 43 percent of the most democratic selections and 18 percent of the least democratic choices were derived from contact with regional representatives.

On the one hand, this relationship between personal experience and democracy could result because experts assume regions with which they have not had contact are less democratic. On the other hand, respondents may not know less democratic regions as well because these areas may offer fewer professional opportunities and their residents may have less contact with the liberal capital. Less democratic regions may be less likely to sponsor academic exchanges, host professional conferences, and send their elites to Moscow. Because reliance on regional materials and the central media was similar across the categories, I deduced that selection of a region as less democratic was not a function of an expert's knowledge about this region. Moreover, I concluded that experts had sufficient knowledge of regions they selected as less democratic.

The respondents in Kyrgyzstan did not select the most and least democratic regions but instead rated all regions, so I ran a correlation of the familiarity and democracy ratings for the Kyrgyzstani survey and, for comparative purposes, also for the Russian survey. The correlations, 0.29 for Kyrgyzstan and 0.14 for Russia, suggest that weak relationships exist. A large portion of this relationship for the Kyrgyzstan survey is attributable to the inclusion of Bishkek. This region is well known to all the respondents because they live in the capital, and it is typically considered highly democratic. Without Bishkek, the correlation falls to 0.20.

Using the familiarity data, I considered the impact of selecting respondents only from the capital cities. Because Russia is such a large country, respondents' distance from a region may influence their evaluation of it. They may think of distant regions as more foreign and exotic than "liberal" Moscow and therefore judge them as less democratic. To test for a geographic bias in the Russian survey, I used statistical regression to compare average familiarity ratings for each region with the region's distance from Moscow. I found that the experts were neither more nor less familiar with regions far from the capital.

In considerably smaller Kyrgyzstan, distance is not an issue, but north–south prejudices are. Those northerners with particularly strong feelings describe southern Kyrgyzstan as economically and culturally primitive and as a potential breeding ground for Islamic fundamentalism. Because Bishkek is located in northern Kyrgyzstan, the northern prejudice toward the south may have resulted in less democratic evaluations of southern provinces. For the Kyrgyzstan survey, I ranked the seven regions based on the average level of familiarity, and the southern provinces fall in the middle. They are better known than two of the northern regions and fall below only the

TABLE A.4. *Familiarity Ranking: Kyrgyzstan*

Familiarity Ranking	Region
1	Bishkek
2	Chui
3	Issik-Kul'
4	Osh
5	Dzhalal-Abad
6	Naryn
7	Talas

Note: This ranking is based on average familiarity scores for each region.

capital city, capital region, and the resort area Issik-Kul', as Table A.4 indicates.

Moreover, despite the prejudice in Kyrgyzstan, the southern provinces, Osh and Dzhalal-Abad, did not receive the lowest democracy scores. In fact, Osh falls in third place after the capital city and the province where the capital city is located. It is not surprising that this province would be the most democratic region in a country where the national government has been supportive of democratic reform. Furthermore, another province, Naryn, falls below the other southern province, Dzhalal-Abad, in the democracy ranking.

Another component of validity is respondents' compliance with my request to use Dahl's definition of democracy in part two of the survey. To check for compliance, I first ran correlations between the rankings based on respondents' own understandings of democracy and their rankings based on Dahl's definition. The correlation for Russia, 0.97, and the correlation for Kyrgyzstan, 0.91, are extremely strong.[8] This may suggest that the respondents used their own definitions for both parts of the survey; however, their handwritten explanations of their selections and ratings suggest that their conceptualizations of democracy are similar to Dahl's definition.

In these explanations, 81 percent of the respondents in Russia and 53 percent of the respondents in Kyrgyzstan wrote at least one of Dahl's eight institutional guarantees. The respondents mentioned the presence

---

[8] In Kyrgyzstan, one respondent did not rate regions based on Dahl's definition, and two others did not use the one-to-ten scale as requested.

of the guarantees as a rationale for labeling a region more democratic and the absence of the guarantees as a reason for their selection of a region as less democratic. Fewer respondents in Kyrgyzstan mentioned components of Dahl's definition because they interpreted the question in the survey differently. Many respondents explained why democracy was weaker or stronger in a region instead of just explaining their choice. For example, many respondents wrote that the multinational character of Bishkek made the region more democratic. (Kyrgyz will often explain that the presence of Russians promotes democracy and development in a region.)

Of Dahl's guarantees, the ones listed most frequently in both surveys were freedom to form and join organizations, freedom of expression, alternative sources of information, and free and fair elections. For example, respondents in Russia and Kyrgyzstan wrote "freedom of speech." Independent media are alternative sources of information, so I counted phrases such as "freedom of press" as examples of this idea. Phrases capturing the idea of freedom to form and join organizations included "free activity of different political organizations," "existence of a developed political party system," and "democratic parties and movements." For free and fair elections, the respondents wrote phrases such as "the democratism of elections."

The experts also took the absence of Dahl's institutions as an indication that a region was less democratic. For instance, the respondents wrote "suppression...of a free press" and "restraining of journalists," suggesting that alternative sources of information were weak. They used the same approach for elections. One expert in Russia noted the "cancellation of local elections." Another in Russia mentioned that there had been single-candidate elections in a region. A third respondent in Russia wrote that "the gubernatorial elections [in Kurgan] were [like] a bad movie."

It is understandable that Dahl's four other guarantees were less popular. The often-cited idea of free and fair elections encompasses the guarantees of eligibility for public office, the right of political leaders to compete for support, and the right to vote; and the first seven guarantees capture the idea of institutions for making policies based on voters' preferences, the final component. Although the experts did not cite all the components of Dahl's definition, they did employ the main tenets of his conceptualization of democracy. Thus, we can conclude that the ranking is based on a standard definition of democracy.

RESULTS

To calculate the aggregate ratings of the regions in Kyrgyzstan, I averaged the ratings that the experts gave each region. For the Russian survey, I subtracted the percentage of respondents who ranked each region as less democratic from the percentage of respondents who ranked each region as more democratic. The results appear in Tables A.5 and A.6. From these tables, I selected the four regions.

The percentages of respondents in Russia who selected each region as more and less democratic appear in Table A.7. The ten highlighted regions are cases that are highly disputed. A significant number of respondents considered the regions more democratic, whereas others regarded the regions as less democratic. I suspect that this is not a by-product of the survey design but an accurate reflection of the mixed nature of political systems in these regions. Take, for example, the city of Moscow. Most respondents selected it as more democratic because of the strength of political pluralism and political freedoms; however, some respondents considered it less democratic because the mayor rules with a strong hand. He is not open to criticism of his own actions, according to the respondents.

It is interesting to note that the less democratic regions are not disputed. The less democratic regions are clearly less democratic in the experts' minds, whereas the more democratic regions also exhibit some nondemocratic characteristics. This anomaly emphasizes that even Russia's most democratic regions are not ideal democracies.

My decision to match socioeconomic characteristics precluded choosing the first and last regions from the rankings. For Russia, I selected the fourth and 56th regions in the ranking instead of the first and 57th. Because the rankings are based on experts' estimates, the difference between using the fourth and 56th regions versus the first and 57th is not likely to have a meaningful impact on the conclusions of the study. For Kyrgyzstan, I chose the third and the last, rather than the first and the last. I did not select the capital city or province because, in any country, these regions tend to be significantly different from the others. The capital city and province are the sites of national

TABLE A.5. *Regional Ratings: Russia*

Ranking	Region	Percentage	Ranking	Region	Percentage	Ranking	Region	Percentage
1	St. Petersburg	94	15	Tomsk	17	33	Rostov	−5
2	Sverdlovsk	73	21	Arkhangel'sk	12	33	Smolensk	−5
3	Nizhegorod	67	22	Kaluga	11	33	Stavropol'	−5
4	Samara	62	23	Kostroma	6	42	Amur	−11
5	Moscow (city)	56	24	Magadan	6	42	Ryazan'	−11
6	Irkutsk	39	25	Tver'	6	44	Tula	−15
6	Kaliningrad	39	26	Moscow (oblast)	2	45	Voronezh	−16
8	Perm'	33	27	Omsk	1	46	Kemerovo	−20
9	Yaroslavl'	28	28	Ivanovo	0	46	Orel	−20
9	Krasnoyarsk	28	28	Khabarovsk	0	46	Tambov	−20
9	Murmansk	28	28	Vladimir	0	49	Kurgan	−26
9	Novgorod	28	28	Volgograd	0	49	Lipetsk	−26
9	Sakhalin	28	28	Vologda	0	49	Saratov	−26
14	Novosibirsk	23	33	Altay	−5	52	Bryansk	−32
15	Chelyabinsk	17	33	Astrakhan'	−5	52	Penza	−32
15	Kamchatka	17	33	Belgorod	−5	54	Krasnodar	−36
15	Leningrad	17	33	Chita	−5	55	Kursk	−68
15	Orenburg	17	33	Kirov	−5	56	Ul'ianovsk	−74
15	Tyumen'	17	33	Pskov	−5	57	Primor'e	−79

Note: The ranking of regions is based on the percentage of respondents who selected a region as most democratic minus the percentage who selected it as least democratic.

TABLE A.6. *Regional Ratings: Kyrgyzstan*

Ranking	Region	Rating
1	Bishkek	8.85
2	Chui	7.85
3	Osh	6.60
4	Issik-Kul'	6.55
5	Talas	6.21
6	Dzhalal-Abad	6.05
7	Naryn	5.11

Note: Experts in Kyrgyzstan rated all the regions of their country on a scale of one to ten, with ten being the most democratic. The rating represents an average of the responses.

government, often the homes of the first reform initiatives, and sometimes the primary conduits to the outside world. The advantage of excluding the capital and its province outweighs any disadvantage of not selecting the absolute first region in the ranking for Kyrgyzstan.

Because I selected my cases from the top and bottom of the Russian ranking, the possibility of the center of the list being less reliable is not a significant concern. Regions in the center may be truly neither the most nor least democratic, but, alternatively, they might simply be less well-known. Experts may not have chosen them simply because they are unfamiliar with them. Two findings challenge this interpretation. First, only two of the 57 regions (Ivanovo and Vladimir) were not chosen by any experts. This suggests that the respondents were familiar with many regions. Second, I found only a moderate relationship between the selections and the level of media coverage. I hypothesized that experts would be most likely to select regions that received the greatest media coverage. Using a rating of media coverage of Russia's regions, I found a correlation of 0.55 between media attention and the respondents' selections.[9]

---

[9] A region's media rating is based on 14 factors of media visibility: a famous politician, "loud" elections, power conflicts, struggles over ownership, large economic projects, international connections, territorial problems and border disputes, criminal activity and corruption, terrorism, political events and visits of nationwide significance, large cultural or sporting events, strikes, environmental and biological catastrophes, and a Constitutional Court decision regarding the region. For a more detailed explanation, see McFaul and Petrov, *Politicheskii al'manakh Rossii 1997*, 135–138.

TABLE A.7. *Russian Survey: More and Less Democratic Rankings (percentage of respondents selecting region as more democratic or as less democratic)*

Ranking	Region	More	Less	Ranking	Region	More	Less	Ranking	Region	More	Less
1	St. Petersburg	94	0	18	Orenburg	17	0	39	Kemerovo	6	26
2	Sverdlovsk	78	5	18	Tomsk	17	0	39	Orel	6	26
3	**Nizhegorod**	78	11	22	Arkhangel'sk	17	5	39	Tambov	6	26
4	**Moscow (city)**	72	16	23	Kaluga	11	0	42	Krasnodar	6	42
5	Samara	67	5	24	Tver'	11	5	43	Ivanovo	0	0
6	Irkutsk	44	5	25	**Khabarovsk**	11	11	43	Vladimir	0	0
6	Kaliningrad	44	5	25	**Volgograd**	11	11	45	Altay	0	5
8	Perm'	33	0	25	Vologda	11	11	45	Kirov	0	5
9	Krasnoyarsk	33	5	28	Pskov	11	16	45	Smolensk	0	5
10	Murmansk	28	0	28	**Rostov**	11	16	48	Amur	0	11
10	Novgorod	28	0	30	Saratov	11	37	48	Ryazan'	0	11
10	Sakhalin	28	0	31	Kostroma	6	0	50	Voronezh	0	16
10	Yaroslavl'	28	0	31	Magadan	6	0	51	Kurgan	0	26
14	Novosibirsk	28	5	33	**Omsk**	6	5	51	Lipetsk	0	26
15	**Moscow (oblast)**	28	26	34	Astrakhan'	6	11	53	Bryansk	0	32
16	Leningrad	22	5	34	Belgorod	6	11	53	Penza	0	32
16	Tyumen'	22	5	34	Chita	6	11	55	Kursk	0	68
18	Chelyabinsk	17	0	34	Stavropol'	6	11	56	Ul'ianovsk	0	74
18	Kamchatka	17	0	38	Tula	6	21	57	Primor' e	0	79

Note: Regions are ordered by more and then less democratic rankings, and, if rankings are identical, by alphabetical order. The bold regions are cases that are highly disputed.

199

The correlation of 0.55 suggests that there is a moderate relationship; however, it does not indicate bias in the experts' evaluations. Regions that are neither the most nor the least democratic may deserve less media attention. True electoral competition, abundant civic activity, and political debates in the most democratic regions may attract the media, and outrageous violations of democratic procedures and civil rights in the least democratic regions may put these provinces in the news. Regions between these two extremes may not be in the media spotlight because there is little political hubbub; therefore, a region's position on the democracy spectrum may influence its level of media coverage.

Appendix B

Alternative Explanations

Chapter 2 considers the influence of interests, resources, and organizational capacity relative to economic autonomy. This appendix considers four other alternative explanations – political opportunity structures, institutions, leadership, and international promotion of democracy. Unlike economic autonomy, none account for the greater degree of self-censorship and government harassment in Ul'ianovsk and Naryn.

POLITICAL OPPORTUNITY STRUCTURES

Scholars have argued that political changes, such as increased access to government institutions and new alliances with government officials, can encourage people to become politically involved.[1] Clearly,

[1] Grzegorz Ekiert and Jan Kubik, "Contentious Politics in New Democracies: East Germany, Hungary, Poland, and Slovakia, 1989–93," *World Politics* 50 (July, 1998), 547–581; Jeff Goodwin, *No Other Way Out: States and Revolutionary Movements, 1945–1991* (Cambridge: Cambridge University Press, 2001); Samuel P. Huntington and Joan M. Nelson, *No Easy Choice: Political Participation in Developing Countries* (Cambridge, MA: Harvard University Press, 1976); Herbert Kitschelt, "Political Opportunity Structures and Political Protest: Antinuclear Movements in 4 Democracies," *British Journal of Political Science* 16 (January, 1986), 57–85; Doug McAdam, "Conceptual Origins, Current Problems, Future Directions," in *Comparative Perspectives on Social Movements: Political Opportunities, Mobilizing Structures, and Cultural Framings*, ed. Doug McAdam, John D. McCarthy, and Mayer N. Zald (Cambridge: Cambridge University Press, 1996); Suzanne Mettler, "Bringing the State Back into Civic Engagement: Policy Feedback Effects of the GI Bill for World War II

by harassing activists, local authorities are not sending the message that they want citizens to be involved in politics. Yet, harassment cannot explain self-censorship in Ul'ianovsk and Naryn. As Chapter 4 enumerates, government punishments in Ul'ianovsk are more common than they are in Naryn, yet self-censorship is greater in Naryn. Moreover, government harassment cannot account for the fact that a few individuals in Naryn nonetheless do challenge local authorities.

INSTITUTIONS

Institutions are often cited as possible influences on democratic development in the former Soviet Union. Institutional theories hypothesize that reformers can design laws regulating elections, legislatures, and other components of democracy in order to enhance the long-term success of this form of government.[2] However, laws regulating activism are too similar in the provinces of each country to account for the differences in officials' and activists' behaviors. In Kyrgyzstan, national laws regulate the media, political organizations, and candidacy, so the regulations in Naryn and Osh are identical. Civic activity in the Russian provinces falls under both federal and provincial rules. In Ul'ianovsk

Veterans," *American Political Science Review* 96 (June, 2002), 351–365; Theda Skocpol, *States and Social Revolutions: A Comparative Analysis of France, Russia, and China* (Cambridge: Cambridge University Press, 1979); Theda Skocpol, Marshall Ganz, and Ziad Munson, "A Nation of Organizers: The Institutional Origins of Civic Volunteerism in the United States," *American Political Science Review* 94 (September, 2000), 527–546; Sidney G. Tarrow, *Power in Movement: Social Movements, Collective Action, and Politics* (New York: Cambridge University Press, 1994); Sidney Verba, Norman H. Nie, and Jae-on Kim, *Participation and Political Equality: A Seven-Nation Comparison* (Cambridge: Cambridge University Press, 1978).

[2] Larry Diamond, "Introduction: In Search of Consolidation," in *Consolidating the Third Wave Democracies*, ed. Larry Diamond (Baltimore: Johns Hopkins University Press, 1997), xxv, xxvii–xxix, xxx; Di Palma, *To Craft Democracies;* M. Steven Fish, "Conclusion: Democracy and Russian Politics," in *Russian Politics: Challenges of Democratization*, ed. Zoltan D. Barany and Robert G. Moser (New York: Cambridge University Press, 2001), 215–252; Michael McFaul, "Russia's Rough Ride," in *Consolidating the Third Wave Democracies*, ed. Larry Diamond (Baltimore: Johns Hopkins University Press, 1997), 82–84; Przeworski, *Democracy and the Market;* Theda Skocpol, *Protecting Soldiers and Mothers: The Political Origins of Social Policy in the United States* (Cambridge, MA: Belknap Press of Harvard University Press, 1992), 47–54. Even Dahl, whose focus in *Polyarchy* is preconditions, allows for the possibility that leaders can increase the chances for democracy through crafting. See Dahl, *Polyarchy*, 46, 121–123, 217, 221.

and Samara, regional laws address only candidacy – not media and NGOs – and these rules are nearly identical.[3]

Differences between candidacy laws in Samara and Ul'ianovsk are insignificant. In Samara, individuals must meet slightly more stringent requirements in order to become candidates. For example, parliamentary candidates in Samara must be 21, whereas in Ul'ianovsk 18-, 19-, and 20-year-olds may run. Individuals hoping to compete for seats in Samara's parliament also must gather more signatures from voters. On the other hand, gubernatorial hopefuls in Ul'ianovsk cannot nominate themselves, whereas their counterparts in Samara can, according to the laws. Table B.1 provides an overview of candidacy regulations.

With respect to campaigning, small differences exist in terms of who can help candidates campaign, who can make donations, the size of campaign expenditures, and the number of regulations imposed on the independent media. (See Table B.2.) For example, members of the military, charities, and religious groups can campaign for gubernatorial candidates in Ul'ianovsk but not in Samara. Similarly, regulations in Samara require that the independent media treat candidates equally in terms of prices demanded and time or space allocated, whereas rules in Ul'ianovsk do not address the nonstate media. Also, Samara bans certain legal entities, such as those with more than 30 percent foreign capital, from making campaign donations, whereas Ul'ianovsk permits these contributions. (See Table B.3.)

Samara law allows parliamentary and gubernatorial candidates to spend considerably more than their Ul'ianovsk counterparts. Gubernatorial candidates in Ul'ianovsk could spend 35 percent of the amount gubernatorial contenders in Samara could. In Ul'ianovsk,

---

[3] The conclusions in this section are based on my analysis of the laws in each region. In Samara, the oblast laws "About the Samara Gubernskaia duma" and "About the election of deputies to the Samara Gubernskaia duma" applied to the December 1997 parliamentary elections, and the oblast law "About the election of governor of Samara oblast" regulated the December 1996 gubernatorial election. Because Ul'ianovsk did not have a legislative body at the time, an administrative statute ("About the election of deputies to the Zakonodatel'noe sobranie of Ul'ianovsk oblast"), instead of an oblast law, governed the December 1995 parliamentary elections. The oblast law "About the election of the governor of Ul'ianovsk oblast" regulated the December 1996 gubernatorial race. See "O Samarskoi gubernskoi dume," No. 154 (1996); "O vyborakh deputatov Samarskoi gubernskoi dumy," No. 268 (1996); "O vyborakh gubernatora Samarskoi oblasti," No. 155 (1996); "O vyborakh deputatov Zakonodatel'nogo sobraniia Ul'ianovskoi oblasti," No. 118 (1995).

TABLE B.I. *Candidacy Regulations in the Russian Regions*

	Samara	Ul'ianovsk
Eligibility		
Parliament	• 21 years of age • Resident of oblast for one year • Eligible to vote • Citizen of the Russian Federation	• 18 years of age • Current resident of oblast
Governor	• 30 years of age • Resident of oblast for one year • Eligible to vote • Completed higher education	• 30 years of age • Resident of oblast for one year
Nominations		
Parliament	• Regional electoral association, voter group, and candidate himself may nominate • Voter groups require 50 citizens, and self-nominations require support of 50 in district	• Regional electoral association, voter group, and candidate himself may nominate • Law does not specify number of supporters
Governor	• Regional electoral association, voter group, and candidate himself may nominate • Voter groups require 100 citizens, and self-nominations require support of 100 in district	• Regional electoral association and voter group may nominate. (Law does not mention self-nominations.) • Law does not specify number of supporters
Signatures		
Parliament	• Signatures from two percent of registered voters in candidate's district • Signatures must be submitted 32 days prior to the election	• Signatures from one percent of registered voters in candidate's district • Signatures must be submitted 40 days prior to the election
Governor	• Signatures from two percent of registered voters, with no more than seven percent from any one territory • Signatures must be submitted 32 days prior to the election	• Signature from 20,000 voters (approximately two percent) • Signatures must be submitted 50 days prior to the election

Sources: "O vyborakh deputatov Samarskoi gubernskoi dumy," No. 268 (1996); "O vyborakh gubernatora Samarskoi oblasti," No. 155 (1996); "O vyborakh deputatov Zakonodatel'nogo sobraniia Ul'ianovskoi oblasti," No. 118 (1995); "O vyborakh gubernatora Ul'ianovskoi oblasti."

TABLE B.2. *Campaign Regulations in the Russian Regions*

	Samara	Ul'ianovsk
Time Period		
Parliament	• From the day candidates register to the evening prior to election	• From the day candidates register to the evening prior to election
Governor	• From the day candidates register to the evening prior to election	• From the day candidates register to the evening prior to election
Financing		
Parliament	• Must manage funds in official account • Total spending limit 10,000 times minimum wage • Provided funds from provincial budget • Contributions from candidate, electoral associations and blocs, physical entities, and legal entities • Limits on contributors (see Table B.3) • Contributions prohibited from foreign states, organizations, and citizens; individuals and entities without citizenship; international organizations and movements; state and military organs; religious associations; charities; and legal entities with more than 30 percent foreign capital, legal entities without a branch or representative in the oblast, physical entities located outside the oblast	• Must manage funds in official account • Total spending limit 500 times minimum wage • Provided funds from provincial budget • Contributions from candidate, electoral associations and blocs, physical entities, and legal entities • Limits on contributors (see Table B.3) • Contributions prohibited from foreign states, organizations, and citizens; individuals and entities without citizenship; international organizations and movements; state and military organs; religious associations; and charities
Governor	• Must manage funds in official account • Total spending limit 20,000 times minimum wage • Provided funds from provincial budget • Contributions from candidate, electoral associations and blocs, physical entities, and legal entities • Limits on contributors (see Table B.3) • Contributions prohibited from foreign states, organizations, and citizens; individuals and entities without citizenship; international organizations and movements; state and military organs; religious associations; charities; and legal entities with more than 30 percent foreign capital, legal entities without a branch or representative in the oblast, physical entities located outside the oblast	• Must manage funds in official account • Total spending limit 7,000 times minimum wage • Provided funds from provincial budget • Contributions from candidate, electoral associations and blocs, physical entities, and legal entities • Limits on contributors (see Table B.3) • Contributions prohibited from foreign states, organizations, and citizens; individuals and entities without citizenship; international organizations and movements; state and military organs; and religious associations
Media		
Parliament	• State and private media representatives who are candidates, campaign managers, or electoral commission members cannot cover the election	• State and private media representatives who are candidates, campaign managers, or electoral commission members cannot cover the election

(continued)

TABLE B.2 *(continued)*

	Samara	Ul'ianovsk
Governor	• Equal amount of free time and space for all candidates in regional state media	• Equal amount of free time and space for all candidates in regional state media
	• Private media must treat candidates equally in terms of allocations and prices	• No regulation of private media
	• State and private media representatives who are candidates, campaign managers, or electoral commission members cannot cover the election	• State and private media representatives who are candidates, campaign managers, or electoral commission members cannot cover the election
	• Equal amount of free time and space for all candidates in regional state media	• Equal amount of free time and space for all candidates in regional state media
	• Private media must treat candidates equally in terms of allocations and prices	• Private media must treat candidates equally in terms of allocations and prices
Other Parliament	• Candidates cannot use the advantages of their employment, such as a government position	• Candidates cannot use the advantages of their employment, such as a government position
	• No giving of free or subsidized services, securities, or money to voters	• No giving of free or subsidized services, securities, or money to voters
	• Literature must contain name of issuer	• Literature must contain name of issuer
	• No literature at polls	• No literature at polls
	• Federal, oblast, and local officials and members of military, charities, religious groups, and electoral commissions cannot campaign	• Federal, oblast, and local officials and members of military, charities, religious groups, and electoral commissions cannot campaign
Governor	• Candidates cannot use the advantages of their employment, such as a government position	• Candidates cannot use the advantages of their employment, such as a government position
	• No giving of free or subsidized services, securities, or money to voters	• No giving of free or subsidized services, securities, or money to voters
	• Literature must contain name of issuer	• Literature must contain name of issuer
	• No literature at polls	• No literature at polls
	• Federal, oblast, and local officials and members of military, charities, religious groups, and electoral commissions cannot campaign	• Federal, oblast, and local officials and members of electoral commissions cannot campaign

Sources: "O vyborakh deputatov Samarskoi gubernskoi dumy," No. 268 (1996); "O vyborakh gubernatora Samarskoi oblasti," No. 155 (1996); "O vyborakh deputatov Zakonodatel'nogo sobraniia Ul'ianovskoi oblasti," No. 118 (1995); "O vyborakh gubernatora Ul'ianovskoi oblasti."

TABLE B.3. *Allowable Campaign Funds in the Russian Regions (as a multiple of the minimum wage)*

Source	Samara		Ul'ianovsk	
	Parliament	Governor	Parliament	Governor
Candidate	100	500	20	200
Electoral associations and blocs	1,000	6,000	40	No limit specified
Physical entities	100 each	10 each	10^a	10 each
Legal entities	1,000 each	300 each	15^a	500 each
TOTAL	10,000	20,000	500	7,000

[a] The law on parliamentary elections in Ul'ianovsk does not specify whether limits for physical and legal entities are by entity or for all entities in that category.

Sources: "O vyborakh deputatov Samarskoi gubernskoi dumy," No. 268 (1996); "O vyborakh gubernatora Samarskoi oblasti," No. 155 (1996); "O vyborakh deputatov Zakonodatel'nogo sobraniia Ul'ianovskoi oblasti," No. 118 (1995); "O vyborakh gubernatora Ul'ianovskoi oblasti."

parliamentary candidates could spend only 5 percent as much as their Samara counterparts. (See Table B.4.) The difference in parliamentary spending is not as great as it seems. The parliamentary elections in Ul'ianovsk were two years earlier than the parliamentary elections in Samara, and candidates have devoted increasingly more resources to elections over time. The differences in gubernatorial limits are more significant because both regions held gubernatorial elections in December 1996.

Although candidates face slightly different challenges in Samara and Ul'ianovsk, overall the legal requirements are no more arduous in one region than in the other. Moreover, the rules related to workplace harassment in both provinces are identical. In Samara and Ul'ianovsk, the parliamentary and gubernatorial electoral laws state that during the election period a candidate cannot be fired without his agreement and he must be able to return to the same rank and type of work.[4]

---

[4] "O Samarskoi gubernskoi dume," No. 154 (1996); "O vyborakh deputatov Samarskoi gubernskoi dumy," No. 268 (1996); "O vyborakh gubernatora samarskoi oblasti," No. 155 (1996); "O vyborakh deputatov Zakonodatel'nogo sobraniia Ul'ianovskoi oblasti," No. 118 (1995); "O vyborakh gubernatora Ul'ianovskoi oblasti."

TABLE B.4. *Allowable Campaign Funds in Ul'ianovsk as a Percentage of Allowable Campaign Funds in Samara*

Source	Parliament	Governor
Candidate	20	40
Electoral associations and blocs	4	No limit specified
Physical entities	10	100
Legal entities	1.5	167
TOTAL	5	35

Sources: "O vyborakh deputatov Samarskoi gubernskoi dumy," No. 268 (1996); "O vyborakh gubernatora Samarskoi oblasti," No. 155 (1996); "O vyborakh deputatov Zakonodatel'nogo sobraniia Ul'ianovskoi oblasti," No. 118 (1995); "O vyborakh gubernatora Ul'ianovskoi oblasti."

A specific institutional explanation that has received considerable attention in post-Soviet studies is center–periphery relations. Even though Moscow and Bishkek were generally supportive of democratization in the 1990s, the national governments' actions cannot account for the strength of democracy in Samara and Osh. The development of democracy in their countries was not the top priority for the national executives, and Moscow and Bishkek had considerably less leverage over these provinces. In Russia, the emphasis of Boris Yeltsin's administration was on winning the support of the regions for its battles with parliament, the communists, and the nationalists.[5] The administration was unlikely to meddle in provinces where the regional leader had joined the bandwagon and obtained votes for Yeltsin and his policies. Loyalty to Yeltsin, not democratic reform, was the yardstick for evaluating regional leaders. In Kyrgyzstan, even though the president can remove regional governors, Askar Akaev also had to worry about the support of regional elites, particularly in the south, where some Uzbeks had called for autonomy. While these demands dissipated, Akaev still needed the support of regional elites. His failure to appoint new regional leaders when he first came to power exacerbated this situation. Also, Moscow and Bishkek were in stronger positions to influence Ul'ianovsk and Naryn than Samara and Osh. Federal assistance accounted for 15.0 percent of Ul'ianovsk's budget income but only

[5] Daniel Treisman, *After the Deluge: Regional Crises and Political Consolidation in Russia* (Ann Arbor: University of Michigan Press, 1999); Slider, "Russia's Market-Distorting Federalism," 447.

1.4 percent of Samara's.[6] In fact, Samara is a donor region, meaning it contributes more to the federal budget than it receives, whereas Ul'ianovsk is a recipient region.[7] Similarly, Naryn received five and one-half times more in federal subsidies per person than Osh oblast.[8]

LEADERSHIP

Another popular explanation for post-Soviet democratic development has been leadership.[9] Democratization studies emphasize the importance of elite understanding of democracy and elite support for the new system of government.[10] Yet, government elites in all four provinces have a clear understanding of democratic ideals. Furthermore, a portion of officials in each province, not just in Ul'ianovsk and Naryn, is unenthusiastic about them.

A regional deputy in Naryn explained, "The general understanding [of democracy] is that for the president, workers, and average people – for all of them there should be one law. There should not be one law for the poor and one law for the rich. [Democracy means] freedom of speech, freedom of opinion, freedom to live as a person wants to live."[11] This description of democracy was typical of provincial elites' understanding of democracy – basically, a political system guaranteeing citizens civil and personal freedoms.[12] Leaders' attitudes toward

---

[6] *Predprinimatel'skii klimat regionov Rossii: geografiia Rossii dlia investorov i predprinimatelei* (Moscow: Nachala-Press, 1997), 269.

[7] East West Institute, *Who Are the Donor Regions?* [e-mail service]. Russian Regional Report. New York: East West Institute, May 27, 1999.

[8] This money came from a grant to equalize economic conditions among the regions – one of two grants regions received from the national level. The other grant was for the salaries of teachers and doctors. These data are from the budget department of the Kyrgyzstani Ministry of Finance.

[9] George W. Breslauer, *Gorbachev and Yeltsin as Leaders* (New York: Cambridge University Press, 2002); Archie Brown, *The Gorbachev Factor* (New York: Oxford University Press, 1996); McFaul, "The Fourth Wave of Democracy *and* Dictatorship."

[10] Robert Dahl, "Development and Democratic Culture," in *Consolidating the Third Wave Democracies*, ed. Larry Diamond (Baltimore: Johns Hopkins University Press, 1997), 34–38; Huntington and Nelson, *No Easy Choice*; Huntington, *The Third Wave*, 257–258; Higley and Gunther, *Elites and Democratic Consolidation*.

[11] Author's interview (29) with a deputy in the oblast parliament, Osh oblast, July 8, 1997.

[12] My conclusions about elites' understandings of democracy and support for democracy are based on interviews I conducted in each region with approximately ten oblast parliamentary deputies and administration officials, at the level of deputy governor. This represents nearly one-third of the top regional elites in each province. To learn

democracy were also similar across the four regions. In each oblast, some governing elites favored democracy, whereas others were opposed to democracy even as an ideal. A communist deputy in Ul'ianovsk defined democracy but then clarified that his party's goal is socialism, not Western democracy. An administrator in Samara expressed the concern that "many paths to democracy can lead to anarchy.... When a person shouts slogans for democracy, this could result in anarchy."[13] Angered by media criticism of him, a member of the Osh administration lamented, "Not everyone has my understanding of democracy: others think 'Everything is possible.' Free speech should be without insult and without personalism."[14] A deputy governor in Naryn expanded upon these complaints: "Mass media can write insults [and] no facts.... [They] write what you do poorly... [And the courts] protect only Akaev and big people [not the lower-level officials]."[15]

During an interview, administrators and deputies can, of course, disguise their true beliefs about democracy, so it is also worth examining their careers and backgrounds. Are these officials members of the democratic movement in one province but not in the other? Were these individuals supporters of the Communist Party? Do current leaders differ more from their communist predecessors in one region versus another? To explore these questions within each pair of regions, let us examine the current party affiliation, Communist Party membership, and former employment of today's government officials.[16]

Most deputies and administration officials in the four regions do not belong to any political party or organization. Of the 25 deputies in Samara, one was nominated by the KPRF and another by the Agrarian Party. In Samara's administration, two officials are unique in terms of

how they understood democracy, I asked, at the end of the interview, "Chto znachit demokratiia? [What does democracy mean?]," prefaced by the comment that the national government in their countries seemed to be trying to create democracies and I was curious what this term meant to them as an ideal. After providing a definition, the officials then offered their thoughts on the benefits and drawbacks of democratic reforms in their countries.

13 Author's interview (145) with an administration official, Samara oblast, February 20, 1998.

14 Author's interview (82) with an administration official, Osh oblast, May 26, 1998.

15 Author's interview (30) with an administration official, Naryn oblast, July 4, 1997.

16 For biographical data, I relied on elites' own descriptions of their lives and checked the material against biographies printed in newspapers during elections, government publications about officials, and accounts by other members of the communities.

party involvement. The director of one department, a position comparable to a deputy governorship, is chair of the oblast branch of the Russian United Industrialists Party and a member of the national council of the party. At the time of my fieldwork, Governor Titov was a deputy chair of NDR, a party popular with government officials.[17] Similarly, in Ul'ianovsk, a few members of parliament are active members of the KPRF, and former Governor Goriachev has been a member of NDR. Goriachev also has led the oblast political organization the Ul'ianovsk Patriotic Union, which unites local government leaders, heads of collective farms, bureaucrats, and some activists, such as defectors from the KPRF. In Kyrgyzstan, political affiliations are even rarer. None of the deputies or administration officials I interviewed in Osh acknowledged involvement with a political organization. In Naryn, an administration official chairs the oblast division of the party of power Ata-Meken, and the chair of the oblast parliament was rumored also to be a member of Ata-Meken, although he denied it. Party affiliation does not suggest that incumbents in some regions are more inclined toward democracy than their counterparts in other regions.

Governing elites' past membership in the Communist Party also does not indicate that there are more reformers in one region as compared with another. In all four oblasts, most members of the elected representative body and executive branch had been members of the Communist Party. Although only 15.6 percent of Soviet adult males were members of the Communist Party, it is not surprising that nearly all the current leaders in the four regions had joined at one time.[18] Current leaders come from relatively elite backgrounds, and in the Soviet Union well-educated individuals tended to join the party to promote their careers and because it was a rite of passage in their circles. For a postcommunist country or region to have few leaders who were once members of the Communist Party, these leaders must be from nonelite backgrounds or relatively young. But, as in most countries, leaders

---

[17] In the winter of 1999, he quit the organization and established his own national political group, *Golos Rossii*.

[18] I use the figure for adult males because most current leaders are men. The figure for the entire adult population was 8.3 percent. From Jerry Hough, *The Soviet Union and Social Science Theory* (Cambridge, MA: Harvard University Press, 1977), 126–127; Robert D. Putnam, *The Comparative Study of Political Elites* (Englewood Cliffs, NJ: Prentice-Hall, 1976), 22–37.

in postcommunist societies tend to be well-educated and middle-aged. Typically, the leaders in the regions joined the Communist Party when they were in their twenties and were completing their military service or higher education. A few joined later in their lives when they began to hold positions of authority in their fields. For example, a deputy in Osh joined the party in 1979 at age 32 when he became head of a transportation depot. Generally, only younger deputies in the four regions have never been party members. For example, in Ul'ianovsk, a deputy who was in his twenties in the 1980s took advantage of the political liberalism of the era and did not join the party. With the demise of the Communist Party, reactions were similar across the oblasts. Some of the current leaders left the party before it was banned, some relinquished their membership when it was banned, and some never left the party in spirit.

In each oblast, some deputies and administrators had been leaders in the Soviet era, suggesting that elite turnover was not significantly greater in one region versus another. Across the four regions, approximately one-third of the deputies I interviewed had been deputies in the Soviet-era legislatures, or they had been top party officials. A few of the highest administrators in each region had governing experience during the Soviet era.

Elite turnover, and understandings of democracy, attitudes toward democracy, party affiliation, and Communist Party membership, do not indicate that government officials are more democratic in one region as compared with the other. Consequently, characteristics of elites cannot account for the greater frequency of government harassment in Ul'ianovsk and Naryn. Also, characteristics of government leaders provide no insight into the issue of self-censorship.

INTERNATIONAL PROMOTION OF DEMOCRACY

The international promotion of democracy in the former Soviet Union and worldwide has also received considerable attention;[19] however,

[19] Susan Burgerman, *Moral Victories: How Activists Provoke Multilateral Action* (Ithaca, NY: Cornell University Press, 2001); Thomas Carothers, *Aiding Democracy Abroad: The Learning Curve* (Washington, DC: Carnegie Endowment for International Peace, 1999); Thomas Carothers, "Aiding Post-communist Societies: A Better Way?" *Problems of Post-communism* 43 (September/October, 1996),

the presence of foreign civic development groups in the regions cannot account for the differences in political engagement.[20] International promotion of democracy is distinct from international factors that contribute to economic autonomy, such as access to international markets and foreign direct investment.

Samara, Ul'ianovsk, Osh, and Naryn were off-limits to most foreign groups until Russia and Kyrgyzstan became sovereign countries. The

15–24; Thomas Carothers, "Democracy Assistance: The Question of Strategy," *Democratization* 4 (Autumn, 1997), 109–132; Thomas Carothers and Marina Ottaway, "The Burgeoning World of Civil Society Aid," in *Funding Virtue: Civil Society Aid and Democracy Promotion*, ed. Marina Ottaway and Thomas Carothers (Washington, DC: Carnegie Endowment for International Peace, 2000); Ann Marie Clark, *Diplomacy of Conscience: Amnesty International and Changing Human Rights Norms* (Princeton, NJ: Princeton University Press, 2001); Dahl, *Polyarchy*, 44, 191, 201; Ann Florini, *The Third Force: The Rise of Transnational Civil Society* (Washington, DC: Carnegie Endowment for International Peace, 2000); Sarah Henderson, *Building Democracy in Contemporary Russia: Western Support for Grassroots Organizations* (Ithaca, NY: Cornell University Press, 2003); Sarah Henderson, "Selling Civil Society: Western Aid and the Nongovernmental Organization Sector in Russia," *Comparative Political Studies* 35 (March, 2002), 139–167; Richard A. Higgott, Geoffrey R. D. Underhill, and Andreas Bieler, *Non-State Actors and Authority in the Global System* (New York: Routledge, 2000); Huntington, *The Third Wave*, 40, 77–78, 87, 89, 91; Keck and Sikkink, *Activists Beyond Borders;* Sanjeev Khagram, James V. Riker, and Kathryn Sikkink, *Restructuring World Politics: Transnational Social Movements, Networks, and Norms* (Minneapolis: University of Minnesota Press, 2002); Linz and Stepan, *Problems of Democratic Transition and Consolidation;* Abraham F. Lowenthal, *Exporting Democracy: The United States and Latin America – Themes and Issues* (Baltimore: Johns Hopkins University Press, 1991); Marina Ottaway, *Strengthening Civil Society in Other Countries: Policy Goal or Wishful Thinking* (Washington, DC: Carnegie Endowment for International Peace, June 24, 2001). Available at http://www.ceip.org/files/Publications/StrengtheningCivilSociety.asp?from=pubauthor; Laurence Whitehead, "International Aspects of Democratization," in *Transitions from Authoritarian Rule: Comparative Perspectives*, ed. Guillermo O'Donnell, Philippe C. Schmitter, and Laurence Whitehead (Baltimore: Johns Hopkins University Press, 1991).

[20] The analysis in this section is based on interviews I conducted with foreign groups in each region, materials provided by the organizations, and in a few cases electronic mail communications with representatives in the regions. Interviews with local NGO leaders and government officials and conversations with citizens corroborated the foreign representatives' accounts. I focused on organizations that maintain a permanent representative in a region. Two other potential international explanations, the "Zeitgeist" and diffusion effects, are also not illuminating. All the provinces experienced regime change during the same era. Also, demonstration effects from other countries or regions influenced the neighboring provinces at the same time. See Huntington, *The Third Wave*, 94, 101–102, 273; Linz and Stepan, *Problems of Democratic Transition and Consolidation*, 75–76.

Red Cross and Red Crescent operated in the Soviet Union, but foreign development organizations did not have access. In the early 1990s, however, international organizations flooded the capitals of Russia and Kyrgyzstan and over time began to work in outlying areas. Table B.5 provides examples of the activities of each of the foreign organizations operating in the four provinces through 1997. Many of the foreign groups run numerous programs, so only some are listed. I listed civic development programs over other types.

The presence of international democracy promoters is strong in Samara as compared with Ul'ianovsk, but foreign organizations did not bring activism to Samara. Instead, these groups chose to work in Samara because local authorities were abiding by new laws and citizens were engaging in democratic activities. For example, the European Union's Technical Assistance to the Commonwealth of Independent States (TACIS) arrived in Samara in 1992, having selected it as one of the organization's six focal regions in Russia.[21] A staff member in Moscow explained, "We work with regions which [sic] are reform-minded."[22] By contrast, there are no international groups in Ul'ianovsk because, as the TACIS official explained, it is considered "a very conservative area" and no one from the region ever expressed an interest.[23] The absence of foreign democracy promoters in Ul'ianovsk is not the cause of weak democracy in the region but a reaction to it. International organizations chose not to set up shop in the region. Foreign

---

[21] The five other regions were Kaliningrad, St. Petersburg, the Urals, Tyumen', and Western Siberia.

[22] Similarly, a representative of Know How in Moscow explained that his staff looks for signs of "some kind of forward-thinking, perhaps in the administration." In selecting regions, the National Democratic Institute for International Affairs (NDI), which also works in Samara, values a "developed democratic process." Author's interview (251) with Boris Iarochevitch, First Secretary, Delegation of the European Commission in Russia, European Union, Moscow, March 11, 1998; author's telephone interview (249) with Heather Christie, Project Assistant, Know How, Moscow, March 6, 1998; author's interview (248) with Dmitrii Valentei, Program Coordinator, National Democratic Institute for International Affairs, Moscow, March 6, 1998.

[23] As in Samara, there are individual foreigners living in Ul'ianovsk. Approximately 100 students, mainly from South Asia and Africa, study at Ul'ianovsk State University, and a Lutheran church is home to foreign pastors. A deputy governor claimed that there was a foreign organization for the elderly and another charitable group in the region, but no one I spoke with was able to help me locate them. Moreover, no one else knew of them. Author's interview (251) with Boris Iarochevitch, First Secretary, Delegation of the European Commission in Russia, European Union, Moscow, March 11, 1998.

TABLE B.5. *International Organizations in the Regions*

Samara

The Know-How Fund	This British organization, along with the British group BEARR Trust, published a directory of NGOs in Samara in 1996. Since 1995, Know-How has also run programs to expose local officials to policy issues and support entrepreneurs.
National Democratic Institute for International Affairs (NDI)	An independent organization affiliated with the Democratic Party in the United States, NDI has held periodic seminars for government, media, and NGO leaders in Samara since 1995.
Open Society Institute (OSI)	Created by American financier George Soros, this institute has worked in Samara since 1994. The organization works with local NGOs to run educational advising centers, textbook programs, and Internet centers; OSI also administers a grant program for civil society projects.
Technical Assistance to the Commonwealth of Independent States (TACIS)	Since 1992, TACIS, a European Union organization, has advised local officials on policy making and supported NGO activity. It has also helped create a business communications center, a wholesale agricultural market, and a medical service in Samara.
United States Peace Corps	Peace Corps volunteers have worked with local NGOs in Samara since 1993, and they have helped create a business center, an educational advising office, and an institute celebrating American culture.

Osh

Aga Khan Educational Program	Since 1997, this program has built a private school in the region and supported Osh State University by providing training and technical equipment.
Doctors Without Borders	This organization runs programs related to venereal diseases, mainly syphilis.
Foundation for International Community Assistance	This American organization provides loans to groups of women to help alleviate poverty. The women establish and run businesses. The organization began working in the oblast in 1995 and gave its first loan in 1996.
German Technical Agency	This German organization has run development programs in Osh oblast.
Mercy Corps International	Since 1995, this U.S. group has worked through local NGOs to provide rice and oil to individuals in return for work. The organization has also lent money to private farmers' organizations so that they can provide services to individual farmers. Mercy Corps provides assistance to local NGOs that focus on community development, and it runs a microcredit program for women.
Osh Institute for Western Education	Begun in 1995 by an American couple, this school offers an English-based certification program in business and computers. The couple also established a medical clinic.
Pharmacists Without Borders	Beginning in 1996, this organization started providing medical assistance in Osh oblast.
Soros Foundation Resource Center	The center opened in 1995, and it runs a grant program for youths to start clubs. It also works with schools and NGOs on educational and health programs. The center serves as an educational advising office as well.
Technical Assistance to the Commonwealth of Independent States (TACIS)	TACIS worked from 1995 to 1997 in Osh oblast supporting livestock breeding and providing credit for agricultural goods.

(continued)

TABLE B.5 *(continued)*

UNESCO/USIS Media Resource Center	Since the mid-1990s, the center has offered training seminars for media outlets, provided computer training, and made office equipment available to journalists.
United Nations Development Programme (UNDP) Poverty Alleviation Project	In 1995, the UNDP began a credit-lending program with local NGOs. The NGOs review business plans and administer loans to groups of people who grow crops, raise animals, or sew, for example.
United Nations High Commissioner for Refugees (UNHCR)	UNHCR opened an office in Osh in 1995. It works with local NGOs on community development programs, such as construction of a village center and distribution of roofing materials to refugees. The organization also helped the government establish a refugee office in the oblast.
United States Peace Corps	Since 1993, Peace Corps volunteers have assisted local NGOs in addition to teaching English or business. Volunteers have worked with an NGO resource center, a community development group, a charity for children, and farmers' organizations.
Naryn	
Counterpart International	This U.S. organization opened an office in Naryn in 1997, and it supports NGOs by training leaders, organizing roundtable discussions, and providing access to office equipment.
Helvetas	In the mid-1990s, this Swiss organization established a business center that provides advice, credit, and marketing assistance. Helvetas also runs a program to encourage women to create businesses.
Pharmacists Without Borders	This organization distributes medicine to local hospitals and monitors its use.
Technical Assistance to the Commonwealth of Independent States (TACIS)	Since 1994, TACIS has helped farmers establish associations, created an agricultural business center, and shared technical skills with farmers.
Turkish School	Nearly 200 male students study in this school from the 7th through the 11th grade. Turkish and Kyrgyz teachers instruct the students, and a Turkish firm funds the school.
United Nations Development Programme/United Nations Volunteer Programme	Since the mid-1990s, these programs have trained local NGOs to create and run credit and savings banks.
United States Peace Corps	Since 1993, Peace Corps volunteers have taught English in the province and completed projects on the side. Projects have included working with a local NGO to support a kindergarten.

Note: This table provides a sample of the programs run by these organizations. Many of them have a large number of projects. Besides the organizations listed, other groups provide periodic humanitarian assistance to Kyrgyzstani regions but do not have permanent representatives in the provinces. For example, Mercy Corps International has donated goods to Osh and Naryn.

Sources: The information in this table is drawn from interviews I conducted with foreign groups in each region, materials provided by the organizations, and, in a few cases, electronic mail communications with representatives in the regions. Interviews with local NGO leaders and government officials and conversations with citizens corroborated the foreign representatives' accounts. I focused on organizations that maintain a permanent representative in a region.

democracy promoters are also not the catalyst for greater activism in Osh. Although there are foreign development groups in both Osh and Naryn, the international organizations arrived earlier and are more numerous, per capita, in Naryn relative to Osh. By the end of 1994, approximately 50 percent of the international groups that have had a presence in Naryn had already begun their projects versus only 15 percent in Osh.[24] Based on its population, Osh oblast should have at least five times as many foreign organizations as Naryn. Yet, Osh has fewer than twice as many international groups. Basically, Naryn oblast is saturated with foreign civic development organizations, yet harassment and self-censorship are more common than in Osh.

---

[24] In both regions, international organizations have run similar programs, and the first projects to encourage civic activism were initiated in 1994 in each oblast. In Naryn, TACIS began helping farmers organize unions. In Osh, the United Nations Educational, Scientific, and Cultural Organization (UNESCO) and the U.S. Information Service established a resource center for journalists.

Appendix C

List of Interviews

Table C.1 provides a list of the interviews I conducted. In addition to the groups noted in the table, I spoke with businesspeople and average citizens. I interviewed businesspeople who were activists, and they are included in the appropriate categories in the table. I also had informal conversations with other businesspeople who were not activists but whom I met while I lived in each region. Similarly, I spoke with average citizens, such as members of the families with whom I lived and their neighbors and friends. I did not enumerate these conversations with businesspeople or average citizens.

TABLE C.1. *Tally of Interviews*

	Samara	Ul'ianovsk	Osh	Naryn	Bishkek	Moscow
Journalists and heads of state and independent media outlets	9	13	10	8	0	0
Political and civic NGO members and leaders	18	15	11	12	1	0
Unsuccessful candidates for oblast office	6	4	3	3	0	0
Deputies in oblast parliaments (successful candidates)	4	7	5	6	0	0
Officials in the oblast administration	2	2	3	2	0	0
Representatives of the electoral commission for oblast elections	1	1	0	0	1	0
Observers of elections to oblast offices[a]	1	1	2	2	0	0
Civil servants (legislative, legal, economic, and NGO experts)	5	5	5	8	0	0
Representatives to/of the oblasts (presidential, parliamentary)	7	2	5	3	0	0
Representatives of international NGOs and GOs	6	0	10	7	3	4
Individuals who provided background information[b]	4	3	1	1	19	1
TOTAL INTERVIEWS[c]	63	53	55	52	24	5

Notes: I also interviewed businesspeople in the regions. They held other positions, such as serving as a leader of an NGO or a media outlet. They are not listed separately in this table. I also had informal conversations with other businesspeople and average citizens.

[a] Election observers include members of electoral commissions, official observers, and journalists who covered the polls.

[b] Three individuals in Samara provided insight into the NGO community in the oblast, and one individual provided background information about international groups in the province. In Ul'ianovsk, two individuals provided information about the lack of foreign groups in the oblast, and one gave an overview of the business climate. One individual in Osh provided insight into the media environment in the region. In Naryn, I interviewed an individual who headed a *raion* electoral commission for national elections, and she offered a comparison of the national and oblast elections and the work of commissions for each. Nineteen scholars, civil servants, and foreign consultants in Bishkek provided information about regional politics, and one scholar of regional politics in Moscow provided information. The input from the 19 individuals in Bishkek was important in initiating the study, because little published information about regional politics in Kyrgyzstan existed at the time.

[c] I interviewed a total of 53 people for Samara, 55 people for Ul'ianovsk, 53 people for Osh, and 48 people for Naryn, as well as the 19 individuals located in Bishkek and the 5 in Moscow. Some people in each oblast had more than one position, so they gave more than one interview. For example, in Samara, four individuals were both representatives of NGOs and unsuccessful candidates. At a few interviews, more than one person was present. For example, for an interview about NGO registration in Ul'ianovsk, two government registration clerks were present.

Appendix D

Measurement of Eight Guarantees of Democracy

Chapters 3 and 4 provided an overview of how I evaluated the extent of democracy in each province. This appendix offers details about that process as well as additional findings – information about media ownership, number of NGOs, and percentage of the vote that winners received in electoral races. The eight guarantees are in the order in which they appear in Chapter 4.

ALTERNATIVE SOURCES OF INFORMATION

My first task in evaluating alternative sources of information was to identify major outlets of local political and economic news in each province. I began by reviewing media registries, purchasing periodicals at kiosks, reading television guides, watching television, and listening to the radio. From this, I compiled a list of the main state and independent newspapers and broadcasting companies in each region. My list, in Table D.1, includes all the "serious" media outlets. Among print media alone, there are 557 outlets registered in Samara and 135 outlets registered in Ul'ianovsk.[1] But few of these provide political or economic news, and most are tabloids. Moreover, the number of media outlets does not reflect the degree to which the right to provide

---

[1] The statistics were reported in "Vperedi Rossii vsei," *Samaraskoe obozrenie*, January 19, 1998, 5.

TABLE D.I. *Sources of Provincial News*

	Media Type	Name of Outlet
Samara	State newspapers	*Volzhskaia kommuna, Samarskie izvestiia*
	Independent newspapers	*Samarskoe obozrenie*
	State broadcasting firms	State Teleradio Company
	Independent broadcasting firms	SKAT-TV, RIO
Ul'ianovsk	State newspapers	*Ul'ianovskaia pravda, Narodnaia gazeta, Emet*
	Independent newspapers	*Simbirskii kur'er, Simbirskie gubernskie vedomosti, Otkrytaia gazeta*
	State broadcasting firms	Volga
	Independent broadcasting firms	Simbirsk-Efir, Gubernskii kanal, Evroproekt
Osh	State newspapers	*Osh zhangirigi, Ush sadosi, EkhOsha*
	Independent newspapers	*Mezon*
	State broadcasting firms	State Teleradio Company
	Independent broadcasting firms	Osh TV, ALMAZ
Naryn	State newspapers	*Tengir too*
	Independent newspapers	none
	State broadcasting firms	Naryn Oblast Radio, Naryn Oblast Television Station
	Independent broadcasting firms	none

alternative information can be exercised. A publication or broadcast is of little use to democracy if it only repeats the government line.

With few exceptions,[2] these media outlets are provincial institutions – not city, county, or national organizations. Most cities and counties in these four regions do have at least one newspaper. However, local governments typically own them, so these publications are not

---

[2] *Simbirskie gubernskie vedomosti* is part of an interregional company. Volga receives federal as well as oblast funds and broadcasts in neighboring regions also. *Mezon* is a republican company but it is based in Osh and focuses on news useful to Uzbeks in Kyrgyzstan, most of whom live in Osh oblast. Almaz is a financially independent branch of a republican station.

alternative sources of information. In a few regions of Russia, the government newspaper of a provincial capital does provide an outside view of provincial politics because the provincial governor and mayor of the capital are in disagreement.

Some national media outlets have correspondents in regions, but even these companies rarely cover oblast politics. Most of the correspondents also work for regional or local media outlets, so they submit stories to the national media infrequently. Moreover, these local and national outlets do not necessarily have large clienteles. Particularly in Kyrgyzstan, national newspapers and broadcast signals do not reach some distant *raions*. In Naryn oblast, for example, the national newspaper *Slovo Kyrgyzstana* sells only about 250 papers.

The independent media outlets in the three regions are independent in the sense that they are not part of a government budget and no government entity owns controlling shares in them. Most of these media outlets have no government ownership and receive no government funds. A couple have sold a small number of shares to a government institution, and one has won a government grant. Several have allowed a government institution to pay for airtime for public announcements or public service programming, such as a review of regional legislative work. Information about ownership comes from my interviews with media representatives, their competitors, media observers, and media reports. Although claims that such information is proprietary made data collection difficult, Table D.2 (see pp. 224–225) provides a nearly complete picture of independent media ownership and financing.

Once I identified the sources of provincial news in the regions and distinguished between state and independent entities, I conducted interviews with at least one representative, and in many cases more than one, from each independent and state media outlet. Representatives included editors-in-chief, presidents of broadcasting companies, and journalists.

FREEDOM TO FORM AND JOIN ORGANIZATIONS

Before I began my fieldwork, I did not know that only groups engaged in political activities faced harassment, so I started to evaluate the freedom to form and join organizations by examining all nongovernmental groups. Identifying all NGOs is difficult, in part because not all NGOs register with the state. To compensate for this, I also relied on the

records of local and foreign NGO support centers, telephone directories, and information obtained from the media, political activists,
and government officials. State registration lists and telephone directories occasionally include defunct, inactive, or governmental groups,
so this numerical estimate of NGOs is inexact. My list appears in
Table D.3 (see p. 226).

From this list, I then interviewed leaders and some members of
all the political organizations that were independent of the government and active at one time. By "political" I mean political parties
and movements and human- and legal-rights organizations. I excluded
some groups that did not meet these criteria based on information they
had provided to the state or to NGO support centers. I excluded other
groups after conducting interviews with their representatives. This process narrowed the count to 12 groups in Samara, 9 in Ul'ianovsk (one of
which is defunct), 6 in Osh, and 1 defunct party in Naryn. Groups that
developed or merged into other groups are not counted separately. For
example, in Samara, numerous leftist groups formed when the Communist Party was outlawed in 1991, but they reunited as the KPRF
once the ban was lifted. I was unable to pose questions related to risk-
taking to one party because of time constraints, so that group is not
included in Table 4.3 about harassment and self-censorship.

In addition to the political organizations, I conducted interviews
with a sample of active, nonpolitical NGOs in each region. I randomly
sampled from the list in Table D.3, selecting again when a group proved
to be inactive or governmental. I interviewed nonpolitical groups until
the total number of NGOs I interviewed in a region reached approximately 15.

ELIGIBILITY FOR PUBLIC OFFICE AND RIGHT OF POLITICAL
LEADERS TO COMPETE FOR SUPPORT

In order to evaluate eligibility for public office and the right of political
leaders to compete for support, I had to overcome two challenges: the
lack of information about candidates in Kyrgyzstan and the difficulty of
finding losing and "discouraged" candidates. Newspapers in Osh and
Naryn did not publish biographies of candidates as did their Russian
counterparts, so I had to rely on interviews with samples of losing
and winning candidates. Had I interviewed all 147 candidates in Osh
and 61 candidates in Naryn, I would not have had the resources to

TABLE D.2. *Ownership and Financing of Independent Media*

Samara oblast

Samarskoe obozrenie

This newspaper is self-financed, although two sets of businesspeople have invested in the media outlet since its inception. The staff would not reveal the identities of the businesspeople but confirmed that they are not government officials. The newspaper is considered the most objective and serious among the political opposition.

SKAT-TV

SKAT-TV is a joint-stock company that earns income through advertising. The president of the firm owns 15 percent of the company's stock – the highest percentage of ownership among individual investors. Nearly 50 percent of the shares are owned by employees of the firm. The oblast administration owns two percent. The president sold shares for interest-free credit because of financial difficulties when he created the company in 1990. Additional shareholders include a cable factory, a construction firm, and a bank. The firm also received a grant from the international nonprofit organization Internews to share reports with other media outlets over the Internet.

RIO

This television and radio company is self-financed, and the staff holds 61 percent of the shares. A competitor alleges that the governor has close ties to the president of RIO, although the company holds the controlling packet of shares. The firm has a contract with the Samara city administration for a specific program, as it does with a tourist company. RIO also won a competition and received a grant from the central government to acquire a new office.

Ul'ianovsk oblast

Simbirskii kur'er

Simbirskii kur'er pays its expenses through advertising, subscriptions, and sales at kiosks. The paper does not make a profit, and journalists receive very low salaries, although they are paid on time.

Simbirskie gubernskie vedomosti

This newspaper is self-financed and is part of an interregional corporation that also owns a television station and *Arbus*, a children's magazine. It has divisions in Moscow, Samara, Nizhegorod, Murmansk, Saratov, and St. Petersburg, among other regions. Moreover, the corporation owns the controlling share in a firm that distributes periodicals to stores and kiosks, according to a competitor. The newspaper's competitors also allege that the newspaper and governor did have a friendly relationship until correspondents began writing about the governor's misuse of funds.

Otkrytaia gazeta	This newspaper is self-financed and is part of the firm RIA Optima, which also has a business magazine and a directory.
Simbirsk-Efir	This company includes television, cable, and radio stations and is financed through advertising and shareholders, including the Ul'ianovsk Automobile Factory.
Gubernskii kanal	Although this broadcast company does not receive funds from the regional government, the oblast administration is one of its few shareholders. The number of shares was not available. For this reason, Gubernskii kanal should perhaps be considered independent or possibly quasi-independent. Other shareholders include Inkombank. Although cooperative, the head of this media company was short on time, so I was able to pose only two-thirds of my questions. Therefore, the experiences of this media outlet are not included in Table 4.2 in Chapter 4.
Evroproekt	This broadcast firm is self-financed through advertising and related businesses such as pagers. Shareholders are a variety of businesspeople.
Osh oblast	
Mezon	Half of the funding for this newspaper comes from earnings through advertisements paid for by candidates during elections and public service announcements paid for by the government. The founders, including the nongovernmental Uzbek National Cultural Center and a private scientific industrial firm, provide the rest of the funds. The newspaper has divisions in Dzhalal-Abad oblast and Andizhan (Uzbekistan).
Osh TV	This television station is self-financed, earning income from paid programming by candidates and businesses and paid congratulatory announcements. The station also received a grant from the Soros Foundation.
ALMAZ	This radio station is part of a republican radio company, but it is financially independent of the republican firm. The station earns money from broadcasting paid congratulatory messages, music orders, and business and electoral candidates' advertisements. The republican company has provided only technical equipment.

Sources: This information comes from my interviews with members of the media and their publications and broadcasts. Interviews with government officials and businesspeople and conversations with average citizens corroborated the information. Details about SKAT-TV's credit and shareholders are drawn from two additional sources: "Patriarkh televideniia Nikolai Fomenko," *Samarskoe obozrenie,* January 19, 1998, 12, 26; U.S. Department of State, *SKAT-TV: Getting the Most from Media Training* (Washington, DC: U.S. Department of State). Available at http://www.internetelite.ru/samarari/english/story.phtml?pic=07. Details about RIO's grant come from "'RIO' bogateet i zapuskaet ezhenedel'nuiu analiticheskuiu programmu," *Samarskoe obozrenie,* January 19, 1998, 4.

TABLE D.3. *Nongovernmental Organizations*

Types of Activity	Russia		Kyrgyzstan	
	Samara	Ul'ianovsk	Osh	Naryn
Sports, games, hobbies	319	83	15	4
Culture, history	30	7	7	5
Education	23	14	9	0
Ethnic	44	17	12	0[b]
Science, art, research	71	11	1	1
Ecology	28	9	14	0
Charity, social development	130	36	86	11
Health, illness	113	32	28	4
Religion, spiritual matters[a]	263	185	14	0
Professions, unions	303	173	117	17
Soldiers, veterans	111	35	15	0
Youth	60	19	11	0
Women	13	7	16	3
Senior citizens	5	1	0	0
Consumer rights	25	7	2	0
Politics	127	74	15	3
Unclear	153	18	18	1
TOTAL	1818	728	380	49
TOTAL PER 10,000 PEOPLE	5.5	4.9	3.0	2.0

Notes: Organizations often fell under more than one category; however, by using the decision rules that follow, I counted each organization only once. The sign ">" should be read "takes priority over." For example, if a group helps both veterans and senior citizens, I counted it under the category "Soldiers and veterans" and not under "Senior citizens." These rules are arbitrary, but because I am using them consistently across the regions, this is of little importance.
Sports, games, and hobbies > Youth.
Veterans > Senior citizens.
Health and illness > Youth.
Politics > Women.
Veterans, Youth > Charity.
Ecology > Culture, history; politics.
Data are from 1997.
[a] "Religion, spiritual matters" does not include places of worship for Osh and Naryn. The category includes only religious organizations.
[b] Although I included ethnic groups in the list for Naryn, the oblast is 98 percent Kyrgyz.

evaluate the other democratic guarantees. It is also likely that it would have taken years to find all the losing candidates.

Nonetheless, I was able to find losing candidates in each of the four regions by living in each place for an extended period of time and "keeping my ear to the ground." In addition to my local hosts and friends in each region, NGO leaders, media representatives, government officials, and media publications and broadcasts were helpful in locating losing and potential candidates. Whereas I randomly selected winning candidates to interview,[3] I interviewed only those losing candidates I could find. Thus, it is likely that I oversampled for notable losing candidates in both regions and party candidates in Russian provinces, where parties are more numerous. I acknowledge this by concluding that it is the most viable candidates and the candidates in key races who typically face harassment. Individuals who are already famous or who have a political group to back them pose a greater threat than unknown, unconnected candidates.

FREEDOM OF EXPRESSION AND RIGHT TO VOTE

Whereas the preceding democratic guarantees focus on limited groups – media outlets, NGOs, and candidates – freedom of expression and the right to vote potentially engage all adult citizens. For this reason, mass survey data would have been useful to enable the public to weigh in on how easily they can exercise these rights. Unfortunately, at the time of my research, no surveys had been conducted that enabled a regional-level analysis of these topics. Within Ul'ianovsk and Samara, survey work was being done; however, the questionnaires did not address these issues. In Kyrgyzstan, in the 1990s survey research was almost nonexistent, with the exception of some economic surveys conducted by international organizations. By this period, survey costs had risen substantially, making it impractical to conduct a survey that would help evaluate only a few of the eight democratic guarantees.

As described in Chapter 3, citizens communicate with officials through visits, letters, and phone calls. The number of letters received per month by an individual legislator ranged from 20 to 50 in Samara and five to ten in Ul'ianovsk. This difference reflects the fact that the constituencies in Ul'ianovsk are half the size. Deputies in Osh receive one or two letters per month, and those in Naryn receive one or no letters per month. The number of letters staff members receive depends

---

[3] Only one winner, a regional parliamentary deputy in Ul'ianovsk, declined to speak with me.

on their responsibilities. In the Russian oblasts, some members of the governor's staff receive 90 letters per month, whereas others receive only a few each month. Officials in Osh recalled receiving an average of 30 to 40 letters from voters each month. In Naryn, officials received anywhere from five to 150 letters per month.

These numbers are based on the deputies' own estimates, the estimates of members of the mass media, and my own observation of contact between citizens and government officials. As in the case of the estimates of visits, data collected by the Gubernskaia duma suggest that the Samara legislators' estimates of letters may be inflated. According to the Duma data, deputies received 710 letters in 1997, meaning that on average each legislator received two letters per month. However, letters that deputies received at their other workplaces or homes are likely not included in these figures.[4]

Phone calls are more difficult to enumerate because deputies and administration officials tend not to record them, and often they ask citizens to put their requests in writing or to come in person. In Samara, a deputy who holds a prominent state position estimated that he and his assistants receive approximately 12 calls per month. In Ul'ianovsk, deputies reported 5 to 60 calls from voters each month. Osh deputies receive one to 20 calls per month. A number of deputies in Osh noted that often a local leader, such as the head of a village council or block committee, would call on behalf of a large group of citizens. Deputies I interviewed in Naryn received 2 to 60 calls per month. Top officials in the four provinces also received calls from residents, and the number varied with the officials' positions.

To evaluate the frequency of protest in each region, two research assistants and I reviewed national and foreign articles about the four provinces. For all four provinces, we used the U.S. publication *Radio Free Europe/Radio Liberty* from 1995 to 1998. For the Russian provinces, we also read the U.S. publication *IEWS Russian Regional Report* (1996–1998) and online versions of the national newspapers *Izvestiia* (1995–1998), *Nezavisimaia gazeta* (1996–1998), and *Obshchaia gazeta* (1996–1998). We also used the foreign e-mail report *Kyrgyz News* (1995–1998) and the online version of the national newspaper *Vechernii Bishkek* (1998) for the Kyrgyzstani regions.

---

[4] "Vestnik Samarskoi gubernskoi dumy," 1 (January, 1998), 26.

TABLE D.4. *Outcomes in Russian Regional Parliamentary Elections*

Electoral District	Samara		Ul'ianovsk	
	Number of Candidates	Percentage Winner Received	Number of Candidates	Percentage Winner Received
1	12	20	3	47
2	8	52	3	48
3	10	34	2	48
4	13	33	5	22
5	10	24	3	34
6	11	31	3	29
7	6	32	3	40
8	9	65	3	43
9	3	36	3	60
10	8	73	4	27
11	5	42	5	15
12	7	55	6	17
13	8	44	4	49
14	4	38	4	10
15	2	78	2	34
16	3	64	7	17
17	3	76	6	16
18	3	39	5	18
19	3	63	3	13
20	5	40	4	22
21	4	52	8	15
22	7	44	7	17
23	3	60	7	14
24	6	52	7	23
25	5	62	7	13

Note: Percentages are rounded.

Sources: Data are based on official election results published in newspapers in each oblast.

Our starting point was limited by the holdings in the online archives and my own collections. Our focus was on national and foreign reports because independent media do not exist in each region. However, I did review editions of regional independent newspapers I was able to obtain from media archives in each region. Each research assistant reviewed the different news sources and coded articles she believed described protest in the region. I then reviewed their findings and compiled a list of protests. We were interested only in those protests directed against the government, not those directed against firms' managers.

FREE AND FAIR ELECTIONS

Candidates in the provincial elections did not sweep the elections. This suggests that violations in ballot counting were not severe. Table D.4 (see p. 229) indicates the outcomes for the parliamentary elections in Samara and Ul'ianovsk. Similar comprehensive data were not available for Osh and Naryn.

INSTITUTIONS FOR MAKING GOVERNMENT POLICIES DEPEND ON VOTERS' PREFERENCES

Whereas the design and operation of formal institutions are relatively easy to measure, effectiveness is more difficult to evaluate at a reasonable cost. Deputies and administration officials I interviewed and citizens I encountered provided their own evaluations. It would have been helpful, however, to have mass survey data on this question. Surveys had not been conducted on this question in these provinces, and, as described in the section on freedom of expression and the right to vote, conducting my own surveys would have been prohibitively expensive. The impact of not having survey data is minimal, however, because the focus of the book is on the process of democracy, not the outcome.

References

English Language Sources

Appel, Hilary. "Voucher Privatisation in Russia: Structural Consequences and Mass Response in the Second Period of Reform." *Europe–Asia Studies* 49, no. 8 (1997), 1433–1449.

B., L. ""Persecution" of Media Decried in Ulyanovsk." *RFE/RL Newsline* (January 29, 1998).

Bacon, Elizabeth E. *Central Asians under Russian Rule: A Study in Culture Change.* Ithaca, NY: Cornell University Press, 1966.

Balzer, Harley. "Managed Pluralism: Vladimir Putin's Emerging Regime." *Post-Soviet Affairs* 19, no. 3 (2003), 189–227.

Barnes, Andrew. "Russia's New Business Groups and State Power." *Post-Soviet Affairs* 19, no. 2 (2003), 154–186.

Beer, Caroline. "Assessing the Consequences of Electoral Democracy: Subnational Legislative Change in Mexico." *Comparative Politics* 33, no. 4 (2001), 421–440.

Belin, Laura, and Peter Rutland. "Regional Press Fights Political Control." *Transition* 1, no. 17 (1995).

Bellin, Eva. "Contingent Democrats: Industrialists, Labor, and Democratization in Late-Developing Countries." *World Politics* 52, no. 2 (2000), 175–205.

Bellin, Eva. *Stalled Democracy: Capital, Labor and the Paradox of State-Sponsored Development.* Ithaca, NY: Cornell University Press, 2002.

Bienen, Henry, and Jeffrey Herbst. "The Relationship between Political and Economic Reform in Africa." *Comparative Politics* 29, no. 1 (1996), 23–42.

Boix, Carles, and Susan C. Stokes. "Endogenous Democratization." *World Politics* 55, no. 4 (2003), 517–549.

Bollen, Kenneth. "Issues in the Comparative Measurement of Political Democracy." *American Sociological Review* 45, no. 3 (1980), 370–390.

Bollen, Kenneth. "Political Democracy: Conceptual and Measurement Traps." *Studies in Comparative International Development* 25, no. 1 (1990), 7–24.

Brader, Ted, and Joshua A. Tucker. "The Emergence of Mass Partisanship in Russia, 1993–1996." *American Journal of Political Science* 45, no. 1 (2001), 69–83.

Bratton, Michael, Robert B. Mattes, and Emmanuel Gyimah-Boadi. *Public Opinion, Democracy, and Market Reform in Africa.* New York: Cambridge University Press, 2005.

Breslauer, George W. *Gorbachev and Yeltsin as Leaders.* New York: Cambridge University Press, 2002.

Brown, Archie. *The Gorbachev Factor.* New York: Oxford University Press, 1996.

Bulletin of the National Bank of the Kyrgyz Republic, 1, no. 13 (1997).

Bunce, V. "Democratization and Economic Reform." *Annual Review of Political Science* 4 (2001), 43–65.

Bunce, Valerie. "Comparative Democratization: Big and Bounded Generalizations." *Comparative Political Studies* 33, nos. 6/7 (2000), 703–734.

Bunce, Valerie. "Comparative Democratization: Lessons from Russia and the Postcommunist World." In *After the Collapse of Communism: Comparative Lessons of Transitions,* edited by Michael McFaul and Kathryn Stoner-Weiss, 207–231. New York: Cambridge University Press, 2005.

Bunce, Valerie. "Regional Differences in Democratization: The East Versus the South." *Post-Soviet Affairs* 14, no. 3 (1998), 187–211.

Bunce, Valerie. "Should Transitologists Be Grounded?" *Slavic Review* 54, no. 1 (1995), 111–127.

Burgerman, Susan. *Moral Victories: How Activists Provoke Multilateral Action.* Ithaca, NY: Cornell University Press, 2001.

Burns, Nancy. *The Formation of American Local Governments: Private Values in Public Institutions.* Oxford: Oxford University Press, 1994.

Business Information Service for the Newly Independent States. *General Investment Opportunities in Osh Oblast.* Washington, DC: Business Information Service for the Newly Independent States, 1997. Available at http://bisnis.doc.gov/bisnis/country/kgosh4.htm.

Business Information Service for the Newly Independent States. *Samara Regional Report.* Washington, DC: Business Information Service for the Newly Independent States, 1999. Available at http://bisnis.doc.gov/bisnis/country/991101samararegrep.htm.

Campbell, Angus, Philip Converse, E. Miller, and Donald Stokes. *The American Voter.* New York: Wiley, 1960.

Carothers, Thomas. *Aiding Democracy Abroad: The Learning Curve.* Washington, DC: Carnegie Endowment for International Peace, 1999.

Carothers, Thomas. "Aiding Post-communist Societies: A Better Way?" *Problems of Post-communism* 43, no. 5 (1996), 15–24.

Carothers, Thomas. "Democracy Assistance: The Question of Strategy." *Democratization* 4, no. 3 (1997), 109–132.

Carothers, Thomas. "The End of the Transition Paradigm." *Journal of Democracy* 13, no. 1 (2002), 5–21.

Carothers, Thomas, and Marina Ottaway. "The Burgeoning World of Civil Society Aid." In *Funding Virtue: Civil Society Aid and Democracy Promotion*, edited by Marina Ottaway and Thomas Carothers, 3–17. Washington, DC: Carnegie Endowment for International Peace, 2000.

Centeno, M. A. "Blood and Debt: War and Taxation in Nineteenth-Century Latin America." *American Journal of Sociology* 102, no. 6 (1997), 1565–1605.

Chavez, Rebecca Bill. "The Construction of the Rule of Law in Argentina: A Tale of Two Provinces." *Comparative Politics* 35, no. 4 (2003), 417–437.

Chehabi, H. E., and Juan J. Linz. "A Theory of Sultanism 1: A Type of Non-democratic Rule." In *Sultanistic Regimes*, edited by H. E. Chehabi and Juan J. Linz, 3–25. Baltimore: Johns Hopkins University Press, 1998.

Chong, Dennis. *Collective Action and the Civil Rights Movement*. Chicago: University of Chicago Press, 1991.

Clark, Ann Marie. *Diplomacy of Conscience: Amnesty International and Changing Human Rights Norms*. Princeton, NJ: Princeton University Press, 2001.

Collier, David, and Steven Levitsky. "Democracy with Adjectives: Conceptual Innovation in Comparative Research." *World Politics* 49, no. 3 (1997), 430–451.

Collier, David, and Steven Levitsky. "Democracy 'with Adjectives': Conceptual Innovation in Comparative Research." In *Working Paper Series: The Helen Kellogg Institute for International Studies*. Notre Dame, IN: University of Notre Dame, 1996.

Collins, Kathleen. "Clans, Pacts, and Politics in Central Asia." *Journal of Democracy* 13, no. 3 (2002), 137–152.

Collins, Kathleen. "The Logic of Clan Politics: Evidence from Central Asian Trajectories." *World Politics* 56, no. 2 (2004), 224–261.

Collins, Kathleen. "The Political Role of Clans in Central Asia." *Comparative Politics* 35, no. 2 (2003), 171–190.

Colton, Timothy J. *Transitional Citizens: Voters and What Influences Them in the New Russia*. Cambridge, MA: Harvard University Press, 2000.

Colton, Timothy J., and Jerry F. Hough. *Growing Pains: Russian Democracy and the Election of 1993*. Washington, DC: Brookings Institution Press, 1998.

Colton, Timothy J., and Michael McFaul. *Popular Choice and Managed Democracy: The Russian Elections of 1999 and 2000*. Washington, DC: Brookings Institution Press, 2003.

Coppedge, Michael, and Wolfgang Reinicke. "Measuring Polyarchy." *Studies in Comparative International Development* 25, no. 1 (1990), 51–72.

Coulloudon, Virginie. "Crime and Corruption after Communism: The Criminalization of Russia's Political Elite." *East European Constitutional Review* 6, no. 4 (1997).

Crowley, Stephen. *Hot Coal, Cold Steel: Russian and Ukrainian Workers from the End of the Soviet Union to the Post-communist Transformations.* Ann Arbor: University of Michigan Press, 1997.

Dahl, Robert. *After the Revolution? Authority in a Good Society.* Rev. ed. New Haven, CT: Yale University Press, 1990.

Dahl, Robert. *Democracy and Its Critics.* New Haven, CT: Yale University Press, 1989.

Dahl, Robert. *Democracy, Liberty, and Equality.* Oslo: Norwegian University Press, 1986.

Dahl, Robert. "Development and Democratic Culture." In *Consolidating the Third Wave Democracies*, edited by Larry Diamond, 34–39. Baltimore: Johns Hopkins University Press, 1997.

Dahl, Robert. *Polyarchy: Participation and Opposition.* New Haven, CT: Yale University Press, 1971.

Dahl, Robert. *A Preface to Economic Democracy.* Berkeley: University of California Press, 1985.

Dahl, Robert. *Toward Democracy – a Journey: Reflections, 1940–1997.* Berkeley: University of California, 1997.

Dahl, Robert. *Who Governs? Democracy and Power in an American City.* New Haven, CT: Yale University Press, 1989.

Dahl, Robert, and Charles Lindblom. *Politics, Economics, and Welfare: Planning and Politico-Economic Systems Resolved into Basic Social Processes.* New York: Harper, 1953.

Dawisha, Karen, and Bruce Parrott. *Russia and the New States of Eurasia: The Politics of Upheaval.* Cambridge: Cambridge University Press, 1994.

Deutsch, Karl W. "Social Mobilization and Political Development." *American Political Science Review* 55, no. 3 (1961), 493–514.

Diamond, Larry. "Introduction: In Search of Consolidation." In *Consolidating the Third Wave Democracies*, edited by Larry Diamond, xv–xlix. Baltimore: Johns Hopkins University Press, 1997.

Diamond, Larry. "Is the Third Wave Over?" *Journal of Democracy* 7, no. 3 (1996), 20–37.

Diamond, Larry. "Thinking About Hybrid Regimes." *Journal of Democracy* 13, no. 2 (2002), 21–35.

Di Palma, Giuseppe. *To Craft Democracies: An Essay on Democratic Transitions.* Berkeley: University of California Press, 1990.

Dogan, Mattei, and John Higley. *Elites, Crises, and the Origins of Regimes.* Lanham, MD: Rowman and Littlefield Publishers, 1998.

East West Institute. *Who Are the Donor Regions?* [e-mail service]. Russian Regional Report. New York: East West Institute, May 27, 1999.

Eaton, Kent. "Designing Subnational Institutions: Regional and Municipal Reforms in Postauthoritarian Chile." *Comparative Political Studies* 37, no. 2 (2004), 218–244.

Ekiert, Grzegorz. "Peculiarities of Post-communist Politics: The Case of Poland." *Studies in Comparative Communism* 25, no. 4 (1992), 341–361.

Ekiert, Grzegorz, and Jan Kubik. "Contentious Politics in New Democracies: East Germany, Hungary, Poland, and Slovakia, 1989–93." *World Politics* 50, no. 4 (1998), 547–581.

Ekiert, Grzegorz, and Jan Kubik. *Rebellious Civil Society: Popular Protest and Democratic Consolidation in Poland, 1989–1993*. Ann Arbor: University of Michigan Press, 2001.

Elazar, Daniel. *Exploring Federalism*. Tuscaloosa: University of Alabama Press, 1987.

Eldersveld, Samuel. "The Comparative Development of Local Political Systems." In *Nation, Power, and Society: Essays in Honor of Jerzy J. Wiatr*, edited by Aleksandra Jasinska-Kania and Jacek Raciborski, 343–355. Warsaw: Wydawnictwo Naukoe Scholar, 1996.

Elster, Jon. *Deliberative Democracy*. Cambridge: Cambridge University Press, 1998.

European Bank for Reconstruction and Development. *Russian Federation 1999 Country Profile*. London: European Bank for Reconstruction and Development, 1999.

European Bank for Reconstruction and Development. *Regional Venture Funds*. London: European Bank for Reconstruction and Development. Available at http://www.ebrd.com/english/opera/Country/ruso5.htm.

European Bank for Reconstruction and Development. *Russia Small Business Fund*. London: European Bank for Reconstruction and Development. Available at http://www.ebrd.com/english/opera/Country/RSBF08.htm.

Fish, M. Steven. "Conclusion: Democracy and Russian Politics." In *Russian Politics: Challenges of Democratization*, edited by Zoltan D. Barany and Robert G. Moser, 215–252. New York: Cambridge University Press, 2001.

Fish, M. Steven. *Democracy from Scratch: Opposition and Regime in the New Russian Revolution*. Princeton, NJ: Princeton University Press, 1995.

Fish, M. Steven. "Democratization's Requisites: The Postcommunist Experience." *Post-Soviet Affairs* 14, no. 3 (1998), 212–247.

Fish, M. Steven. "Islam and Authoritarianism." *World Politics* 55, no. 1 (2002), 4–37.

Fitzpatrick, Sheila. *The Russian Revolution*. 2nd ed. Oxford: Oxford University Press, 1994.

Florini, Ann. *The Third Force: The Rise of Transnational Civil Society*. Washington, DC: Carnegie Endowment for International Peace, 2000.

Fox, Jonathan. "The Difficult Transition from Clientelism to Citizenship." *World Politics* 46, no. 2 (1994), 151–184.

Freedom House. *Freedom in the World.* Freedom in the World Series. New York: Freedom House, 1978–2002.

Friedgut, Theodore H., and Jeffrey W. Hahn, eds. *Local Power and Post-Soviet Politics.* Armonk, NY: M. E. Sharpe, 1994.

Frug, Gerald. *Local Government Law.* St. Paul, MN: West, 1988.

Frye, Timothy. "Markets, Democracy, and New Private Business in Russia." *Post-Soviet Affairs* 19, no. 1 (2003), 24–45.

Frye, Timothy, and Ekaterina Zhuravskaya. "Rackets, Regulation, and the Rule of Law." *Journal of Law Economics and Organization* 16, no. 2 (2000), 478–502.

Gasiorowski, Mark. "The Political Regimes Project." In *On Measuring Democracy: Its Consequences and Concomitants,* edited by Alex Inkeles, 105–122. New Brunswick, NJ: Transaction Publishers, 1991.

Gel'man, Vladimir. "Regime Transition, Uncertainty and Prospects for Democratisation: The Politics of Russia's Regions in a Comparative Perspective." *Europe–Asia Studies* 51, no. 6 (1999), 939–956.

Gibson, James L. "The Russian Dance with Democracy." *Post-Soviet Affairs* 17, no. 2 (2001), 101–128.

Gleason, Gregory. *The Central Asian States: Discovering Independence.* Boulder, CO: Westview Press, 1997.

Golosov, G. V. "Electoral Systems and Party Formation in Russia: A Cross-Regional Analysis." *Comparative Political Studies* 36, no. 8 (2003), 912–935.

Golosov, Grigorii. *Political Parties in the Regions of Russia: Democracy Unclaimed.* Boulder, CO: Lynne Rienner Publishers, 2004.

Goodwin, Jeff. *No Other Way Out: States and Revolutionary Movements, 1945–1991.* Cambridge: Cambridge University Press, 2001.

Gorin, Sergey. "Protest Rally for Press Freedom Staged in Ulyanovsk." *Russian Regional Report* 3, no. 4 (1998).

Gurevitch, M., and J. Blumler. "Political Communications Systems and Democratic Values." In *Democracy and the Mass Media: A Collection of Essays,* edited by Judith Lichtenberg, 269–289. Cambridge: Cambridge University Press, 1990.

Gurr, Ted R. *Why Men Rebel.* Princeton, NJ: Princeton University Press, 1970.

Gutmann, Amy. "Freedom of Association: An Introductory Essay." In *Freedom of Association,* edited by Amy Gutmann, 3–32. Princeton, NJ: Princeton University Press, 1998.

Hadenius, Axel. *Democracy and Development.* Cambridge: Cambridge University Press, 1992.

Haggard, Stephan, and Robert R. Kaufman. *The Political Economy of Democratic Transitions.* Princeton, NJ: Princeton University Press, 1995.

Hagopian, Frances. *Traditional Politics and Regime Change in Brazil.* Cambridge: Cambridge University Press, 1996.

Hahn, Gordon M. "The Impact of Putin's Federative Reforms on Democratization in Russia." *Post-Soviet Affairs* 19, no. 2 (2003), 114–153.

Hale, Henry E. "Explaining Machine Politics in Russia's Regions: Economy, Ethnicity, and Legacy." *Post-Soviet Affairs* 19, no. 3 (2003), 228–263.

Hale, Henry E. "Why Not Parties? Electoral Markets, Party Substitutes, and Stalled Democratization in Russia." *Comparative Politics* 37, no. 2 (2005), 147–166.

Hanson, Philip. "Samara: A Preliminary Profile of a Russian Region and Its Adaptation to the Market." *Europe–Asia Studies* 49, no. 3 (1997), 407–429.

Hayek, Friedrich A. von. *The Road to Serfdom*. Chicago: University of Chicago Press, 1980.

Held, David. *Models of Democracy*. 2nd ed. Stanford, CA: Stanford University Press, 1996.

Heller, Patrick. "Degrees of Democracy: Some Comparative Lessons from India." *World Politics* 52, no. 4 (2000), 484–517.

Hellman, Joel S. "Winners Take All: The Politics of Partial Reform in Postcommunist Transitions." *World Politics* 50, no. 2 (1998), 203–234.

Henderson, Sarah. *Building Democracy in Contemporary Russia: Western Support for Grassroots Organizations*. Ithaca, NY: Cornell University Press, 2003.

Henderson, Sarah. "Selling Civil Society: Western Aid and the Nongovernmental Organization Sector in Russia." *Comparative Political Studies* 35, no. 2 (2002), 139–167.

Higgott, Richard A., Geoffrey R. D. Underhill, and Andreas Bieler. *Non-State Actors and Authority in the Global System*. New York: Routledge, 2000.

Higley, John, and Michael Burton. "The Elite Variable in Democratic Transitions and Breakdowns." *American Sociological Review* 54, no. 1 (1989), 17–32.

Higley, John, and Richard Gunther. *Elites and Democratic Consolidation in Latin America and Southern Europe*. Cambridge: Cambridge University Press, 1992.

Hough, Jerry. *The Soviet Union and Social Science Theory*. Cambridge, MA: Harvard University Press, 1977.

Hough, Jerry F. *The Logic of Economic Reform in Russia*. Washington, DC: Brookings Institution Press, 2001.

Howard, Marc Morjé. *The Weakness of Civil Society in Post-communist Europe*. Cambridge: Cambridge University Press, 2003.

Human Rights Watch. *Human Rights Watch World Report*. New York: Human Rights Watch, 1996.

Huntington, Samuel P. *The Clash of Civilizations and the Remaking of World Order*. New York: Simon and Schuster, 1996.

Huntington, Samuel P. *Political Order in Changing Societies*. New Haven, CT: Yale University Press, 1968.

Huntington, Samuel P. *The Third Wave: Democratization in the Late Twentieth Century*. The Julian J. Rothbaum Distinguished Lecture Series, Vol. 4. Norman: University of Oklahoma Press, 1991.

Huntington, Samuel P., and Joan M. Nelson. *No Easy Choice: Political Participation in Developing Countries*. Cambridge, MA: Harvard University Press, 1976.

Huskey, Eugene. "Kyrgyzstan: The Fate of Political Liberalization." In *Conflict, Cleavage, and Change in Central Asia and the Caucasus*, edited by Karen Dawisha and Bruce Parrott, 242–276. Cambridge: Cambridge University Press, 1997.

IEWS Russian Regional Report, selected issues.

Inkeles, Alex. "The Modernization of Man." In *Modernization: The Dynamics of Growth*, edited by Myron Weiner, 138–150. New York: Basic Books, 1966.

International Studies of Values in Politics Project. *Values and the Active Community: A Cross-National Study of the Influence of Local Leadership*. New York: Free Press, 1971.

Jacob, Betty M., Krzysztof Ostrowski, and Henry Teune. *Democracy and Local Governance: Ten Empirical Studies*. Honolulu: University of Hawai'i, 1993.

Jacobs, Andrew. "Newark Relives Day of Machine in Mayor's Race." *New York Times*, April 9, 2002, 1, 28.

Jay, Antony. *The Oxford Dictionary of Political Quotations*. Oxford: Oxford University Press, 1996.

Johnson, Chalmers A. *Revolutionary Change*. Boston: Little Brown, 1966.

Jones Luong, Pauline. *Institutional Change and Political Continuity in Post-Soviet Central Asia: Power, Perceptions, and Pacts*. Cambridge: Cambridge University Press, 2002.

Kalicki, Jan H. "Caspian Energy at the Crossroads." *Foreign Affairs* 80, no. 5 (2001), 120–134.

Kazemi, Farhad, and Augustus Richard Norton. "Hardliners and Softliners in the Middle East: Problems of Governance and the Prospects for Liberalization in Authoritarian Political Systems." In *Democracy and Its Limits: Lessons from Asia, Latin America, and the Middle East*, edited by Howard Handelman and Mark A. Tessler, 69–89. Notre Dame, IN: University of Notre Dame Press, 1999.

Keane, John. *The Media and Democracy*. Cambridge: Polity Press, 1991.

Keck, Margaret E., and Kathryn Sikkink. *Activists Beyond Borders: Advocacy Networks in International Politics*. Ithaca, NY: Cornell University Press, 1998.

Kelley, David, and Roger Donway. "Liberalism and Free Speech." In *Democracy and the Mass Media: A Collection of Essays*, edited by Judith Lichtenberg, 66–101. Cambridge: Cambridge University Press, 1990.

Kesselman, Mark, and Donald B. Rosenthal. *Local Power and Comparative Politics*. Beverly Hills, CA: Sage Publications, 1974.

Key, V. O., and Alexander Heard. *Southern Politics in State and Nation.* Knoxville: University of Tennessee Press, 1984.

Khagram, Sanjeev, James V. Riker, and Kathryn Sikkink. *Restructuring World Politics: Transnational Social Movements, Networks, and Norms.* Minneapolis: University of Minnesota Press, 2002.

Khamidov, Alisher. "Kyrgyz–Tajik Border Riots Highlight Building Inter-Ethnic Tension in Central Asia." EurasiaNet, 2003. Available at http://www.eurasianet.org/departments/insight/articles/eav010803.shtml.

King, Charles. "Post-Communism: Transition, Comparison, and the End of "Eastern Europe"." *World Politics* 53, no. 1 (2000), 143–172.

King, Gary, Robert O. Keohane, and Sidney Verba. *Designing Social Inquiry: Scientific Inference in Qualitative Research.* Princeton, NJ: Princeton University Press, 1994.

Kitschelt, Herbert. "Political Opportunity Structures and Political Protest: Antinuclear Movements in 4 Democracies." *British Journal of Political Science* 16 (1986), 57–85.

Kohli, Atul. *Democracy and Discontent: India's Growing Crisis of Governability.* Cambridge: Cambridge University Press, 1990.

Konitzer-Smirnov, A. "Incumbent Electoral Fortunes and Regional Economic Performance during Russia's 2000–2001 Regional Executive Election Cycle." *Post-Soviet Affairs* 19, no. 1 (2003), 46–79.

Kullberg, Judith, and William Zimmerman. "Liberal Elites, Socialist Masses, and Problems of Russian Democracy." *World Politics* 51, no. 3 (1999), 323–358.

Kurtz, Marcus J. "The Dilemmas of Democracy in the Open Economy: Lessons from Latin America." *World Politics* 56, no. 2 (2004), 262–302.

Kurtz, Marcus J. *Free Market Democracy and the Chilean and Mexican Countryside.* Cambridge: Cambridge University Press, 2004.

Kurtz, Marcus J. "Free Markets and Democratic Consolidation in Chile: The National Politics of Rural Transformation." *Politics and Society* 27, no. 2 (1999), 275–301.

Kyrgyz News, e-mail service, selected issues.

"Kyrgyzstan Confronted by Narcotics Nightmare as Drug Trade Booms." EurasiaNet, 2004. Available at http://www.eurasianet.org/departments/insight/articles/eav031904.shtml.

Kyrgyzstan Development Gateway Project. *Investment Projects.* Bishkek: State Committee of the Kyrgyz Republic on Foreign Investments and Economic Development, July 14, 2000. Available at http://kyrgyzinvest.org/en/economy/invest_projects.htm.

Kyrgyzstan Development Gateway Project. *Regions.* Bishkek: State Committee of the Kyrgyz Republic on Foreign Investments and Economic Development. Available at http://kyrgyzinvest.org/en/country/regions.htm.

Lamis, Alexander P. "The Two-Party South: From the 1960s to the 1990s." In *Southern Politics in the 1990s*, edited by Alexander P. Lamis, 1–49. Baton Rouge: Louisiana State University Press, 1999.

Lane, David S., and Cameron Ross. *The Transition from Communism to Capitalism: Ruling Elites from Gorbachev to Yeltsin*. 1st ed. New York: St. Martin's Press, 1999.

LaPalombara, Joseph, and Myron Weiner, eds. *Political Parties and Political Development*. Princeton, NJ: Princeton University Press, 1966.

Levitsky, Steven, and Lucan A. Way. "The Rise of Competitive Authoritarianism." *Journal of Democracy* 13, no. 2 (2002), 51–65.

Lichtenberg, Judith. "Foundations and Limits of Freedom of the Press." In *Democracy and the Mass Media: A Collection of Essays*, edited by Judith Lichtenberg, 102–135. Cambridge: Cambridge University Press, 1990.

Lichtenberg, Judith. "Introduction." In *Democracy and the Mass Media: A Collection of Essays*, edited by Judith Lichtenberg, 1–21. Cambridge: Cambridge University Press, 1990.

Lilley, Jeffrey. "Eastern Model: Democratic Norms under Assault in Russian Far East." *Far Eastern Economic Review* (April 7, 1994), 28.

Lindblom, Charles. *Politics and Markets: The World's Political Economic Systems*. New York: Basic Books, 1977.

Linz, Juan J., and Amando de Miguel. "Within-Nation Differences and Comparisons: The Eight Spains." In *Comparing Nations: The Use of Quantitative Data in Cross-National Research*, edited by Richard L. Merritt and Stein Rokkan, 267–319. New Haven, CT: Yale University Press, 1966.

Linz, Juan J., and Alfred C. Stepan. *Problems of Democratic Transition and Consolidation: Southern Europe, South America, and Post-communist Europe*. Baltimore: Johns Hopkins University Press, 1996.

Lipset, Seymour M. "The Social Requisites of Democracy Revisited: 1993 Presidential Address." *American Sociological Review* 59, no. 1 (1994), 1–22.

Lipset, Seymour M. "Some Social Requisites of Democracy: Economic Development and Political Legitimacy." *American Political Science Review* 53, no. 1 (1959), 69–105.

Lipset, Seymour M., and Stein Rokkan. *Party Systems and Voter Alignments: Cross-National Perspectives*. International Yearbook of Political Behavior Research. New York: Free Press, 1967.

Lowenthal, Abraham F. *Exporting Democracy: The United States and Latin America – Themes and Issues*. Baltimore: Johns Hopkins University Press, 1991.

Lubin, Nancy, and Barnett R. Rubin. *Calming the Ferghana Valley: Development and Dialogue in the Heart of Central Asia*. New York: Century Foundation Press, 1999.

Madison, James. *The Federalist Papers: Alexander Hamilton, James Madison, John Jay*, no. 10. New York: New American Library, 1961.

Marsh, Christopher. "Measuring and Explaining Variations in Russian Regional Democratisation." In *Russian Politics under Putin*, edited by Cameron Ross, 176–197. Manchester: Manchester University Press, 2004.

McAdam, Doug. "Conceptual Origins, Current Problems, Future Directions." In *Comparative Perspectives on Social Movements: Political Opportunities, Mobilizing Structures, and Cultural Framings*, edited by Doug McAdam, John D. McCarthy, and Mayer N. Zald, 23–40. Cambridge: Cambridge University Press, 1996.

McAuley, Mary. "Politics, Economics, and Elite Realignment in Russia: A Regional Perspective." *Soviet Economy* 8, no. 1 (1992), 46–88.

McCarthy, John D. "Constraints and Opportunities in Adopting, Adapting, and Inventing." In *Comparative Perspectives on Social Movements: Political Opportunities, Mobilizing Structures, and Cultural Framings*, edited by Doug McAdam, John D. McCarthy, and Mayer N. Zald, 141–151. Cambridge: Cambridge University Press, 1996.

McCarthy, John D., and Mayer Zald. "Resource Mobilization and Social Movements: A Partial Theory." *American Journal of Sociology* 82, no. 6 (1977), 1212–1241.

McFaul, Michael. "The Fourth Wave of Democracy *and* Dictatorship: Noncooperative Transitions in the Postcommunist World." *World Politics* 54, no. 2 (2002), 212–244.

McFaul, Michael. "Russia's Rough Ride." In *Consolidating the Third Wave Democracies*, edited by Larry Diamond, 64–94. Baltimore: Johns Hopkins University Press, 1997.

McFaul, Michael. *Russia's Unfinished Revolution: Political Change from Gorbachev to Putin*. Ithaca, NY: Cornell University Press, 2001.

McMann, Kelly M., and Nikolai V. Petrov. "A Survey of Democracy in Russia's Regions." *Post-Soviet Geography and Economics* 41, no. 3 (2000), 155–182.

Mereu, Francesca. "Defending Press Freedom No Easy Chore in Regions." *The Russia Journal*, June 24, 2000. Available at http://www.russiajournal.com/weekly/article.shtml?ad=3115.

Mettler, Suzanne. "Bringing the State Back into Civic Engagement: Policy Feedback Effects of the GI Bill for World War II Veterans." *American Political Science Review* 96, no. 2 (2002), 351–365.

Mikhailov, Valentin. "Regional Elections and Democratisation in Russia." In *Russian Politics under Putin*, edited by Cameron Ross, 198–220. Manchester: Manchester University Press, 2004.

Mill, John Stuart. *Considerations on Representative Government*. New York: Prometheus Books, 1991.

Mill, John Stuart. *On Liberty with the Subjection of Women and Chapters on Socialism*, edited by Stefan Collini. Cambridge: Cambridge University Press, 1989.

Miller, Arthur H. "Comparing Citizen and Elite Belief Systems in Post-Soviet Russia and Ukraine." *Public Opinion Quarterly* 59 (1995), 1–40.

Moore, Barrington. *Social Origins of Dictatorship and Democracy: Lord and Peasant in the Making of the Modern World*. Boston: Beacon Press, 1966.

Moraski, Bryon J. "Electoral System Design in Russian *Oblasti* and Republics: A Four Case Comparison." *Europe–Asia Studies* 55, no. 3 (2003), 437–468.

Moses, Joel. "Soviet Provincial Politics in an Era of Transition and Revolution, 1989–91." *Soviet Studies* 44, no. 3 (1992), 479–509.

Moses, Joel C. "Political–Economic Elites and Russian Regional Elections 1999–2000: Democratic Tendencies in Kaliningrad, Perm and Volgograd." *Europe–Asia Studies* 54, no. 6 (2002), 905–931.

Moses, Joel C. "Voting, Regional Legislatures and Electoral Reform in Russia." *Europe–Asia Studies* 55, no. 7 (2003), 1049–1075.

Munck, Gerardo L. "The Regime Question: Theory Building in Democracy Studies." *World Politics* 54, no. 1 (2001), 119–144.

Munck, Gerardo L., and Jay Verkuilen. "Conceptualizing and Measuring Democracy: Evaluating Alternative Indices." *Comparative Political Studies* 35, no. 1 (2002), 5–34.

Norris, Pippa. *A Virtuous Circle: Political Communications in Postindustrial Societies*. Cambridge: Cambridge University Press, 2000.

O'Brien, Kevin J. "Rightful Resistance." *World Politics* 49, no. 1 (1996), 31–55.

O'Donnell, Guillermo. "Illusions About Consolidation." In *Consolidating the Third Wave Democracies*, edited by Larry Diamond, 40–57. Baltimore: Johns Hopkins University Press, 1997.

O'Donnell, Guillermo. "On the State, Democratization and Some Conceptual Problems: A Latin-American View with Glances at Some Postcommunist Countries." *World Development* 21, no. 8 (1993), 1355–1369.

O'Donnell, Guillermo. "State and Alliances in Argentina, 1956–1976." *The Journal of Development Studies* 15, no. 1 (1979), 3–33.

O'Donnell, Guillermo, Philippe C. Schmitter, and Laurence Whitehead. *Transitions from Authoritarian Rule*. 4 vols. Baltimore: Johns Hopkins University Press, 1986.

Offe, Claus, and John Keane. *Contradictions of the Welfare State*. Cambridge, MA: MIT Press, 1984.

Oi, Jean C. *State and Peasant in Contemporary China: The Political Economy of Village Government*. Berkeley: University of California Press, 1989.

Olson, Mancur. *The Logic of Collective Action: Public Goods and the Theory of Groups*. Cambridge, MA: Harvard University Press, 1971.

OMRI Daily Digest, selected issues.

Orttung, Robert W. *From Leningrad to St. Petersburg: Democratization in a Russian City*. 1st ed. New York: St. Martin's Press, 1995.

Ottaway, Marina. *Strengthening Civil Society in Other Countries: Policy Goal or Wishful Thinking*. Washington, DC: Carnegie Endowment for International Peace, June 24, 2001. Available at http://www.ceip.org/files/Publications/StrengtheningCivilSociety.asp?from=pubauthor.

Pereira, Luiz Carlos Bresser, José María Maravall, and Adam Przeworski. *Economic Reforms in New Democracies: A Social–Democratic Approach*. Cambridge: Cambridge University Press, 1993.

Peterson, Paul E. *City Limits*. Chicago: University of Chicago Press, 1981.

Petro, Nicolai N. *Crafting Democracy: How Novgorod Has Coped with Rapid Social Change*. Ithaca, NY: Cornell University Press, 2004.

Petrov, Nikolai. "Regional Models of Democratic Development." In *Between Dictatorship and Democracy: Russian Post-communist Political Reform*, edited by Michael McFaul, Nikolai Petrov, and Andrei Ryabov, 239–267. Washington, DC: Carnegie Endowment for International Peace, 2004.

Pipes, Daniel. *In the Path of God: Islam and Political Power*. New York: Basic Books, 1983.

Polat, Abdumannob. "Can Uzbekistan Build Democracy and Civil Society?" In *Civil Society in Central Asia*, edited by M. Holt Ruffin and Daniel Clarke Waugh, 135–157. Seattle: University of Washington Press, 1999.

Popkin, Samuel L. *The Reasoning Voter: Communication and Persuasion in Presidential Campaigns*. Chicago: University of Chicago Press, 1991.

Przeworski, Adam. *Democracy and the Market: Political and Economic Reforms in Eastern Europe and Latin America*. Cambridge: Cambridge University Press, 1991.

Przeworski, Adam, Michael E. Alvarez, Jose Antonio Cheibub, and Fernando Limongi. *Democracy and Development: Political Institutions and Material Well-Being in the World, 1950–1990*. New York: Cambridge University Press, 2000.

Przeworski, Adam, and Fernando Limongi. "Modernization: Theories and Facts." *World Politics* 49, no. 2 (1997), 155–183.

Putnam, Robert D. "Bowling Alone: America's Declining Social Capital." *Journal of Democracy* 6, no. 1 (1995), 65–78.

Putnam, Robert D. *Bowling Alone: The Collapse and Revival of American Community*. New York: Simon and Schuster, 2000.

Putnam, Robert D. *The Comparative Study of Political Elites*. Englewood Cliffs, NJ: Prentice-Hall, 1976.

Putnam, Robert D., Robert Leonardi, and Raffaella Nanetti. *Making Democracy Work: Civic Traditions in Modern Italy*. Princeton, NJ: Princeton University Press, 1993.

Raczka, Witt. "Xinjang and Its Central Asian Borderlands." *Central Asia Survey* 17, no. 3 (1998), 373–407.

Remick, Elizabeth J. "The Significance of Variation in Local States: The Case of Twentieth Century China." *Comparative Politics* 34, no. 4 (2002), 399–418.

Remmer, Karen L., and François Gelineau. "Subnational Electoral Choice: Economic and Referendum Voting in Argentina, 1983–1999." *Comparative Political Studies* 36, no. 7 (2003), 801–821.

Remmer, Karen L., and Erik Wibbels. "The Subnational Politics of Economic Adjustment: Provincial Politics and Fiscal Performance in Argentina." *Comparative Political Studies* 33, no. 4 (2000), 419–451.

RFE/RL Newsline, selected issues.

Richards, Alan, and John Waterbury. *A Political Economy of the Middle East.* 2nd ed. Boulder, CO: Westview Press, 1996.

Rokkan, Stein. *Citizens, Elections, Parties: Approaches to the Comparative Study of the Processes of Development.* Oslo: Universitetsforlaget, 1970.

Rose, Richard. "How Muslims View Democracy: Evidence from Central Asia." *Journal of Democracy* 13, no. 4 (2002), 102–111.

Rubin, Jeffrey. *Decentering the Regime: Ethnicity, Radicalism, and Democracy in Juchitâan, Mexico.* Durham, NC: Duke University Press, 1997.

Rueschemeyer, Dietrich, Evelyne Huber Stephens, and John D. Stephens. *Capitalist Development and Democracy.* Chicago: University of Chicago Press, 1992.

Ruffin, M. Holt, and Daniel Clarke Waugh. *Civil Society in Central Asia.* Seattle: University of Washington Press, 1999.

Rustow, Dankwart A. "Transitions to Democracy: Toward a Dynamic Model." *Comparative Politics* 2, no. 3 (1970), 337–363.

Salamon, Lester M., and Stephen Van Evera. "Fear, Apathy, and Discrimination: A Test of Three Explanations of Political Participation." *The American Political Science Review* 67, no. 4 (1973), 1288–1306.

Salisbury, Robert. "An Exchange Theory of Interest Groups." *Midwest Journal of Political Science* 13, no. 1 (1969), 1–32.

Samara Region Administration. *Samara Region Administration: Economy and Business.* Samara Region Administration. Available at http://www.adm.samara.ru/econom/invprjen.asp.

Samara Research Group. "Two Military-Industrial Giants." In *The Russian Enterprise in Transition: Case Studies,* edited by Simon Clarke, 275. Cheltenham: Edward Elgar, 1996.

Samara State University. *Samara Region: Investments.* Samara State University. Available at http://www.samara.ru/business/indexen.asp.

Samara State University. *Samara Region: Small Business.* Samara State University. Available at http://www.samara.ru/investments/smallen.asp.

Sanyal, Bishwapriya. *Cooperative Autonomy: The Dialectic of State–NGOs Relationship in Developing Countries.* Geneva: International Institute for Labour Studies, 1994.

Schamis, Hector E. "Distributional Coalitions and the Politics of Economic Reform in Latin America." *World Politics* 51, no. 2 (1999), 236–268.

Schamis, Hector E. *Re-Forming the State: The Politics of Privatization in Latin America and Europe.* Interests, Identities, and Institutions in Comparative Politics. Ann Arbor: University of Michigan Press, 2002.

Schumpeter, Joseph. *Capitalism, Socialism, and Democracy.* New York: Harper and Brothers, 1942.

Schwartzman, Simon. "Regional Contrasts within a Continental-Scale State: Brazil." In *Building States and Nations: Analyses by Region,* edited by S. N. Eisenstadt and Stein Rokkan, 209–231. Beverly Hills, CA: Sage Publications, 1973.

Shapiro, Ian. *Democracy's Place.* Ithaca, NY: Cornell University Press, 1996.

Skocpol, Theda. *States and Social Revolutions: A Comparative Analysis of France, Russia, and China.* Cambridge: Cambridge University Press, 1979.

Skocpol, Theda. *Protecting Soldiers and Mothers: The Political Origins of Social Policy in the United States.* Cambridge, MA: Belknap Press of Harvard University Press, 1992.

Skocpol, Theda, Marshall Ganz, and Ziad Munson. "A Nation of Organizers: The Institutional Origins of Civic Volunteerism in the United States." *American Political Science Review* 94, no. 3 (2000), 527–546.

Slider, Darrell. "Russia's Market-Distorting Federalism." *Post-Soviet Geography and Economics* 38, no. 8 (1997), 445–460.

Smelser, Neil J. *Theory of Collective Behavior.* New York: Free Press of Glencoe, 1963.

Smith, Steven S., and Thomas F. Remington. *The Politics of Institutional Choice: The Formation of the Russian State Duma.* Princeton, NJ: Princeton University Press, 2001.

Snyder, Richard. "After Neoliberalism: The Politics of Reregulation in Mexico." *World Politics* 51, no. 2 (1999), 173–204.

Snyder, Richard. *Politics after Neoliberalism: Reregulation in Mexico.* Cambridge: Cambridge University Press, 2001.

Solnick, Steven L. "Gubernatorial Elections in Russia, 1996–1997." *Post-Soviet Affairs* 14, no. 1 (1998), 48–80.

Solnick, Steven Lee. *Stealing the State: Control and Collapse in Soviet Institutions.* Cambridge, MA: Harvard University Press, 1998.

Specter, Michael. "A Few Miles Apart, 2 Russias Contend for Nation's Future." *New York Times*, May 25, 1996, 1.

Sperling, Valerie. *Organizing Women in Contemporary Russia: Engendering Transition.* Cambridge: Cambridge University Press, 1999.

Staniszkis, Jadwiga. "Political Capitalism in Poland." *East European Politics and Societies* 5, no. 1 (1991), 127–141.

Stark, David. "Recombinant Property in East European Capitalism." *American Journal of Sociology* 101, no. 4 (1996), 993–1027.

State Commission on Foreign Investment and Economic Assistance. *The Kyrgyz Republic: Osh Regional Economic Strategy.* Bishkek State Commission on Foreign Investment and Economic Assistance, 1996.

Stone, Clarence N. *Regime Politics: Governing Atlanta, 1946–1988.* Lawrence: University Press of Kansas, 1989.

Stoner-Weiss, Kathryn. *Local Heroes: The Political Economy of Russian Regional Governance.* Princeton, NJ: Princeton University Press, 1997.

Sunstein, Cass R. *Democracy and the Problem of Free Speech.* New York: The Free Press, 1993.

"Sweetly Flows the Volga." *The Economist*, June 5, 1999, 62.

Tamir, Yael. "Revisiting the Civic Sphere." In *Freedom of Association*, edited by Amy Gutmann, 214–238. Princeton, NJ: Princeton University Press, 1998.

Tarrow, Sidney G. *Power in Movement: Social Movements, Collective Action, and Politics.* New York: Cambridge University Press, 1994.

Terry, Sarah Meiklejohn. "Thinking About Postcommunist Transitions: How Different Are They?" *Slavic Review* 52, no. 2 (1993), 333–337.

Teune, Henry. "Local Government and Democratic Political Development." *The Annals of the American Academy of Political and Social Science* 540 (1995), 10–23.

Tocqueville, Alexis de. *Democracy in America.* Vols. 1, 2. Vintage Classics. New York: Vintage Books, 1990.

Treisman, Daniel. *After the Deluge: Regional Crises and Political Consolidation in Russia.* Ann Arbor: University of Michigan Press, 1999.

Truman, David. *The Governmental Process.* 1st ed. New York: Knopf, 1951.

United Nations. *Global Illicit Drug Trends: 2001.* New York: United Nations, 2001.

United Nations Human Development Programme in Kyrgyzstan. *National Human Development Report for the Kyrgyz Republic 1999.* Bishkek: United Nations Human Development Programme in Kyrgyzstan, 1999. Available at http://www.undp.bishkek.su/english/publications/nhdr1999/chapter_5.html.

United Nations International Drug Control Programme. "UN Drug Programme to Launch Regional Law Enforcement Project Linking Kyrgyzstan, Tajikistan and Uzbekistan." Press Release, May 2, 1997.

U.S. Department of State, *SKAT-TV: Getting the Most from Media Training* (Washington, DC: U.S. Department of State). Available at http://www.internetelite.ru/samarari/english/story.phtml?pic = 07.

Verba, Sidney, Norman H. Nie, and Jae-on Kim. *Participation and Political Equality: A Seven-Nation Comparison.* Cambridge: Cambridge University Press, 1978.

Verba, Sidney, Kay Lehman Schlozman, and Henry E. Brady. *Voice and Equality: Civic Voluntarism in American Politics.* Cambridge, MA: Harvard University Press, 1995.

Volga-Dnepr Airlines. *Volga-Dnepr Airlines: Company Background.* Ul'ianovsk: Volga-Dnepr Airlines. Available at http://voldn.ru/compbarc.htm.

Walder, Andrew G. *Communist Neo-Traditionalism: Work and Authority in Chinese Industry.* Berkeley: University of California Press, 1986.

Way, Lucan A. "Pluralism by Default in Moldova." *Journal of Democracy* 13, no. 4 (2002), 127–141.

Weber, Max. *Economy and Society: An Outline of Interpretive Sociology.* Berkeley: University of California Press, 1978.

White, Stephen, Richard Rose, and Ian McAllister. *How Russia Votes.* Chatham, NJ: Chatham House Publishers, 1997.

Whitehead, Laurence. "International Aspects of Democratization." In *Transitions from Authoritarian Rule: Comparative Perspectives*, edited by

Guillermo O'Donnell, Philippe C. Schmitter, and Laurence Whitehead, 3–46. Baltimore: Johns Hopkins University Press, 1991.

The World Bank. Gonca Okur. [e-mail correspondence]. Development Data Group, The World Bank. November 8–15, 2002.

The World Bank. *2001 World Development Indicators*. [CD-ROM]. Washington, DC: The World Bank. November 1, 2001.

Zakaria, Fareed. "The Rise of Illiberal Democracy." *Foreign Affairs* 76, no. 6 (1997), 22–43.

Zhong, Yang, and Jie Chen. "To Vote or Not to Vote: An Analysis of Peasants' Participation in Chinese Village Elections." *Comparative Political Studies* 35, no. 6 (2002), 686–712.

Foreign Language (Kyrgyz, Russian, Uzbek)

"Aldangan va khurlangan otakhonlar onakhonlar." *Mezon,* April 24–May 1, 1998, 3.

Arianina, O. "Za slovom-delo: sel'chane blagodariat Kosyreva, a tot nameren pomogat' im eshche bol'she." *Volzhskaia kommuna,* November 18, 1997, 1.

Bunce, V. "Elementy neopredelennosti v perekhodnyi period." *Polis* 1 (1993), 44–51.

EkhOsha, selected issues.

Emet, selected issues.

Gel'man, Vladimir, Sergei I. Ryzhenkov, and Michael Brie. *Rossiia regionov: transformatsiia politicheskikh rezhimov.* Moscow: Ves' Mir, 2000.

Ishina, S. "Oleg D'iachenko: 'Ia gotov rabotat' po 16 chasov v sutki." *Volzhskaia kommuna,* November 12, 1997, 1.

Ivanov, I. "Viacheslav Chernavin: 'nastoiashchaia izvestnost' zarabatyvaetsia dobrymi delami, a ne skandalami: interv'iu po povodu." *Volzhskaia kommuna,* December 2, 1997, 2.

"Kandidaty v deputaty Samarskoi gubernskoi dumi: Tatishchevskii okrug N 13." *Volzhskaia kommuna,* December 2, 1997, 3.

Kirsanova, V. "Andrei Kislov: 'Moia programma ne gotovilas' k vyboram. Ia po nei zhivu'." *Volzhskaia kommuna,* November 26, 1997, 1–2.

"Leon Koval'skii: 'Vybirat' nado delo, a ne obeshchaniia'." *Volzhskaia kommuna,* December 5, 1997, 1, 5.

McFaul, Michael, and Nikolai Petrov, eds. *Politicheskii al'manakh Rossii 1997: sotsial'no-politicheskie portrety regionov.* Vol. 2. Moscow: Tsentr Karnegi, 1997.

Mezon, selected issues.

Moliakova, L. "Vybory-97: v narode govoriat: 'Kogda trudno, vpered vykhodiat muzhchiny, a esli ochen' trudno – ikh zameniaiut zhenshchiny'." *Volzhskaia kommuna,* December 2, 1997, 2.

Narodnaia gazeta, selected issues.

"Nastoichivoe trebovanie." *Pravozashchita: Samarskii biulleten'* 2 (1997).

Nekipelov, V. "Vybory-97: Leon Koval'skii – eto vser'ez." *Volzhskaia kommuna*, December 3, 1997, 1–2.

Neverova, V. "Oleg D'iachenko: esli oblast' zarabatyvaet bol'she, ona i dolzhna zhit' luchshe." *Volzhskaia kommuna*, November 14, 1997, 4.

"O dinastiiakh, svivshikh gnezdyshko na Molodogvardeiskoi, 187." *Grazhdanskaia initsiativa* 15 (1997), 4.

"O Samarskoi gubernskoi dume," No. 154 (1996).

Osh zhangirigi, selected issues.

Otkrytaia gazeta, selected issues.

"Otradnenskii izbiratel'nyi okrug N 23: N. P. Gavrilin: kazhdyi dolzhen zanimat'sia svoim delom: monolog s pristrastiem'." *Volzhskaia kommuna*, December 2, 1997, 5.

"O vyborakh deputatov Samarskoi gubernskoi dumy," No. 268 (1996).

"O vyborakh deputatov Zakonodatel'nogo sobraniia Ul'ianovskoi oblasti," No. 118 (1995).

"O vyborakh gubernatora Samarskoi oblasti," No. 155 (1996).

"O vyborakh gubernatora Ul'ianovskoi oblasti."

Patreov, A. "Kandidat: chto skazhesh', predsedatel'?" *Volzhskaia kommuna*, November 12, 1997, 1.

"Patriarkh televideniia Nikolai Fomenko." *Samarskoe obozrenie*, January 19, 1998, 12, 26.

Petrov, A. "Kontakt: chto khorosho dlia 'semerki'. . ." *Volzhskaia kommuna*, November 18, 1997, 1.

Petrov, A. "Kto v plenu u reform?" *Volzhskaia kommuna*, November 14, 1997, 1.

"Pravo na otkaz." *Pravozashchita: Samarskii biulleten'* 3 (1997).

Predprinimatel'skii klimat regionov Rossii: geografiia Rossii dlia investorov i predprinimatelei. Moscow: Nachala-Press, 1997.

"Proigravshie na vyborakh mashut kulakami posle draki." *Samarskoe obozrenie*, January 19, 1998, 7.

Regional'naia elita: kto est' kto. Moscow: SNIK Tsentre, 1998.

Regiony Rossii, 1999: statisticheskii sbornik. Vol. 2. Moscow: Goskomstat Rossii, 1999.

Riblin, G. "Kontakt: u dobra – svoi zakony." *Volzhskaia kommuna*, November 25, 1997, 1.

"'RIO' bogateet i zapuskaet ezhenedel'nuiu analiticheskuiu programmu." *Samarskoe obozrenie*, January 19, 1998, 4.

Rubtsov, V. "Pokhvistnevskii izbiratel'nyi okrug N 24: Gennadii Kirdiashev: 'Interesy sel'chan v Dume smogut zashchitit' tol'ko deputaty-agrarii . . .'." *Volzhskaia kommuna*, December 2, 1997, 5.

Rusanov, Oleg. "Ia ne khochu voevat'." *Pravozashchita: Samarskii biulleten'* 3 (1997).

Samarskaia oblast': 1996 ofitsial'nyi spravochnik. Samara: Fedorov, 1997.

Samarskie izvestiia, selected issues.

Samarskoe obozrenie, selected issues.

"Sarancha." *Grazhdanskaia initsiativa* 15 (1997), 1, 2.

Savin, A. "Vybory-97: vse li metody khoroshi?" *Volzhskaia kommuna*, November 28, 1997, 1.

Savina, L. "Kandidat: u sela k Dume – svoi schet." *Volzhskaia kommuna*, November 21, 1997, 1.

Simbirskie gubernskie vedomosti, selected issues.

Simbirskii kur'er, selected issues.

Slavin, A. "Prazdnik mitingu rozn'." *Volzhskaia kommuna*, November 11, 1997, 1.

Sobranie zakonodatel'stva Samarskoi oblasti. Vols. 1, 2. Samara: Samarskaia gubernskaia duma, 1997.

"Svad'ba pod predsedatel'stvom." *Volzhskaia kommuna*, December 3, 1997, 1.

Tengir too, selected issues.

Ul'ianovskaia pravda, selected issues.

Ush sadosi, selected issues.

"Vestnik Samarskoi gubernskoi dumy." 1, no. 3 (1998).

Volzhskaia kommuna, selected issues.

"Voprosy, otvety…i prazdnik." *Volzhskaia kommuna*, December 2, 1997, 1.

"Vperedi Rossii vsei." *Samaraskoe obozrenie*, January 19, 1998, 5.

"Vybory-97: Vladimir Lumpov: 'vy predlagaete-ia deistvuiu'." *Volzhskaia kommuna*, November 14, 1997, 2.

Vybory glav ispolnitel'noi vlasti sub"ektov Rossiiskoi Federatsii, 1995–1997. Moscow: Tsentral'naia Izbiratelnaia Komissiia Rossiiskoi Federatsii, 1997.

Zakonodatel'noe sobranie Ul'ianovskoi oblasti. *Informatsionni biulleten'* (March 1996–October 1997), Ul'ianovsk: Zakonodatel'noe sobranie Ul'ianovskoi oblasti, 1997.

Zhelezhniakov, V. "Vybory-97: Vasilii Ianin, mer Syzrani, kandidat v deputaty gubernskoi dumy po Syzranskomu izbiratel'nomu okrugu N 17. 'Moskva ishchet prezidenta cherez sud. A on zdravstvuet v Samare'." *Volzhskaia kommuna*, November 18, 1997, 2.

Index